FINDING THE SINGING SPRUCE

SOUNDING APPALACHIA
Travis D. Stimeling, Series Editor

TITLES IN THE SERIES

JASPER
WAUGH-QUASEBARTH

FINDING THE SINGING SPRUCE

MUSICAL INSTRUMENT MAKERS AND APPALACHIA'S MOUNTAIN FORESTS

WEST VIRGINIA UNIVERSITY PRESS / MORGANTOWN

ISBN 978-1-959000-00-6 (paperback) / 978-1-959000-01-3 (ebook)

Library of Congress Cataloging-in-Publication Data
Names: Waugh-Quasebarth, Jasper, 1990– author.
Title: Finding the singing spruce : musical instrument makers and Appalachia's mountain
        forests / Jasper Waugh-Quasebarth.
Description: First edition. | Morgantown : West Virginia University Press, 2023. | Series:
        Sounding Appalachia | Includes bibliographical references and index.
Identifiers: LCCN 2023010641 | ISBN 9781959000006 (paperback) | ISBN 9781959000013
        (ebook)
Subjects: LCSH: Musical instruments—Social aspects—West Virginia. | Musical instrument
        makers—West Virginia. | Musical instruments—Construction—West Virginia. |
        Forest products—Economic aspects. | Forest products—Environmental aspects. |
        Tonewoods.
Classification: LCC ML3917.U6 .W38 2023 | DDC 784.19754—dc23/eng/20230412
LC record available at https://lccn.loc.gov/2023010641

Cover and book design by Than Saffel / WVU Press
Cover image courtesy of the author

Listen to the story told by the reed,
of being separated.
"Since I was cut from the reedbed,
I have made this crying sound.
Anyone apart from someone he loves
understands what I say.
Anyone pulled from a source
longs to go back."

—Rumi, *Masnavi*, Book 1

CONTENTS

LIST OF ILLUSTRATIONS

ACKNOWLEDGMENTS

This book has a social life of its own, just as the instruments and makers that it seeks to describe. It has been influenced, shaped, crafted, advised, and inspired by so many people and places. It is held by a meshwork of love, support, creative expression, critical thought, and being that it could not have survived without.

The makers profiled in this book and their families—Paolo and Erica Marks, John Preston, Christopher Zambelli, Travis Holley, Eddie Fletcher, Catalin Murgoci, Mihai and Ana Filip—have all opened their homes, workshops, and lives to me despite facing enormous challenges throughout the years we've worked together. I treasure your friendship, companionship, and your open and curious minds.

This work would not have been possible without the tireless support of Ann Kingsolver. Her determination, compassion, and love of fostering relationships have made this work and my life richer. Her mentorship—along with the writing group she led—encouraged, challenged, and opened me up to new ideas. Hsain Ilahiane, Ron Pen, and Monica Udvardy have all left their imprint on this project, offering clear suggestions and guidance over the years. Their care, commentary, and excitement led to funding from the Department of Anthropology and the Appalachian Center at the University of Kentucky, the Lambda Alpha Anthropology Honor Society, and the Wenner-Gren Foundation, which has financially sustained this project.

My Appalachian studies community—Dwight Billings, Kathryn Newfont, Shaunna Scott, Kenton Sena, Shane Barton, Emma Kiser, Mary Beth Schmid, Henry Bundy, Tammy Clemmons, Julie Shepherd-Powell, Tom Hansell, Sarah Craycraft, Jordan Lovejoy, Sophia Enriquez, Jacob Kopcienski, Lee Bidgood,

Katherine Ledford, Theresa Burriss, Travis Stimeling, and in particular, Kathryn Engle and Zada Komara—supported me and opened my eyes to new ways of seeing the region and the world. They exemplify the gracious humility, keen intellect, and energetic enthusiasm found in the Appalachian studies community that provides a continual aspiration.

The community of folklorists from Ohio State University has taught me new ways to approach my work in collaboration and reciprocity. I thank Cassie Patterson, Katey Borland, and the students and community partners of the Ohio Field School for all they have brought to my work. A Global Arts and Humanities Discovery Theme Faculty Fellowship at Ohio State gave me the necessary time, resources, and collegial feedback to finish this project. I'm grateful for the support of that program and my fellow members. Brian Harnetty, Mary Hufford, Mark-Anthony Arceño, and the Department of Comparative Studies have also all contributed valuable feedback and enthusiasm that brought this work forward.

An emerging group of tonewood scholars has provided new insights and a unique intellectual resonance for this work. In particular, this book rests upon the incredible scholarship of Kathryn Dudley, José Martinez-Reyes, Chris Gibson, Andrew Warren, Aaron Allen, and Jared Beeton, without whom I would never have seen the forest for the trees. My colleagues at the Smithsonian Institution—in particular Paul Taylor, Rob Pontsieon, and Jared Koller—have supported this work in various ways, often giving me platforms to bring this research to new communities of collaboration throughout the world.

A few of my friends in West Virginia—Mary, Gil, and Thurston Willis, Maureen Conley, and Carter Zerbe—have been around my entire life and made a home for me at the loneliest of times during this project. My Lexington family always has my back and pushes me to be both lighthearted and conscientious of the world around me. Trevor Merrion and Sebastian Arze have been my consistent companions in fieldwork throughout the years, pushing me to new understandings of music and the world, helping me to find my feet in the world, and to understand who I was.

My parents, Brenda Waugh and Chris Quasebarth, my siblings, Elexa Waugh-Quasebarth and Dashiell Quasebarth, and my extended family have been the foundation and bedrock upon which all of this is based. They've traveled with me, made fieldwork connections, and shown up at academic conference panels hundreds of miles from their homes. The connections we've made through this project continue to blossom. My grandparents fostered the love of community, place, music, and craft in all of us. Thank you, Grandma Nancy, for your love of craft and open heart. Thank you, Grandpa Norval, for your love of music and West Virginia. Thank you, Grandpa Werner and Grandma Elaine, for the encouragement to travel over the mountains and throughout the world. And thank you, Grandma Gladys, Grandaddy Oren, and Aunt Ann, for providing the home that sheltered me during my research. My work and this book are challenged and inspired by the legacy that my ancestors have left behind.

Thank you, Céline, for sharing your life and so many of the experiences in this book with me.

Finally, I offer gratitude to the land and forests that have rooted this work, my life, and my family for many more years than the length of this project. Every sentence in this text reflects a step taken in, to, and from the Allegheny Mountains, where I have felt the earth reach up and take ahold of my being. I thank those who have sustained and stewarded these forests through the millennia, listening for what wisdom they might pass along.

"IT WILL GET IN YOUR BLOOD"

Christopher Zambelli, a Randolph County, West Virginia, guitar maker, and I were seated at the small card table in his shop where he often set up for small tasks and the work of selecting wood for guitar projects. The open window blew warm, humid summer air into the shop as we contemplated a thin plank of spruce in consideration for the top on the guitar project we had just embarked upon. He asked me to count the reddish rings of the "winter growth" streaked through the otherwise creamy color of a piece of red spruce. Using the lead of a pencil to move along the parallel lines, I calculated 180 rings in the plank, which was about ten inches wide, and Chris was noticeably disappointed. His head dropped slightly to his chest, joining the image of a quilt above the words "Jackson Mill Arts and Crafts Festival" on his T-shirt. My calculation conflicted with what he had been telling customers, that the tree dated from around "Constitution Days" in the eighteenth century.

He had been given permission by the National Forest to cut this old-growth tree in 1998 to promote the West Virginia northern flying squirrel habitat, yet he noted his conflicting thoughts on conservation, saying that "people have to live on this land, too." However, he was amazed that the Forestry Service had requested it, given the age of the stand of trees and the fact that they often limit permits to large timber companies. Realizing that the wood had aged for almost twenty years after it had been cut and that the thin plank had material removed from both edges, I excitedly calculated that indeed, as Chris had suggested, the tree must have been at least two hundred years old when he cut it.

After at least 218 years since the red spruce had sprouted on a mountaintop

Fig. I.1. Guitar maker Christopher Zambelli grading red spruce tops

in Pocahontas County, West Virginia, overlooking the headwaters of the Elk, Gauley, and Williams Rivers, the top would be fashioned in the style of a C.F. Martin-style dreadnought guitar and be shipped to the out-of-state customer. Bearing silent witness to generations of forest communities, waves of human immigration, and extensive timber extraction, the spruce would become a guitar soundboard, the crucial component to making the instrument sing.

A couple of weeks later, as the work on the guitar progressed into its construction, Chris and I chatted about my recent hike to the peak Red Spruce Knob, the highest local mountaintop. As he had not been before, I described the mountaintop covered in red spruce, a climax species that shades out competitors and grows in thick stands along the ridges of the Alleghenies. Beams of sunlight cut narrow channels through the deep shade cast by the towering canopy of spindling spruce branches, and spruces surrounded me at every stage of life, from the green seedling poking out of mossy humus to their fallen ancestors still clinging to the rocky soil left after fires consumed the topsoil in the early twentieth century. Unlike the spruce that was now taking shape in the guitar, these spruces had returned with Civilian Conservation Corps efforts to replant trees in the 1930s, with the peak still bearing the concrete pad, remnant of the tower once used to watch for forest fires. The resulting feeling in this restored landscape is one of quiet openness and a plaintive, pensive shade, even on the brightest day. The stillness struck me as I searched for a tree that might, one day, be the right size and shape for some artisan to draw song from its lively tissue. While I was working with Chris, he had made his own affection for red spruce no secret, offering both scientific and affective reasons for his use of the material and encouraging me to use it in my own future guitars. With a knowing yet approachable tone that characterized his teaching, he said, "I told you, it will get in your blood."

Musical instrument making gets in one's blood both through embodied and affective means. It both creates strong emotional ties to the materials and processes of the work and shapes the bodies and dispositions of those engaged in the craft. The competing scales and understandings of time or temporalities of tree life, human life, and economic transaction, the compulsion to keep making despite adverse economic circumstances, the joy of bringing sound to seemingly silent life and bringing life to seemingly dead and inert matter, and the forest and human history bound through the fibers of wood are all articulated through the relationships between makers, environments, and materials that the craft embodies. This book explores these connections and relationships by exploring crafters' endeavors to find song in wood and meaning in their work.

With no intent to categorize or describe an archetypical West Virginia instrument maker or reify the category of Appalachian craftspeople, I have tried through this project to represent a broad range of makers, drawing lines of common experience while also pointing to differences among the many people making instruments. I have also searched for examples of makers from the historical record and have sketched here their presumed habits and livelihoods, based on that evidence, to hint at the history of instrument making in West Virginia. While some controversy does exist about how West Virginia artisans or craft should be defined, it is not my intention to define a distinctly "West Virginia" or Central Appalachian tradition among instrument makers but rather to elucidate the experiences of those who live in the Mountain State.[1]

From 2014 to 2018, I conducted ethnographic and contextual archival research in West Virginia with people engaged in or connected to the craft of musical instrument making, aimed at understanding the meaning of the work undertaken by makers and its connection to the state's vast forest environments.[2] This research began with interviewing musical instrument makers, as

Fig. I.2. The spruce forest on the summit of Red Spruce Knob

well as people working in tourism and heritage, timber and forestry, and musicians. I began with identifying known musical instrument makers through existing contacts and their web presence and continued through "snowball sampling," or connecting with makers that they knew and interviewing them. I conducted these interviews almost exclusively with makers in West Virginia to control for different experiences due to influencing state policies and institutions, as well as my initial interest in the impact of the state-based regional identity. Working with a fairly small population, I made my best effort to contact and interview as many instrument makers as time and resources permitted.

I conducted maker biographies through interviews and apprenticeship to complement the participant observation, a hallmark of ethnographic research, which revealed other biographical elements that play a crucial role in the production and value of instruments and instrument materials, such as migration, employment, education, apprenticeship, and kinship. I collected artifact biographies of instruments and tonewood to understand their changing symbolic and economic positions through their transformation and exchange.[3] I visited the sites of cutting trees and logs, talked to foresters at log yards while selecting wood, processed tonewood in the shop, made instruments, and finally discussed the possible futures of musical instruments and tonewood. This analysis drew out the significance of transactions and transferals of materials, instruments, styles, and technologies, as well as their place in or relation to the forest landscape. Together, these biographies allowed me to conceptualize genealogies of makers and instruments and explore how makers position themselves and instruments within histories of craft, music, and the natural resource economy in the region, which is explored throughout the book.

Ultimately, I found that ethnographic apprenticeship was the best way to engage in the kind of participant observation necessary to explore my questions regarding how instrument makers develop relationships through their craft. In the craft of instrument making, I found that non-verbal, extended temporal relationships arise between makers, the materials they use, and the forest environment in which they live. I found these relationships could not be documented merely through interviewing or more extensive participant observation committed to the study of a larger population. Thus, I dedicated periods of months-long apprenticeship research to a guitar maker, Christopher Zambelli of Beverly, West Virginia; a violin maker, Paolo Marks of Lobelia, West Virginia; and an instrument maker and tonewood cutter, John Preston of Lewisburg, West Virginia, from 2016 through 2018.[4]

Though many ethnographers—if not all—are involved in a pursuit of learning from and with those whom they interview, observe, hang out with, document, and speak with and for, apprenticeship involves relationship building between a mentor and a student through the attempted mastery and demonstration of a specific skill or set of skills toward a manifest end. Exploring questions of the materials of production in work settings and the possibility of upsetting power hierarchies of expertise, I embraced apprenticeship as a primary method for research on craft labor, material environments, and the meaning of work.[5] Deeply involved in the work, I became an apprentice musical instrument maker, which opened up the worlds of relation in and beyond instrument shops.[6] By working with makers, I began to see how the craft becomes embodied within artisans, and it also planted the seeds for collaboration beyond the workshop.[7]

In the following chapters, I draw on this ethnographic research to explore the relationships at work across the craft of musical instrument making in forest environments. Through interviews and narratives of the construction of instruments, I tell the stories of the diverse work practices of the craft, tracing the movement of musical tonewood, such as spruce, through regional and global trade networks into the shops of makers and to the finished products of singing, lively instruments. Exploring differences between making techniques, forest landscapes, aesthetic decisions, and livelihood situations, I describe musical instrument craft within the everyday processes of the instrument shop and the globalized context of historical processes and contemporary political economic circumstances. Fundamentally, I argue that the wood materials used in instrument craft and the placed environments of forests contribute to attempts to find meaning through work in a region where labor and landscape are often commoditized, devalued, and stripped of placed meaning and sustainability.

Scholars have frequently bundled such processes of stripping away meaning from the world as *disenchantment*, or the processes through which mysteries of the world are increasingly rationalized or bureaucratized.[8] For example, we may think of the steady trend toward financializing the world in terms of dollars and cents, such as the practice of monetizing the ecosystem "services" of ecological actors. Early social scientists regarded this process as one inevitably tied to so-called modernizing practices, but more recent writers have challenged us to think of the ways in which *enchantment* or *re-enchantment* of social worlds can persist despite the rationalizing processes of our economic and political systems, or be salvaged from them.[9] This book enjoins such scholarship by exploring how makers seek to re-enchant their worlds through their work and connections to environmental and social communities.

I have found the metaphor, model, and language of *meshworks* to be useful in conceptualizing these connections. Scholars have used this term to describe how people are entangled in both hyperlocal social and material interactions and in response to global processes that touch down in specific places throughout the world.[10] We may think of how climate change, for instance, both impacts and is impacted by thousands of diverse, everyday relationships people foster with each other, covering a broad variety of beings and things. Taken together and expressed through the local ways in which people encounter the world, these relationships constitute the notion of *place* that so affectively ties us to the spaces we inhabit in the world. Through their craft, instrument makers are drawn into and make global *meshworks* of musical instrument craft, industrial production, governance, and forest ecology. Their work touches on nodes of *placed* interaction all around the globe. A world of music is created through the intersections and ties of instrument making to transnational movements, trends, and historical processes.

In North America, other scholars of musical instrument craft have explored how guitar makers persist in keeping artisanal values alive while navigating complex international legal frameworks, large instrument-making corporations both set the standards for the craft and also manipulate global tonewood markets to their ends, and small makers look for possibilities of new materials in the ecological ruin of our time.[11] Another recent work, by cultural geographers Chris Gibson and Andrew Warren, follows the flow of guitar woods from forests to sawmills and finally factories while charting the deeply historical and often iniquitous environmental impacts of making instruments.[12] This book builds upon these findings and others by exploring how makers in Appalachia navigate the historical and emerging processes in the mountain forests that surround them—or in their own backyards, so to speak. It speaks to the diverse sets of relationships that constitute meaningful work that emerge from environments, social communities, historical traditions, and the tensions that emerge between the various kinds of craft encompassed by musical instrument making, or *lutherie*.[13]

Chapter 1, "West Virginia's Musical Instrument Makers," sketches a landscape of instrument makers across West Virginia, with interviews from ethnographic fieldwork that considers the commonalities and breadth of diversity that exist across the range of makers encountered during the period I conducted research, as well as those discovered through archival research. Through excerpts from ethnographic interviews, newspaper clippings, and census data, I discuss the central commitments and practices of musical instrument makers and their diversity through time and place. Readers will get a sense of the importance of music and musical instruments in Appalachian communities in both the everyday lived experiences and the representations of Appalachian music in development efforts and regional representation. Readers will also understand how conceptions of craft labor have changed in Appalachia at large through the nineteenth and twentieth centuries, challenging misconceptions about the histories of specific instruments and craft traditions.

Chapter 2, "Craft at Home in the Mountain Forest," dives deep into the theoretical underpinnings of this research to question what we mean when we talk about craft, work, economy, and human actors' connections to the landscapes and environments we are entrenched in. I situate this text in relevant histories and scholarship on the place of music, craft labor, and place in Appalachian forests. This chapter also frames the work through a political ecological understanding of the forest of the Allegheny Mountains of Appalachia, drawing out the threads of connection between the craft of musical instruments, extractive timber practices, forest communities, and the history enmeshed in the forest landscape. A broad background on the concepts of labor re-enchantment, meshworks that make up local and global connections between makers and their environments, and the influential qualities of craft materials on makers' practices anticipates the following chapters that attend to individual makers.

Chapter 3, "A Red Spruce Guitar," follows the process of building an acoustic dreadnought steel-string guitar, typical of old-time and bluegrass musicians, with guitar maker Christopher Zambelli of Beverly, West Virginia. The reader follows along from the planning stages of the guitar through its completion and place in the world as a lively, singing instrument. I focus on Chris's use of red spruce and its impact as a local species used in local craft and its preeminence in the "golden era" of major instrument manufacturers. This focus addresses the intersections of labor made meaningful by place and local environments, as well as the continuing impact of designs, traditions, and modes of manufacture established by large companies that persist in small craft shops today. This chapter also introduces the reader to the fuzzy edges of scientific research encountered in musical instrument shops, where subjectivities of musical tone are understood through processes of sound transmission and cellular structures and where uncertainties in outcome are mitigated by careful attention to minute processes. By following the construction of the guitar from red spruce logs to singing guitar, readers will understand how labor becomes meaningful in relationships with environments, materials, and personal commitments.

Chapter 4, "Bringing Cremona Violins to Lobelia," looks at the craft of violin making through my apprenticeship with Paolo Marks, a violin and mandolin maker from Pocahontas County, West Virginia. I consider the meaning of the craft as articulated through personal philosophies of "knowing" craft materials and the history of making violins entrenched in European traditions that still inspire violin makers to innovate today. In contrast to the previous chapter, chapter 4 focuses on production with hand tools and long-established techniques of maintaining correspondence between maker and materials that result in successful instruments.

In Chapter 5, "Tonewood from the Old World and the New," readers explore the world of the production and sale of musical tonewood, the base material of making musical instruments. By exploring work with John Preston, a tonewood manufacturer in West Virginia who also imports analogous species of trees from the mountain forests of Romania, this chapter problematizes the categorization of the work of tonewood and tonewood cutters. By looking at how the process simultaneously produces commodities and noncommodities, relies on and critiques the cycles of timber extractions, and promotes locality while importing globally, the chapter asks the reader to examine how people make sense of seeming contradictions in economy and ecology. The long-term relationships cultivated with the craft material and other workers involved in the craft process are crucial to understanding this work, and thus the chapter rounds out the two previous case studies. By following the importation of wood into the forests of West Virginia from Romania, we can understand how Appalachian people and forests are highly connected to global meshworks of economy and ecology.

In the conclusion, "Succession in Craft and Forest," I ask the reader to think of processes of succession that exist in the craft and the future of labor and forests in Appalachia. As I worked through making tonewood and musical instruments with makers, these questions continually came up in our discussions while working on instruments, playing music, and through the other daily tasks that come up side by side with craft labor. Though craftwork is often posited as timeless, our work was always happening in specific historical moments where people were drawing on their knowledge of their livelihoods and environment to conceptualize the future of their work and the region. As divisive political issues, environmental stresses, life events, and the flows of material culture passed through the shops and the meshworks from which instruments emerge, makers had to change their practices, causing moments of critical reflection about the role of the craft in their lives and the craft work in the world. The craft of musical instrument making extends from the relationships built between the maker and the wood into a world of changing relationships between human, nonhuman, and institutional forces that bear on the task of finding song within wood and meaning in work.

CHAPTER 1

WEST VIRGINIA'S MUSICAL INSTRUMENT MAKERS

ON THE PAGE AND ON THE SHELF

The propensity of early scholars to focus on the eccentricities of Appalachia makes it difficult to sketch with accuracy the history of musical instruments and musical instrument makers in the region. Scholarly documentation tends toward the strange and peculiar, like early wooden-ringed banjos, cigar-box fiddles, and other homemade versions of popular instruments, alongside various versions of modified or improvised instruments of many shapes and varieties, as seen, for example, in the Museum of Appalachia's catalog, *Musical Instruments of Southern Appalachia*.[1] Given the history of interest in these kinds of instruments—that is, the tradition of searching for the "traditional"—my work was often misunderstood as research into the traditional instruments of Appalachia, though I was interested in a much larger picture of instrument makers.[2]

Archival photographs, catalogs of mail-order services, and the record of instrument manufacturers and dealers in West Virginia that I encountered in my research suggested that inexpensive, industrially produced instruments were available to West Virginians as soon as their lowland counterparts, and they were certainly not only limited to banjos and dulcimers. My own great-grandfather's set of pre–World War II harmonicas in Pocahontas County served a polyphonic reminder of the interconnectedness of Appalachian places with diverse musics and markets. In an interview in his house in Pocahontas

County, banjo and fiddle player Mike Burns told me about his experience learning fiddle tunes from the previous generation of players: "The old-timers had lower-quality instruments. Some banjos had plastic rims and some fiddles had screw-in tuners instead of tuning pegs. . . . [They were instruments bought from] Sears for ten to twelve dollars, handed down to the next generation."[3] These catalog instruments served just as well as the homemade or craft-made instruments in continuing musical traditions at home in the mountains. However, their availability did cause me to question how many people may have been making instruments and making a livelihood from the craft historically.

Given the booms and busts of industrial production and extractive industry in West Virginia, I expected to find instrument makers in service to the state's population, especially at times of relative prosperity and high population. By cross-referencing lists of known makers from museum collections, regional scholarship, newspaper articles, and local oral history with occupational data from census rolls from the late nineteenth to the mid-twentieth centuries, I was able to determine that there were few instrument makers who were able to depend on making instruments for their entire livelihood, a similar situation to today. Yet, there were many instrument makers who made a few instruments for themselves or family members in the state. Milnes's detailed investigation of dulcimer makers throughout the state points to a large tradition of makers who produced a few instruments, and anecdotal records accompanying music collections frequently make mention of an instrument made by a family member.[4] Few examples exist of craftspeople who only made or repaired instruments, such as Arthur Wilkinson of Clarksburg, whose occupation is listed as "repairing stringed instruments" in the 1940 census, or folks working in closely related trades who are known to have made instruments, such as Edward McEwen of Lewis County, who was listed as a "Repairman // Furniture shop" in the 1930 census. More common is to find that known makers, like Dr. Charles D. Rohr of Lewis County, were listed by their occupation—in this case, a medical doctor.[5]

Despite the proliferation of relatively simple "folk instruments" in historical documentation and museum collections that come to stand for their time, makers were certainly aware of skilled techniques of making and selecting wood that are the hallmark of an engaged relationship with the craft. The *Clarksburg Telegram* of April 7, 1893, informed the readers of the process by which old makers selected and processed wood.[6] While the following excerpt is slightly hyperbolic and has minor errors in the facts, the basics of tonewood selection are there for prospective makers and reflect the methods of instrument makers and tonewood producers today:

> The great violin makers all lived within the compass of one hundred and fifty years. They choose their wood from great timbers fell in the South Tyro, and floated down in rafts: pine and maple, sycamore, pear and ash. They examined these to find streaks and veins and freckles, valuable superficially when brought out by varnishing. They learned to tell the dynasty of the pieces of wood by touching them. They weighed them thus: they struck them and listened to judge how fast or slow or how resonantly they would vibrate in answer to strings. Some portions of the wood must be porous and soft, some of close fiber. Just the right beam was hard to find; when found it can be traced all through the violin of some great master, and after his death in those of his pupils. The piece of wood was taken home and seasoned, dried in the hot Brescia and Cremonia [sic] sun. The house of Stradivarius, the great master of all, is described as having been as hot as an oven. Tone wood was there soaked through and through with sunshine. In this great heat the oils thinned and simmered slowly and penetrated far into the wood, until the varnish became a part of the wood itself. The old violin makers used to save every bit of the wood, when they found what they liked, to mend and patch and inlay with it. So vibrant and so resonant is the wood of good old violins that they murmur and echo, and sing in answer to any sound—Detroit Free Press.

For a prospective instrument maker in a time before wide availability of instructional books or Internet forums and videos, this short vignette would give many of the key elements of selecting wood for making successful instruments.

Using methods like these, some makers, like I. W. Allison of Charleston, were well known not only in West Virginia but throughout the United States for their finely crafted violins, and they mentored other local makers.[7] Allison and Charleston-based maker Harold Hayslett are profiled in the illustrious *Violin Makers of the United States*, alongside other noted American violin and bow makers.[8] Hayslett would go on to win several national awards for his instruments. Others combed through historical documentation to attempt to replicate the techniques of storied makers, such as J. E. Hedrick of Charleston, West Virginia, who made front-page news in the *Charleston Daily Mail* on May 27, 1935, for his efforts to copy Cremonese instruments using archival information and photographs. The owners of A. A. Hay's Pastime bowling alleys in Fairmont, West Virginia, claimed to have had a Stradivarius violin that was made in 1713 and brought to West Virginia in the early eighteenth century bearing "the name of Antonius Stardivarious [*sic*] lettered on the inside and also the name of Elias Coe, of Fairmont, who repaired the instrument in 1908."[9]

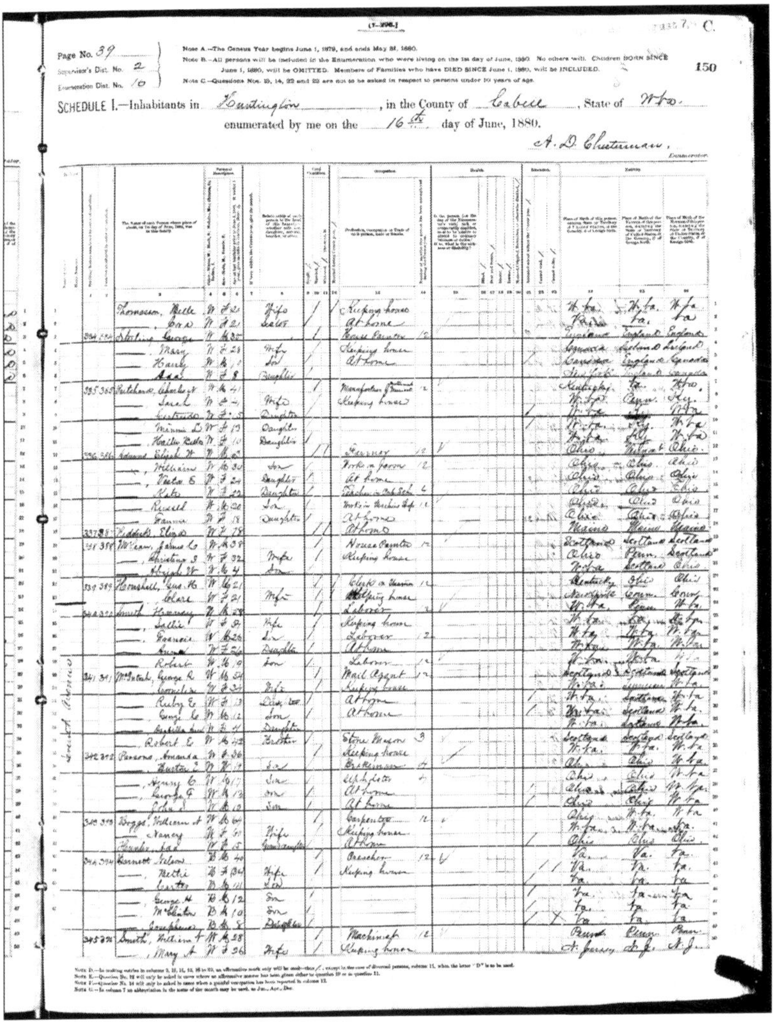
Page No. 39
Supervisor's Dist. No. 2
Enumeration Dist. No. 10
150
SCHEDULE 1.—Inhabitants in Huntington, in the County of Cabell, State of W Va. enumerated by me on the 16th day of June, 1880.

Fig. 1.1. Census record showing "Manufacturer of Musical Instruments" Charles Pritchard as the third household entry

Coexisting alongside this craft practice and knowledge were two examples of factory production that do not exist today in West Virginia: Charles Pritchard of Huntington, a "Manufacturer of Musical Instruments" according to the 1880 Census record, and W. A. Cantrell of Charleston, who owned the American Violin Company in the early twentieth century. Little is known of Pritchard's shop, but some of his instruments exist in museum and private collections, bearing the marks of instruments made for mass consumption. They are painted with faux grain to emulate a finer piece of rosewood or a tropical species of hardwood, and there are notes stenciled below the strings to aid prospective players in the tuning of the instrument. The impact of this potentially mass-produced series on Appalachian instruments is pronounced, as the hourglass pattern of the instrument has also greatly influenced the production of mountain, or Appalachian, dulcimers in the twentieth and twenty-first centuries.[10]

W. A. Cantrell, conversely, bears little in the way of a legacy of instruments, but he left behind considerably more documentation of his efforts at mass production of instruments in West Virginia. As the owner of the American Violin Company that operated out of Charleston, he was issued a charter for $75,000 on November 19, 1915, having recently applied for a permit to expand the plant on Pennsylvania Avenue and Charleston Street (now Washington St.) on the West Side.[11] I was not able to locate any employees of the factory in the census records or any other public record, but Cantrell was well represented in the local press, suggesting that his acumen for public relations outweighed his ability to foster the production of musical instruments. The violin factory and its owner generated semiregular news on the production of instruments or Cantrell's search for wood for violins.

Cantrell was known to buy tonewood in other parts of West Virginia, searching for the quality and quantity to feed his burgeoning enterprise. An August 8, 1916, article describes his arrival in Beckley, "in the interest of this company to buy timber for the manufacture of violins. . . . Already the sales of their product is taxing the capacity of the plant."[12] He claimed to have registered a patent for violin production machinery that could automatically produce violins with a range of violin tones that were not dependent on the wood used in the process, though I could find no record of such a patent. In the one interview, he promoted his company's mechanization as allowing an American enterprise to compete with the proliferation of handmade, imported products:

"The violin industry," said Mr. Cantrell, "has been house and hand industry in Italy, Germany, and Austria, and those countries have had an exclusive monopoly of the business. Violins have never been manufactured by machinery until our company undertook it. We have succeeded in accomplishing this, and we produce by machinery a violin of as fine tone as any violinmaker can turn out with his hands. This has not been easy of accomplishment, but at least we have succeeded after overcoming many seemingly insurmountable obstacles at the cost of many years and many thousands of dollars. There are 300,000 violins imported into the United States each year, representing a value of $2,500,000. When our present plant, as planned, is completed, we will be able to turn out daily fifty thoroughly tested instruments of the finest tone grade.'"[13]

Cantrell's claims intertwine with the threads of tensions still at work in global and local markets for musical instruments today. While Cantrell's concern was to outcompete the craft production at work within factories of Central Europe in the early twentieth century, some of today's makers voice concern about their craft production in contrast to cheap, mechanized factory production abroad.[14] Today, there are no examples of this kind of factory production in West Virginia. Makers whom I encountered and interviewed in this study practiced a wide variety of techniques and backgrounds in creating an array of musical instruments, but they were usually made by themselves in small shops at small scales of production. Ironically, however, the legacy of factory production of instruments in the United States, especially guitars and mandolins, leaves many instrument makers attempting to replicate factory processes in their own shops. Nevertheless, the undergirding principles of today's craft musical instrument makers are rarely in tune with Cantrell's concern at capturing a large slice of the global market for musical instruments. Rather, the legacy of craft work as a singular mode of production, which is intrinsically tied to the crafter's identity and place in the social world, impacts the motivations and meaning of the work of building musical instruments.

The rampant rise of industrial modes of production in the nineteenth century, including those proposed by Mr. Cantrell, were met with criticism and nostalgia by artists, social critics, and writers, such as John Ruskin and William Morris, who were concerned with the stripping away of the meaning of labor and the quality of material production.[15] They constructed a notion of "craft" as a meaningful, deliberate, alternative labor displaced by modernity, a conception that persists in our popular and theoretical understanding of particular kinds of labor and material production today.[16] Underscoring the importance of contemplation through work and critiquing the division of labor in industrial production, these thinkers believed that meaning in life derives from labor that brings together design and execution of physical creation.[17] This movement, directly and indirectly, influences the motivations and identity of nearly every instrument maker I have talked to, and it demonstrates that crafting is more often a response to larger political and economic trends than a vestige of past practices. In the following section, I engage with the craft and crafters where they are in ways that do not replicate images of Appalachia as a vestigial holdout of craft practices but instead as a response to current global processes of labor, aesthetics, and environment.

IN SHOPS, FAIRS, AND FESTIVALS

Given the limits of ethnographic fieldwork and sampling strategies, I could not interview all instrument makers encountered or to whom I was referred in my years of fieldwork. I could not talk to all of West Virginia's instrument makers; some passed away before we had a chance to meet, some moved away to seek opportunities elsewhere, some declined to be part of the project, and there may be others not publicly known to be instrument makers in the state—though they might excel in the craft. Those I encountered include makers of predominantly wooden acoustic instruments—the primary focus of this book—such as guitars, violin family instruments, banjos, mandolins, and dulcimers. But there are also makers excelling at electric instruments, such as the jazz basses of Roger Morillo; flutes and wind instruments, such as the transverse flutes of John Gallagher; or the steelpans (steel drums) of the school of crafters following the legacy of Ellie Mannette, such as Glenn Rowsey. While instruments that feature heavily in Appalachian string band music are certainly common, they by no means represent the full extent of instruments that makers in West Virginia craft and encounter in their careers.

Crafters are keenly aware of how their craft is simultaneously symbolically valorized and economically denigrated, and they are willing to go to uncertain lengths to protect it. Negotiating markets of authenticity can be a paramount goal of some kinds of craftwork in order to resist the de-skilling discourses and regimes of capitalist production that emulate, compete with, supply, and demand the authenticity of craft objects.[18] In the craft of musical instruments, where the influence of large musical instrument enterprises is indelible, makers at once resist the modes of production in factories while embracing the iconic forms of notable factory instruments, buying parts from factory production and making parts and source wood for factory production.

The concept of tradition or authenticity of instruments and instrument craft was certainly important to a large of group of makers I interviewed. Generally, I found that makers, with a few exceptions, who had moved to

West Virginia from elsewhere were more likely to consider concepts of tradition and authenticity in West Virginia and Appalachia important, remarking that the craft had to be learned through grounded knowledge of hundreds of years of tradition and be an expression of personal, creative fulfillment. Others were more ambivalent toward the terminology and did not seem to consider the terms and categories salient in their craft. Ultimately, I found that demarcating a category of "native" or "local" West Virginian was not especially useful, as makers who had moved from other parts of the United States or other countries were as likely to demonstrate similar skills, outlook, and prestige as makers born in the state. Some makers who were originally from out of state were likely to draw distinctions between themselves and other West Virginians, perhaps trying to more explicitly practice perceived West Virginian or Appalachian styles, venting frustrations about how people may not recognize "Appalachian" instruments at craft festivals as their regional heritage, or asserting a specific lineage or style of making that tied them to the craft in absence of a placed genealogy.[19]

Getting to the point where a maker can demonstrate these kinds of expression depends on various strategies for acquiring and practicing the knowledge of instrument making. Formal degree-granting institutions, schools of lutherie, classes aimed at perpetuating cultural heritage, a range of apprenticeship relations, informal advising relationships, and self-teaching through books, instrument collections, online resources, and experimentation are among the strategies makers shared with me.[20] Each maker had likely employed a variety of these methods in the pursuit and practice of the craft. Informal relationships among makers seemed to be an important method of sharing new ideas and techniques, as well as soliciting advice, though some makers referred to new tools, such as the YouTube channel, as the best materials. Several times during interviews, I would hear a phone ring in a shop and a maker would patiently explain to the voice at the other end of the line a technique or strategy and then relay to me that so-and-so is making an instrument and often calls up asking for advice.

These mentor relationships were common among makers and were sometimes formalized through the West Virginia Folklife Apprenticeship Program that occasionally partnered makers with students and apprentices. Nevertheless, the community of West Virginia makers is not particularly cohesive. Instrument makers do not tend to have a comprehensive knowledge of makers throughout the state, unless they work in a business or heritage organization targeting instrument makers. They are, however, curious about others' work and making processes, as suggested by violin maker Paolo Marks:

Fig. 1.2. Flute maker John Gallagher in his shop in Elkins, WV

"I talk to a few, but it's really isolating to be here. I guess you could be isolated anywhere, but to be in Cremona or Brooklyn now, where there's a dozen violin makers within ten square miles, there's more possibility to see each other's work. On the Internet, I can see other makers' work. It would be nice to talk to other makers and see what they are doing." When I asked flute maker John Gallagher about his connection to other makers, he responded that his identity as a musician was a great source of connection. He replied, "I guess I am [connected with other makers], but I feel so isolated to tell you the truth, because— I think I would feel more part of the community if I had more interactions. As a community as something active, I don't really feel like a community in that regard. More as a musician than a maker."

This feeling of isolation is not so much a product of the physical environment—although as Paolo pointed out, there is certainly a lower concentration of makers than you might find in a major metropolitan area. Rather, most instrument makers work by themselves in small shops at their homes or nearby their homes, devoting long hours of seclusion to the detailed and messy labor necessary to produce instruments. The shops of makers tend toward intimate spaces, combining personal interests, social spaces, home life, and work life.

Frequently, they will be primarily organized for large machinery in one space and then small machinery and hand tools by a workbench. Wood and other materials are kept stacked and sorted on shelves in the shop on in nearby outbuildings. Varieties of sawdust accumulate in forgotten, fragrant piles, begetting a sense of warm stillness. Other instruments in various states of repair or some just kept as "wall-hangers" compete for visual space with posters of famous musicians and instruments, and a nearby almost-ubiquitous dusty speaker is plugged into a corner. Frequently, these shops are in basements, garages, rooms, or outbuildings, meaning that a visit to a shop is usually a visit to a home. Thus, the private space of a home often becomes a public space, where clients bring instruments to repair or try instruments in progress, friends may come to visit during work, neighbors might ask for help with a tool, musicians might gather to play, dogs wander in and out, and family members poke their heads in for a household query.

This interaction between the private and the public also reflects the role of the work at home and the work done outside the home or shop. Makers are frequently reliant on other household members for necessities such as food preparation and child care, as well as economic necessities such as health insurance, usually taking shape through normative gendered practices. However, because workshops are generally situated in or near the homes, male makers, who make up the overwhelming majority of makers in West Virginia, may also do concurrent household labor while their partners or spouses may be working in wage or salaried positions outside the house, presenting an opportunity to "unmake" gender through work practices and an inversion of the gendered public/private spheres of domestic and waged labor.[21]

On the other hand, workshops are usually situated away from the main house in spaces that divide the work of making instruments from the domestic labor of the household, articulating a separate space not only for the messy work of woodworking but also a physical separation from household labor. I found that visitors, such as potential customers or interviewers, are usually welcomed directly to the shop space rather than the domestic space, reinforcing or even curating such spaces as explicitly gendered and distinct from the labor practices that support them in the larger household setting.

In these spaces, makers work in a range of formal and informal connections in attempting to draw a living from the craft. With no corollaries existing to the owners of production in the nineteenth and early twentieth centuries, there are few exceptions to the lone maker working in their shop to refine their designs and their instruments. Mannette Musical Instruments in Morgantown is operated as an association between steel drum makers rather than a factory enterprise, with the makers sharing workspace and tasks among their areas of expertise. Andrew White, also of Morgantown, had licensed out his designs to be mass-produced by Korea-based company Artec Sound Co., but he still kept a shop to make custom guitars by hand and set up guitars imported to the United States when I visited him in 2014. The financial outlay of materials, machinery, and tools generally leaves the work to those with capital to incur these costs or social capital to borrow, barter, or receive tools, though there are young makers who make do with little in the way of materials and tools other than what is at hand. A few makers fondly described making their first instruments with hand tools in their homes or apartments with few specialized tools or machinery, though they were appreciative of their gradual accumulation of machinery that sped laborious processes and relieved aching backs, arms, and hands.

Very few makers are able to make a livelihood by constructing instruments alone. Almost all makers rely on repair work to fill in the gaps between instruments, embracing the challenges presented by unique repairs or instruments and abiding the everyday repairs required by the living stresses of musical instruments. Often makers will have had another line of work, be retired or semi-retired, or make instruments in addition to their regular work. They may bring skills from other crafts or industrial work, such as guitar maker Bob Thompson and mandolin maker Glenn Cecil, who worked at the Kaiser Aluminum factory in Ravenswood; famed violin maker Harold Hayslett, who worked as a pipe fitter for Union Carbide; and Reed Krack, who worked as a stone carver before transitioning to musical instruments. However, former doctors like Bob Rose of Elkins, policemen like Jim Morris of Hampshire County, and high school teachers such as Don Kwalek of Inwood also took up the craft both as a hobby and to provide ancillary income. A smaller group was long committed to instrument craft, having learned young through schooling and apprenticeship and extended the craft throughout their career, such as Glenn Rowsey of Morgantown and Paolo Marks of Pocahontas County.

The possibilities of *who* is able to practice the craft of instrument making are undergirded by bias inflected by popular representations of makers—that is, largely white, male, and middle-class makers—but also historical labor practices and processes that influence the ability of men to practice the craft and make a livelihood from it. I often found that those who can rely on a safety net through a retirement fund or employed spouses, for example, were likely to be engaged in the craft full time. Others might have to accommodate the work in their spare time or put it off for years. While some makers describe trying to find time to draw the thread of their craft labor as ancillary to their livelihood and cash income, others may resist seeing the craft as labor, preferring to conceptualize it through the social bonds and personal well-being that it instills. The in-depth knowledge needed to practice the craft and the vast assemblage of hand tools, machines, and craft materials required often precludes many would-be makers from practicing in the absence of a family member or close acquaintance with access to basic knowledge and tools. As these productive relationships are influenced by gendered, classed, and racialized social ties to other workers in woodworking-related fields, it can present a major obstacle for those who wish to take up the craft.

With respect to musical instrument makers, inequalities normally manifest through the exclusion or invisibility of women in small-scale production of the craft. Anthropologist Kathryn Dudley points to the performance of American, masculine identities and "whiteness" as a perceived self-reliance in production, making the craft attractive to white, male workers. Meanwhile, echoing trends of the neoliberal employment of women in manufacturing, women are simultaneously employed at higher rates in factory guitar production, where they are paid less than men coworkers, viewed as docile, dependable workers by management, and considered bearers of tradition by factory visitors.[22]

During my fieldwork, I witnessed conversations about these national trends through panels on women in instrument makers at an international guitar-makers convention and an international violin-makers convention. Panelists and speakers pointed to the exclusion of women from mentor relationships, bias against the capabilities of women makers, and the hurdles of employment presented by sexual and gender-based harassment. One guitar maker from the United States told the room that she could no longer share expensive table space at conventions with male colleagues as prospective customers would automatically assume that the man would be the maker and she was only there to support him. The maker also pointed out that the gendered networks that exclude women are worked inversely by women consumers who often seek out women makers with whom they feel a gendered affinity. Nevertheless, as the major demand for such instruments is driven by white men with expendable income, gendered barriers of inclusion certainly present an obstacle for people other than middle-class, white men to make a livelihood through the craft.

The risk inherent in the attempts of instrument makers to derive a livelihood from the affective craft is thus highly contingent on their relation to a social safety net guaranteed by former employers or the state and the potentially disenchanted domestic and external labor of the household, especially that of women. Makers dependent on craft labor as their main source of income, rather than another household member, a retirement or pension, or state support through grants or exposure, respond to risk in different ways. They may have to take on added burdens of dealing in craft materials listed in national and international legal protections, compete with makers who can sell their crafts at the cost of materials, invest more fully in self-promotion through travel and digital presence, and find new ways to access and procure specialized tools. "Branding" oneself becomes a central struggle for many makers who either wish to solely focus on the craft or view such branding as contradictory to the craft practice.[23] Thus, other household members often intervene to do the labor of maintaining websites, Facebook pages, and other branding presences, doing the work of selling the finished craft.[24]

Navigating these uncertainties is not wholly exercised through the craft practice but also through the larger meshworks of political, economic, and social processes that contribute to the livelihood of makers. Gendered labor extends through the craft and into other elements of personal relationships, households, and communities. Makers who have been employed in waged labor may see retirement time as a time to seek out meaningful work, while other members of the household may have to keep up their unpaid household labor in support of the craft, as they may have done for waged labor. In this way, the work can assume a taken-for-granted "flexibility" in practice that is reliant, making the work of others less flexible. In my interviews, it was not uncommon for a maker to tell me that their wife or someone else in the household dealt with the housekeeping as well as the bookkeeping for their instrument business. Craft labor, with its uncertainties and tenuous futures, must often be supported by other kinds of wage and household labor.

Such structural hurdles about the possibilities of starting the practice are compounded by the economic realities of continuing the practice. Competition with imported and domestic factory-made instruments, the maintenance of the business of craft, and the lack of a safety net for craft makers all limit their possibilities. During an interview at the West Virginia String Band Festival, maker Jim Morris explained,

> I think the number-one challenge is if people think they're going to be able to make a living at it, they're probably wrong. Because you're not going to be able to get compensated adequately for the amount of time and care that you put into it. I think most of the people that are happy doing crafts are ones that already have or still have a job and they're able to do this as a fun hobby, something they really love doing. And they sell a few here and sell a

few there just to finance the materials and pay for the materials they used. But I think that if anybody went into it thinking, okay I'm going to start making a bunch of banjos and selling them to make money, then they are in the clouds somewhere, because it's just not going to happen. There's too many cheap banjos coming from other places in the world. And people say, "Why should I pay $500 for that handcrafted banjo when I can pay $150 for one that came from China or came from somewhere else?"

Tish Westman, a dulcimer and bowed psaltery maker, described her years working and traveling to craft shows with a mobile shop that she and her husband could use to replenish their stocks before they could rely on the craft to make a living. "You're not going to have a large clientele that's going to come through and drop two or three hundred dollars on an impulse. So, being aware of what your market is, scheduling your market to fit your needs, and being prepared with the right amount of inventory. I'd say that's a big challenge. We've been doing it for long enough that we know kind of what we're doing. We make a living out of it."

In his shop in Elkins, John Gallagher described the precariousness that comes without any protections for small makers in West Virginia:

> You're really kind of an outsider when you are an instrument maker because most people have careers or jobs. And most people go somewhere to work, either a college or a coal mine or a factory or a business, and somebody is providing them employment, you know. In that situation, I'm providing my own employment and that's more precarious in some ways because there's nobody guaranteeing me a paycheck and I don't have a union to represent me or a company to look out for me, to the extent they do these days, which is not very much.

Particularly, the challenges of running a business or "having to keep track of the taxes and paperwork—all the chores to operate a business," as one guitar maker put it, are difficult to manage given the intensive efforts of the craft. Bob Smakula, an instrument repairer, articulated that the legal side of operating a business was crucial with the challenges of using regulated materials: "You know, I use ebony, rosewood, and a lot of mother of pearl in the restorations I do. And if I was a builder, I would use the same things. And all of a sudden, stuff that was perfectly legal when I started in the seventies, when I thought, 'Yeah, making instruments is going to be a fun way to make my

Fig. 1.3. Maker Tish Westman at a state craft festival

living,' it's now turning into a regulatory nightmare." With a constantly evolving legal and regulatory framework, the legality of practicing the craft can be precarious without a careful attention to and understanding of environmental and shipping regulations.

Despite such hurdles, makers reliably expressed to me that even though the craft was no sure way to make a living, if one could succeed, there would be no better vocation. As Bill Hefner, a guitar maker from Mill Point stated, "I'd like anyone making instruments to know, they got the best job there is." So, what is the drive to continue to "make" for instrument makers? Why do they invest a significant amount of money and time into this work? Why is it "the best job there is"?[25]

Makers speak to the compulsion of the craft, the fact that it "gets in your blood" and sparks an internal drive to continue to create and bring life to the materials they work with. Charged with emotional and affective energy, this compulsion can be a source of inspiration as well as an alienating feeling, as Jim Morris described in our interview:

> The other problem facing a lot of craftsmen is people thinking you're strange or weird; family members won't talk about it, because you're doing something that you feel compelled to do that they don't understand, you know, so they're going to want you to spend less time doing whatever craft you're doing and more family time. That's me talking personally [laughs]. And, if I don't, I feel like something's going to explode up there if I don't get that idea out of my head. And I think anybody that's pretty passionate about what they're doing, probably the reason that they're passionate is the idea is in there and it's burning and they have to do it. Otherwise, you'll go crazier than you already are. And I suspect—I know myself for a fact and [it is true for] a lot of other people—if they never made a penny doing a craft, they would still be doing it. They'd still be making baskets or making furniture or whatever it is they're doing. So the bottom line isn't to think about it as going to a job or as a way to make money. The way to think about it is, here's an idea and I can make this idea come to life. You know, it's like bringing something to life almost. If you want to call an inanimate object alive. I believe there's life in them 'cause it's part of you and part of people's lives, when they play music especially.

Still others describe this drive as a way to fulfill your personal potential.[26] Craft is a practice of self-improvement through continually refining a material form that can always be furthered, worked upon, and maintained. Christopher Zambelli of Beverly, West Virginia, talked about how the practice of instrument craft is innately personal and transformative:

> Well, in a lot of jobs, you sometimes peak out on whatever you are doing, and there's no room for further advancement or whatever, unless you get a

Fig. 1.4. Guitar maker Bill Hefner in his workshop in Mill Point, WV

promotion or something. And you are structured and dictated by that working environment. So, in this business, there's a huge difference in being able to control what you want to do and evolve more so. So yeah, there's much more potential to expand your skills and develop your own potential more so. From that standpoint, it gave me an opportunity to really explore other skills that I have, you know. And you're not confined to certain [things], as far as limiting your potential. Much more, as you well know from your own experience, once you complete that instrument, if it turns out successful there's that connection you've gained. You're a bit more in unison with your potential then, so that becomes more of a personal attachment to your work. Definitely, you are more associated with the outcome and you have more connection with it. And that's the motivating factor for me and most other people who do the work. So it's having that personal involvement and starting something from the beginning to the end, and having that attachment. And sometimes, in some work that you do, you don't see the connection to it. You don't see the outcome; you don't fully see or have the association with the completed [instrument].

This sentiment and drive are also articulated through the music that comes from the completed musical instrument, which embodies a tone specific to a preferred musical style for makers themselves or their clients. While not all makers are musicians, being a musician and part of a practicing community of musicians means that many makers connect their craft to their social relationships, feeling an obligation to create instruments for the people they play with. Pete Hobbie, a banjo and guitar maker from Hampshire County, relayed this sentiment while I interviewed him at a small music festival. As groups of people filtered in and out of the nearby circle of musicians, Pete patiently answered my questions, though I could see his anxiety to join his fellow musicians: "I'm not a businessman as much as I just enjoy the music, you know. That's my main motivator. It's just that my passion for the music has gotten me interested in building my own instruments and that sort of thing. I have instruments out there that I've sold to people I don't know as well, but most of the things I've made stay pretty much in my immediate musical family."

Entrenched in the practice of participatory "jams," where people of varying locales and skills would join together in a seemingly repetitive round of melodic "old-time" music, Pete's drive to continue the craft was about building community and participation in musical acts. Like other persistent, participatory Appalachian musical forms, such as contra dance and shape note song, the jams are spaces that evoke a communitarian tradition of Appalachian music that accepts players of all skill levels and has little in the way of hierarchy. People not familiar to the group are invited to call out tunes, and on one occasion the players in the circle took turns purposefully playing poorly to ease the tension created by playing in front of a group of skilled musicians. I found these highly participatory realms of musical production that rely on common repertoires and repetitive melodies central to the desire for instruments made by West Virginia makers.[27] While some makers do appeal to the wish to own an instrument as a souvenir testament to their experiences in these spaces when they cooperate with tourist spaces, such as the Appalachian String Band Festival, others see their work in these spaces as an extension fulfilling a need for the music community—that is, to have instruments that excel in producing musical tone and connect to local makers. Having an instrument make its way into a jam space is inviting musicians to remark on the instrument, compare their own to it, and potentially request one of their own. Further, the repetitive nature of the music and rote familiarity with the melody provide an ideal ground by which to judge the musical excellence of a particular instrument.

Finally, in concert with these social, personal, and musical motivations are the relationships that makers cultivate and practice with their craft materials and the landscape that surrounds them, a central theme of this book. Knowing all the materials used throughout the entire crafting process—including how they extend to the forest landscape—constitutes a primary concern for many makers. Some learn to monitor trees and forests for potential tonewood, and all learn to know the specific qualities of the range of woods employed in making the acoustic instruments. These are integral parts of the craft and ultimately serve to imbue the craft and the musical instrument with placed significance.

Bob Worth, a dulcimer maker living in Beckley when I interviewed him at his home shop in 2014, described the importance of having a social relationship with the wood that extends from the source to the musician:

> I knew who cut the trees and sawed the trees, so I have a connection there. It's not coming from some outlet, you know, in North Carolina or Texas somewhere, you know. And the closer I can get to where the wood came from, that's important to me. I developed a relationship with [a sawyer] over a number of years. He was always glad that someone had the interest in the wood that he sawed, and he would talk for hours about it. You know, I was—I would want to go up there and get some wood. It was never a five-minute visit. It was a three-hour visit. [laughs] And see, there's that community. There's that human connectedness. And he would love to see the things that I make because where the tree—he knew exactly where the tree came from—Greenbrier County somewhere. Um, so I can tell people that this walnut came from Greenbrier County. And people, people want to know that, and a few occasions, I have made things for people that the wood came from their property. So I know exactly where it came from. And those people know that.

Marty Fair, who practices in Loudon County, Virginia, nearby the West Virginia border, and has shared shop space with West Virginia makers, echoed this sentiment, bringing it even closer to home. Looking out his shop window, he said,

> It's different if you cut down a stump in your yard and it's huge and you whittle something out of it rather than cutting down an acre of Brazilian rain forest and taking a mahogany tree and shipping it over. You want to conserve as much as you can, but it becomes less of an issue. Probably, if you're in Brazil and there's mahogany growing all around, they probably have a similar sort of feeling about it as I would have going out here. I've got

these poplar trees, which I'm thinking one of these days, I'm going to probably start making as many parts as I can out of poplar and, you know, take
one of these trees down every five years. It would probably give me enough.

IN CONTEXT

Touching on music and craft, musical instrument makers fall between two
dominant representations of Appalachian people in American popular culture. As enduring images in the social imaginary of Appalachian culture,
representations of craft labor and music often follow the common Janus-
faced projections of Appalachia in American public thought, representing
Appalachian people and practices as both deprecating images of unemployed
and impoverished "hillbillies" and industrious "mountaineers" exercising
American ideals of moral labor and vaunted traditions.[28] Craft and music are
interrelated with the social construction of a place called Appalachia and a
distinct Appalachian culture, as well as the construction of state and regional
identity in West Virginia.[29] Images and scenes of handcrafted objects and
musical traditions placed generations back in American musical genealogy
fix Appalachian artisans and musicians into categories of "contemporary ancestors" or bygone objects and assert a narrative of an enduring preindustrial culture heritage.[30] Yet as scholarship has shown, Appalachia as a social
construction and the images and sounds of supposed preindustrial craft and
music traditions have roots in enjoining, reacting to, and resisting practices
of industrialization and postindustrialization.[31]

Joining the rich documentary tradition of music and craft of Appalachia,
I think critically about the constructed categories of Appalachian music and
craft while acknowledging their importance to some practitioners as meaningful modes of belonging. Through interviews with makers, I recognized the
contemporary global issues at stake in instrument making while witnessing
the ongoing social roles of music and place in Appalachian communities in
local "jams" and music and craft festivals. Though those that play acoustically
driven music are likely to have played in such jams and experienced this participatory form of music making, not all music groups in Appalachia are this
way. Appalachian music is the historical confluence of various global processes
of migration, displacement, and exploitation that brings musical elements of
Indigenous North America, West Africa, and Western, Central, and Eastern
Europe into a broad stylistic milieu that cannot be defined as the sole inheritance of any particular group of people.[32] Appalachian musicians and instrument makers respond to these historical, global processes through place-based

understandings that sometimes privilege narratives and trajectories of craft and music entrenched in popular visions of Appalachia; for example, highlighting Scotch-Irish elements of music at the expense of other influences. While musicians and player-makers each employ these categories and practice such repertoires, the music is remade through performance that can reinforce stereotypes of Appalachian traditional music as white, timeless, and national patrimony, with little concern to how silenced people may value ideas of tradition or heritage.[33]

Music and the instruments that make it persist as salient themes of cultural heritage and provide a large cultural draw for tourists. The Vandalia Gathering in Charleston, the Augusta Heritage Festival in Elkins, and the Appalachian String Band Festival in Clifftop, West Virginia, are but a few draws for regional, national, and global audiences and participants in instrument and band contests. Instrument makers, as well as other craftspeople, often participate in these events primarily as musicians, but they also embrace the space as a place to connect with clients through repairs and sales of instruments. These music festivals largely promote acoustic string band music that is not solely representative of the state's musical history or active musical practices, yet they draw tourists and visitors seeking what are promoted as authentic Appalachian music experiences, largely read as white, northern European musical traditions.[34]

Yet, musical expression in Appalachia is also a site of contesting exploitative and marginalizing discourses and practices, particularly that of labor. Music has figured heavily in labor movements in Appalachia as both a unifying chorus, such as the famed labor song "Which Side Are You On," and sometimes a lone cry for justice, for example, the work of Sarah Ogan Gunning.[35] From enduring ballads such as "John Henry" to emerging classics like Sturgill Simpson's "Old King Coal," work is a major theme of music in a region where labor practices and their continuing impacts continue to influence the music of Appalachia. West Virginia's telling history of labor movements and power has been a wellspring of musical expression, political consternation, and work patterns since the state's inception in 1863. The mass employment of enslaved labor in Charleston salt mines, abject conditions of certain mining and timber towns, and the resultant armed conflicts between labor unions, private interests, and state military are a few steadfast examples of labor conflict and musical expression in the state.[36]

A less common source of musical inspiration is craft work, another major discursive field in which Appalachian musical instrument makers operate. Quilting, wood carving, weaving, wildcraft, and many other forms have come to stand as symbols for Appalachian culture and people, symbols that often bely the history and diversity of practices on the ground. As historians of Appalachian craft have noted, many distinctly Appalachian craft traditions find their roots not necessarily in hundreds of years of steeped intergenerational practices, but rather in early twentieth-century attempts to develop the area's economy through tourist attraction.[37] This inheritance of cultural tourism intrinsically tied to craft in Appalachia often embraces primitive stereotypes, emphasizes premodernity, and promotes craft traditions in opposition to the modern, (post)industrial culture of the greater Untied States. While this is not uncommon across social groups in the United States, Appalachia has been fixed to function as a "traditional culture" for the wider United States, which continues to inform how Appalachian craftspeople navigate the world and the markets for their products.[38] This inheritance informs how music and craft—and those who practice both at the center of this book—affect the implementation of craftwork and music into the future of Appalachia's economic world.

Successes in projects such as Virginia's Crooked Road, a network that connects sites of musical importance to local businesses and attractions, have spurred an interest in pushing Appalachian musical traditions as a key aspect of experience economy. The Mountain Music Trail, running along U.S. Route 219 through the Allegheny Mountains of Appalachia, is a recent effort that attempts to market Appalachian music, musicians, and venues to prospective tourists. Following suit, a 2015 West Virginia public radio show asked, "Could new twists on traditional music help revive Appalachia's economy?"[39] A 2014 Kentucky government study also promoted music and the craft of musical instrument making as gateways to entrepreneurship in the region, and artisan entrepreneurship has also been promoted by state-sponsored and private nonprofit initiatives in West Virginia, such as the Tamarack Foundation and the Mountain Made Foundation, since the early 1990s.[40]

Inspired by these efforts, the state persists in nominal support for craft and music heritage as economic development. Now, "informal economies" of craft production recalling the aesthetics of past agrarian livelihoods and situated in households are approached by the state as opportunities for economic growth.[41] They persist in encouraging entrepreneurial modes of development that rely less on the underlying meaning of craft work and more on measurable metrics of "job" creation.[42] Craft economic development is normally phrased in two ways: as development for artisan households with ancillary income from the sale of craft to a tourist market and development for the state economy through sales to state-based institutions and related tourist spending in other fields.

When considering economy as larger and less measurable than jobs created, wages produced, and increases in gross domestic product, the revitalization of craft and foodways in West Virginia, as in Appalachia and the United States as a whole, has an important role to play. However, while carrying a great deal of symbolic import, the contributions of craft labor and music are not seen as a real economic development and are normally cast instead as heritage preservation or something that is ancillary to the *real* economic draws of job creation. Craft not in service toward a market enterprise in West Virginia is undervalued and usually couched within an additive bonus for visitors to the state rather than production for West Virginians themselves.

While these perspectives are important to crafters and the state institutions that support them, policies and evaluations based solely in economic knowledge phrased through income often miss the whole picture and distill the experiences of crafters into quantifiable and digestible demographics. These obscure the other kinds of value that craft contributes to the material circumstances and meaning of people's lives, such as craft as spiritual fulfillment, interpersonal relationships, environmental connections, and unalienated work, which I explore throughout this text.

With specific regard to labor, this valorization of work is largely directed at forms of gendered productive labor that have dominated West Virginia, especially the extraction of coal, the timber industry, and agriculture.[43] More recent forms of production like factory work and natural gas extraction do not carry the same symbolic weight but are cast by government officials as the future of a post-coal economy, as compared to other kinds of devalorized labor, especially in settings that do not conform to typical models of economic development. Given anxiety about the decline, tensions arise around what the future of the state's economy will be. Will West Virginia be reliant on corporations and enterprises from outside of the state to provide wages and growth? What role will skilled, craft labor play in the future economy, and how will workers be trained? What will the gendered dynamics of the workforce be? What are the real impacts of tourism on the state's economy and well-being? Can work that relies on an image of West Virginia's primeval, forested mountains coexist with large-scale extraction of clear-cutting and pipelines? Working in West Virginia, I found that such questions were likely to be met with lively conversation and multiple viewpoints in private spaces, while more public spaces gave way to statements of hopeful optimism that belied the complexity of the future. It is in this context of work and music that I encountered many instrument makers in the state in person and in the historical record to learn about their lives, their work, and the social relationships that bring song to seemingly silent matter.

The example above, like that of Chris's warning that the craft and wood will get into your blood, illustrates how the materials of the craft are not simply raw materials ushered into a productive process but an important social element of what compels makers to continue to craft instruments. Through time-intensive interactions with forests—responding themselves to centuries of human interaction—and the wood materials that come from them, maker and material relationships form a core aspect of producing affective meaning in the work of creating musical instruments. Bringing what is largely considered by Western epistemologies to be inert, inanimate commodities stripped of agency—along with their bark and leaves in the case of musical tonewood—to life through song is a process of affectivity and emergent meaning-making.

Instrument craft is a process of affective "re-enchantment" of the materials and agentive work of making musical instruments.[44] Rather than a vestigial holdout of generations of artisans quietly stoking the fire of craft in isolation, the "magic" of making instruments is an attempt to capture what has been lost through generations of disenchanted labor and material environments. The social theorist Max Weber posited that labor and the material world would be continually disenchanted through modern bureaucratic and scientific means toward rational goals.[45] However, in examining instrument craft in this book, I consider the possibilities of coexistent "re-enchantment" of craft, work, labor, and livelihoods through the small-scale practice of this craft. In Appalachia, it is precisely because these attempts occur in the wake of extractive industry and reframing postindustrial futures that we find the attempts to re-enchant labor as so important.[46] In these spaces, the re-enchantment is a meaningful relationship with craft material in tension with commodified material and rationalized labor, rather than the historical persistence or resistance of craft production that may have the propensity to continue to cast people who live in Appalachia into the parochial contexts to which they have often been assigned. In this book, I discuss how re-enchantment exists alongside disenchanting processes, but also how it takes form through navigating the uncertainties and improbabilities of making a musical instrument "sing." Through the next three chapters, I demonstrate how the rediscovery of semi-mythic traditional practices, self-realized scientific practices, and relationships between makers, materials, and environments make the work of makers meaningful and give voice to wooden musical instruments.

CHAPTER 2

CRAFT AT HOME IN THE MOUNTAIN FOREST

As we sat in his shop escaping the summer heat in 2014, electric bass special-ist Roger Morillo and I tacked back and forth from English to Spanish as we talked about the similarities between his home community in the mountains of Táchira State in Andean Venezuela and his more recent home in St. Albans, West Virginia. He drew on his experiences living in mountain environments and attributed the uniqueness of wood craft in the mountains to his impres-sion of the freedom that mountaineers have to create and find meaning from their material environment. "It's the environment and traditions that we have," he said, leaning back into his steel folding chair. "Remember, in the past, these people used to get into the woods. They would build their own house, especially with woodworking. Then they're thinking, 'I'm going to build my own kitchen cabinet' and after that say, 'I'm going to build my own banjo because I want to be happy sitting in the house that I built, on the chair that I already built, playing the instrument that I already built. I made everything by myself.'" For Roger, this was an expression of an essential characteristic of every mountaineer all over the world: "They want to be free."

He extended this connection between material environment and the per-sonality of crafters:

No one instrument plays, and sounds, and looks like another one. I have not found one builder that can build two instruments exactly like the other. Building stuff with your hands makes what you are building unique, because you are working with your hands. Even big factories, they can't guarantee the instruments will be the same because they are using wood. Wood was alive. They change. They have water going through them. And that's what makes wood so powerful to the human being because it was another kind of living creature that you are working with.

This reminded him of a "beautiful phrase" he had read in a book, and he began searching for it in a nearby closet. He returned with the book and thumbed through its pages, finally arriving at the passage. "In Latin it sounds like, '*Viva fui in silvis. Sum dura occisa securi. Dum vixi tacui, Mortua dulce cano*.' It means, 'I was alive in the forest. I was cut by the cruel ax. In life I was silent. In death I sweetly sing.' " He looked up from the book and began speaking animatedly. "Isn't that beautiful? You can make a singing tree. You can make a tree sing. That's the magic! You can make that wood alive from our human perspective. I believe from the tree's perspective, it's awful; but from our own perspective, we say it's beautiful. We treat the wood totally different than anyone treats it. That makes the craft of making musical instruments totally different. Totally. Totally. Totally different."

Fig. 2.1. Roger Morillo in his shop in St. Albans, WV

Roger's thoughts on specific relationships instrument makers create with their mountain forest environments and wood materials resonate across the experience of other makers in West Virginia. While not all suggest that the environment determines a particular outlook on livelihood and connections to forests and trees, most makers acknowledge the unique impacts created by building singing instruments from trees. West Virginia's forest environment enables an indelible impact of forests and timber on the livelihoods and worldview of its inhabitants. Owing to the close work with wood and biography of trees found in its grain patterns and material composition, instrument makers find unique "ways of knowing" the material and the environment from which it emerges. In this chapter, I engage the biography of forests and trees through an environmental history of West Virginia's mountain forests and critically evaluate the relationships that people in the Mountain State have sustained with them over centuries. Providing context of the multiplex ways people have come to know and use forest resources and bridging this context with useful theoretical concepts will inform the search for singing instruments in the practice of the craft detailed in later chapters.

THE FOREST AND TIMBER OF WEST VIRGINIA AND THE ALLEGHENIES

West Virginia is the third most forested state in the United States and has the highest mean elevation east of the Mississippi River, meaning that we find makers surrounded by mountain forest environments, regardless of the physical community in which they are making.[1] The mountain and forest environment is critical to the region's identity and is the source of contestation, negotiation, and imagination. West Virginia's beckoning slogan of "Wild and Wonderful" speaks to this imagination in its romanticizing description, but a closer attention to the history of managing forest ecologies shows a forest both young and manipulated. A tangled mesh of human livelihoods, institutional policies, and ecological processes, the forest environment is a space of competing, coexisting, complementary, and contradictory approaches and logics.[2]

The forest has changed immensely over the past two hundred years. The once plentiful varieties of megafauna have been eradicated, with some species having been reintroduced, such as whitetail deer and black bear. Other species such as beavers, fishers (*Martes pennant*), and river otters have been reintroduced after the destruction of their habitat in the early twentieth century. Trout are now stocked in streams and waterways that were once the spawning grounds of many varieties of native brook trout. Introduced species have effectively eliminated major species, as in the case of the chestnut blight (*Cryphonectria parasitica*) and the more recent emerald ash borer (*Agrilus planipennis*), while plants such as black locust (*Robinia pseudoacacia*), autumn olive (*Elaeagnus umbellate*), and Japanese honeysuckle (*Lonicera japonica*) have remade the floral landscape.

The stories of making instruments that follow in this book take place in forests of the Allegheny Mountains of West Virginia.[3] In these ancient mountains, the forest surrounds. It blankets and contains. Roads, patchy farms and fields on bottomland, some bald peaks (grazing land for cattle, horses put out to pasture, or sheep ewes, pronounced occasionally like the greeting "yo"), clear-cuts, and the occasional strip mine form the occasional breakages in the enveloping forest canopy. Slender trees overlap their branches, split out from blasted rock formations, line the roadsides, and bristle up the mountain slopes. The forest is at once a viewshed to passing motorists, a watershed for eight rivers, a shelter to campers and hikers, a playground to mountain bikers, skiers, kayakers, and climbers, an easement for pipelines, a habitat to a vast array of flora and fauna, a garden and range for foragers and hunters, and a raising crop of timber monitored and harvested on regular cycles.

The Allegheny Mountains stretch roughly from southern West Virginia through midwestern Pennsylvania, with the Allegheny Front forming a physical boundary along the border of Virginia and West Virginia. The mountains flatten into the Allegheny Plateau, which runs through the middle of West Virginia into Ohio, Kentucky, and western Pennsylvania, comprising what the Appalachian Regional Commission refers to as North Central and North Appalachia. The Monongahela National Forest in West Virginia and the George Washington and Thomas Jefferson National Forests in Virginia are an olive sprawl across maps of the Allegheny Front that represent their millions of acres of forest.

Though several counties fall along the Alleghenies in West Virginia, the makers whom I follow in subsequent chapters live and work in what I refer to as the Allegheny Region of West Virginia, which includes Greenbrier, Randolph, and Pocahontas Counties, with these three counties comprising about 3,000 of the state's 24,181 square miles in area. Randolph and Pocahontas are among the most forested counties in the state at 90 and 91 percent respectively, and the more agricultural Greenbrier County is 78 percent forest, similar to the state average.[4] They are all among the least populated counties, and Pocahontas has the lowest population density of any county in West Virginia, with only ten

Fig. 2.2. The forests of the Allegheny Mountains in West Virginia

people per square mile.[5] These counties are demarcated as State Forest Legacy Priority Areas by the state Division of Resources given the high intensity of private timber harvest by small and large companies, the importance to major water systems, and the protection of species of concern.

LISTENING FOR VOICES IN THE FOREST'S PAST

Forests, and the myriad beings and processes that create them, are a central social and economic presence in the area. The variety of constituent beings creates competing interests about the future and use of forest spaces, especially as resources for economic development. In 2016, as I drove to the shop in Randolph County where I was apprenticing with a guitar maker, I passed a large sign proclaiming in red letters, PROTECT YOUR RIGHTS. PROTECT YOUR FUTURE. NO BIRTHPLACE OF RIVERS NATIONAL MONUMENT, illustrating its creator's antipathy for a local effort to designate national forest wilderness land as a national monument. The Birthplace of Rivers movement sought to create a national monument to protect forests and waterways, as well as create opportunities to bolster ecotourism. The movement dwindled during my fieldwork, as its supporters hoped a letter-writing campaign would prompt President Barack Obama to include it in his last additions under the Antiquities Act. Conversely, opposition rallied around perceptions of further intrusion by federal government into the forest, restricting timber economic development and access for hunters.[6] The election of Donald Trump that same year, who promised to restrict land protected under the Antiquities Act, confirmed the sign's demands and defeated the efforts of local water rights activists, environmentalists, and tourism beneficiaries.

These efforts were part of a long-term vision to promote the area's natural and cultural heritage by turning an already protected wilderness area into a more marketable tourist destination. Appealing to nature lovers, musicians, environmental activists, economic development, and hunters and fishers, in their view, they sought to bring the confluence of economic development, heritage, and the mountain forest to the birthplace of rivers. Yet, the issues of the federal government's role in adjudicating local land tenure politics and potentially further regulating the usage of the forest proved to be a difficult sell for many of the county's residents and local politicians. The overlapping layers of forest usage and politics point to the multivalent nature of this forest, where different points of view and ways of knowing the forest, human or otherwise, fundamentally changed how the forest is viewed and used.[7] The history and everyday enactment of myriad interests, practices, and policies comprise a crucial context to understanding the work of instrument makers in the Mountain State and their connections to the materials at hand.

This watershed moment was not the first in which the mountain forests of the Alleghenies and the rivers that feed them intersected with a larger political economic estuary. As eight rivers flow from this birthplace to the Ohio River, Mississippi River, and the Gulf of Mexico, they course down the western slopes of the Eastern Continental Divide. In the "Proclamation of 1763," King George III of England proclaimed that lands west of this ridgeline were to be protected lands for Native Americans (specifically the Haudenosaunee allies of the British in the Seven Years' War) and stripped the promised western land grants from British veterans of that war. However, subsequent treaties and conflicts opened up land throughout what is now West Virginia to Euro-American speculators and settlers, while large enterprises and landholders sought to solidify their claims in the river valleys of the Alleghenies.[8]

Before the arrival of these speculators and settlers, Native American groups, including the Cherokee, Shawnee, Moneton, and Haudenosaunee, among many others, lived in and from the forests. They managed their growth and composition through fire and other means to promote mast trees and passable undergrowth suitable for hunting large game.[9] Yet, the land was more than the "hunting ground" usually ascribed to Native groups, having a political history of contention, competition, and meaning making between and among Native Americans and European settler colonists.[10] With trees far surpassing in number and size those in the increasingly denuded landscapes of Europe and flatlands of the Eastern Seaboard of North America, such forests would have included the large American chestnut (*Castanea dentata*), maples (*Acer* spp.), mast-bearing oaks (*Quercus* spp.), red spruce (*Picea rubens*), pine (*Pinnus* spp.), hickory (*Carya* spp.), eastern hemlock (*Tsuga canadensis*), and beech (*Fagus grandifolia*), as well as a host of other hardwood and softwood species.[11] Mast species provided essential food sources for wild and domesticated fauna, supporting large animals like elk and bison, as well as the burgeoning droves of livestock let loose to forage the forest commons upon colonization by European settlers and those they enslaved.[12] Variations in climate, elevation, and orientation to sunlight created great variation in the local composition of forests. While hardwoods might proliferate at lower altitudes, red spruce prospered at altitude, dominating ridgelines and coves in thick numbers, shading out competitors, and maturing at sixty to ninety feet tall and two to four feet in diameter.

Incapable of seeing the forest lands as inhabited and managed as resources for American Indian communities, eighteenth-century land acquisition enterprises eyed the mountains with a promise of capital gain. The Greenbrier Company, which had surveyed 50,000 acres of forest and flatlands prior to the Proclamation, sponsored tenants to assure their claims to the Greenbrier River Valley, while they lobbied the nascent United States federal government to negotiate treaties with American Indian groups and open land for settlement.[13] In establishing the large land grants, surveyors and tenants used "witness trees" or "corner trees" as monuments to demarcate the lines of property.[14] The "General Andrew Lewis Oak" in Marlinton stood well into the twentieth century, a holdout against the extensive deforestation occurring in the surrounding mountainsides, and other witness trees have been used to calculate the approximate makeup of the forest.[15]

Despite large tracts of absentee ownership, the acquisition and tenure of land was the main goal, so trees were valued as markers, housing, and providers of autumnal mast for free-grazing animals. Local history maintains that a companion of the Lewis Oak, a hollow sycamore, sheltered Stephen Sewell from his friend Jacob Marlin through a dispute as they scouted land in the river valley in the 1750s and established the earliest Euro-American settlements.[16] Local and regional interpretations of this history tend to emphasize personal narratives like these of early settling families in the area over the larger looming presence of massive, corporate landholdings that lay in the hands of private, absentee owners, a practice that continues through to today.[17]

Euro-Americans moving into the area may have harbored mixed feelings toward a forest that provided optimal hunting and foraging, yet also represented a hostile and seemingly impenetrable environment.[18] While turkey, deer, elk, bison, and bear accompanied the forest mast and a great variety of edible forest greens, fruits, and fungi provided supplemental food for people, wolves and mountain lions fed into European conceptions of untamed wilderness that presented danger in addition to opportunity. As the major extensive, extractive economic activity, timbering was an essential aspect of life in the mountains in the eighteenth and nineteenth centuries. Yet it was not until the mechanization of the late twentieth century, with its efficient railroads and sawmills, that industrial timber exploitation reached its apex in the region.

THE TIMBER INDUSTRY IN WEST VIRGINIA

West Virginia, and Appalachia at large, contributed heavily to the rapidly industrializing United States through iron ore, coal, oil, gold, and timber. Estimates suggest that southern Appalachia provided 30–40 percent of all timber products to the United States during this time.[19] Timber companies replaced skidders and railroads with horses and oxen in drawing logs to mills. More labor-intensive pit saws and rail-splitters, as well as large band saws in some sawmills, were used to increase productive capacity. From 1880 until 1920, 30 billion board feet of timber were cut out of the mountains in West Virginia across 8.5 million acres of old-growth forest, accounting for about 85 percent of the state's total forested area.[20] As a single board one inch thick and twelve inches wide, this volume of wood would wrap around the circumference of the earth 227 times.

Large landowners cast the necessity of developing the timber industry as the only way to develop the mountain economies, insisting on the development of railroad infrastructure to bring in consumer commodities and take out timber resources.[21] Companies pitted timber extraction against all other kinds of development and livelihoods, including subsistence agriculture, and encouraged political and economic incentives to support such companies, including limiting the power of small landowners to sue for damages and compelling towns and local governments to buy shares of companies.[22] In debating the development of the land, political discourse situated mountain people as backward and incapable of stewarding the forest, either to justify the development of land by timber interests or its conservation as wilderness.[23] Those who privileged the development of timber resources dominated and pushed logics that assessed the forests primarily through their exchange value as commodities measured in board feet of timber. Land was thus developed for timber extraction, prioritizing extractive infrastructure and technologies such as railroads and skid lines, and diminishing the issues of conservation being addressed in other parts of Appalachia and the United States at the time.[24]

The pace at which forests were rendered into commodities required more workers than local communities could supply, though cash wage labor was a significant draw for local people with increasingly small farm partitions.[25] Waves of immigration into the region fueled the work of cutting trees, while companies heavily recruited workers from other parts of the United States, North America, and Europe. The most skilled laborers were the sawyers and saw sharpeners who commanded the highest daily wages, given the precision and familiarity with materials necessary to complete their work, and companies often recruited these workers, citing the need for the requisite skill.[26] Other jobs would have included drivers, wheelmen, cooks, and the supporting labor of families that enabled timber workers to spend long periods in the forest. The timber industry dominated the region's labor and livelihood, which was by no means isolated from global circulations of labor and migration, as companies recruited southern Europeans in particular to clear and grade mountainsides for railroad tracks. By 1910, 45 percent of Pocahontas County workers worked explicitly in the timber industry.[27]

My ancestors cut their living from the timber in the Alleghenies at this time, working either directly in the industry or in support of it, navigating the everyday patterns of life in the forest at the turn of the twentieth century. Writing from a timber camp in Spruce, West Virginia, in March 1905, my great-great-great-grandfather described the encompassment of social and economic life in the timber industry:

> Dear wife, I will write to you again. I came up here Sat. met several that I know. I could get several jobs besides driving a team. I could get a job on the log train firing or breaking or I could fire the big mill day or night to several other jobs. They work day and night to run two crews of men Sunday Monday to every other day rain or shine. I like the place very well I guess . . . more info here after a while. I did not like Marlinton at all. I would not stay there a month for the entire place. It is a bout 13 miles from here to Cass by the railroad. You just ought to been up here Sunday they had a little

war but no body killed. It was fun to watch there was a bout . . . shots fired in a minute it was between the whites and Italians. The Ital shot once and that was down the road from home. Well I am getting sleepy now and will close with a good night kiss. if I don't mail this tomorrow I will write more tomorrow night. good night wife Floyd.

Such stories show that despite the seemingly monolithic charge through mountain forests for timber, timber camps and communities were places of complex feelings of attachment and detachment to place, negotiations of labor, and active constructions of belonging and race.

My great-great grandfather, Marvin Dunbrack, came of age in this setting, beginning his work in the timber industry by carrying water for a sawmill when he was ten years old in 1907. In an oral history conducted by Robert P. Alexander, a historian of Cass, West Virginia, and the timber industry, he offers an account that demonstrates what laboring in the timber industry looked like to my grandfather:

I asked the mill foreman, of course, they paid two dollars a day for doggin', and slacks were a dollar seventy-five. And I asked the foreman for the job of doggin'. And West said, "Marvin, that's a man's job." And I said, "Well, I'm a boy, but if I do a man's job will you pay a man's wages?" And he said, "Certainly will." So I went on the carriage and went to work there. Now I was on the carriage on my thirteenth birthday. And they gave me two dollars a day and that was a lot of money. Twenty cents an hour."[28]

TONEWOOD IN THE APPALACHIANS

While the timber boom attracted workers like my great-great-grandfather with cash wages and fed the timber and paper pulp markets for the burgeoning industrial and bureaucratic political economy in the United States, the high quality of wood also attracted buyers of specialty woods. In addition to large, durable hardwoods, red spruce from West Virginian forests was highly sought after for its strength and light weight, and it was shipped globally.[29] Large buyers bought directly from timber cutters and mill owners in West Virginia, who established towns around sawmills and paper mills, or they bought through dealers in nearby cities such as Cincinnati and Pittsburgh.[30]

As the forests of the Adirondack Mountains and other northeastern forests were cut over earlier than the Alleghenies (and with them, the northeastern stands of red spruce), the musical instrument industry of the northeastern

United States looked to West Virginia as the next closest source of high-quality timber for musical instrument tonewood—in particular, red spruce. The July 12, 1917, front page of the *Pocahontas Times*, the local newspaper, ran a request stating, "Anyone having good clear quarter sawed spruce suitable for fiddle backs might inquire at this office. We have an inquiry for 60,000 feet." Though this inquiry is strange in that it requests spruce for fiddle backs, which are typically made of maple, the request for 60,000 board feet shows the presence of a heavy demand for instrument wood, as this amount would be capable of producing about 30,000 violin backs when accounting for waste. While I was not able to locate the ambitious source behind this request, the demand for West Virginia red spruce at the height and initial decline of the timber boom is demonstrable through the records of C.F. Martin & Co. and the Gibson Mandolin-Guitar Mfg. Co. Ltd., then and now giants of instrument manufacture in the United States.

Correspondence between C.F. Martin, its customers, and a supplier, the Acme Veneer and Lumber Co. of Cincinnati, shows that they used and were interested in continuing to buy red spruce from West Virginia. A letter dated December 17, 1923, to a customer states that "it is very likely that the soundboard of this instrument is of Appalachian Spruce, probably from West Virginia, which forms the greater part of our supply. . . . We consider it best for all-around use in guitar construction." Earlier correspondence between the company and its suppliers points to the diminishing supply of timber coming from West Virginia due to overharvesting. A January 10, 1923, letter from the company states, "Our source for supply since the Pennsylvania Spruce gave out many years ago has been Cincinnati, which is the market for West Virginia Spruce, but this supply is becoming uncertain and unreliable in quality." In a response dated January 22, 1923, the Acme Veneer and Lumber Company advised that "Spruce logs are very hard to secure and the prospect of getting logs in the near future is not good. Therefore, if you are going to use this Spruce right along we believe it would be well for you to order a quantity of this material."[31]

Gibson, one of C.F. Martin's principal competitors and peers in establishing the trends of American acoustic instruments, also sourced red spruce from West Virginia for their iconic mandolin-family instruments. A Gibson specification sheet from the early twentieth century denotes that the finest quality of spruce, used in their F4 and F5 mandolins, H4 mandolas, and K4 mandocellos, was sourced from West Virginia. Compared to spruce sourced from Oregon, the West Virginia spruce shows their finest grading in grain density, acceptable angle of grain runout, uniformity, clear color, and matching sets. In the case of the Martin and Gibson instruments, the use of the spruce from West Virginia coincided with the exploitation of the forests, but it also set a precedent for the wood to be highly desirable for future instruments, as they used red spruce during their "golden eras" of production.[32] However, as these spruce forests gave out in the early twentieth century, tonewood sources—like all timber production—shifted steadily westward until they finally settled on the coasts of the Pacific Northwest. There, Sitka spruces (*Picea sitchensis*) became and remain the most popular tonewood for guitar tops.[33]

CHANGING FORESTS, CHANGING PEOPLE

With few regulatory protections, the forests were overcut, largely for timber and paper pulp. Without trees to capture heavy rainfall, the region experienced massive flooding, while lightning strikes and train embers sparked remnant slash to burn wildfires that raged across the barren landscape. In 1911, the U.S. Congress authorized the Weeks Act, which gave the federal government the power to buy land to protect headstreams to manage water quality and mitigate flooding. The United States government first bought a 7,200-acre tract of land as the Monongahela Purchase in 1915 and then expanded the area to the Monongahela National Forest in 1920, which gradually expanded to today's 919,000 acres. Through the New Deal and the implementation of the Civilian Conservation Corps, the federal government employed about 55,000 young men to reforest the national forest lands and develop the burgeoning tourism infrastructure. This drive toward economic development, conservation, and recreation was later amended by the Multiple-Use Sustained-Yield Act of 1960, which guaranteed that forest land would be administered equally for outdoor recreation, range, timber, watershed, and fish and wildlife purposes to "best meet the needs of the American people," as well as guaranteeing a sustained yield of renewable resources without "impairment of the productivity of the land."[34] Through various administrations, interpreting and executing these restrictions has changed the face of forest landscapes and the communities that are encapsulated by them.[35]

Dependent on cheap labor, accessible timber stocks, and regular demand for timber, the booms and busts of the timber economy produced a large outmigration from the region in the mid-twentieth century to other areas in West Virginia and surrounding states. In an interview, Pocahontas County arborist Ken Beezely pointed to the abrupt end and short span of this boom: "The region from the Greenbrier [River] in most of Pocahontas County had thirty-two commercial sawmills that were producing millions of board feet a week. By 1939, there were three." Timber companies, sawmills, and manufacturers dependent on cheap timber (such as clothespin and leather factories) closed shop, and many searched for work and opportunity outside of the Alleghenies.

However, this wave of migration was accompanied by a smaller in-migration of urban and suburban young people attempting to re-enchant their livelihoods by seeking an agrarian lifestyle stripped of modern industrial consumption; they were often known as "back-to-the-landers." The Appalachian region at large provided an ideal landscape, with its low property values driven by out-migration and lower economic productivity.[36] These in-migrants sought out local knowledge on the production of the material capacity needed to sustain their imagined livelihoods and leisure from native residents, frequently adopting the material modes of production of music, art, and food craft.[37] These new arrivals were certainly a major force in keeping agricultural, craft, and music lifeways open and alive during out-migrations. Jim Morris, the cigar-box violin maker from Hampshire County, praised this spirit of tradition in an interview at the Appalachian String Band Festival. "Thank goodness for the hippies that came around and were interested in living off the land and were interested in how did they do it back then. And a lot them didn't stick with it, but they wrote it down, and they made notebooks, and they documented it, so that was really important stuff."[38]

A parallel drive to recapture what was lost in the past occurred in some of the highest peaks of West Virginia when guitar makers from Tennessee sought to find red spruce trees. They had heard that Martin and Gibson had used the wood during their "golden ages" and knew that red spruce's light weight and cross-grain stiffness allowed makers to play louder while sustaining optimal tone. With this information in mind, in 1989, guitar maker Ted Davis explored the spruce forests on U.S. Forest Service land, looking for appropriate candidates for tonewood. Inspired by what he encountered, he and John Arnold, another Tennessee guitar maker, began yearly trips to the spruce forests in the Alleghenies, finding trees on public and private land. Throughout the 1990s, they built relationships with local timber companies, marked trees for future use, and began to spread the word about the fantastic tonewood in the mountain forests of West Virginia. Their work helped reintroduce red spruce into the conversation among guitar and violin makers, creating a new trend toward the material with both artisan and industrial producers.

While the forest land has gone through contestations of common defenses that worked to establish wilderness areas and protection against clear-cutting in the Monongahela National Forest, today cutting in national forest land is restricted due to threatened species and changing regulations on timber yield.

Most cutting takes place instead on private land, where few regulations on environment mitigation and yield increase profit margins. The regulations for cutting on private land are primarily concerned with mitigating erosion and water quality, so few regulations exist for which trees are cut and how harvests happen. Signs advertising for the purchase of any standing timber or timberland are common throughout the region. Yet, as land ownership studies have found, timberland ownership is dominated by Timber Investment Management Organizations (TIMOs) that manage forestland on behalf of investors—including large international interests—and timber companies that cut on owned and leased land (West Virginia Public Radio 2010). Managed by foresters with registered forest plans, these lands are free to be harvested in whichever technique is judged most suitable for the parcel of land, including clear-cuts or a selection of harvest methods. The resulting profit-motivated logic generally optimizes harvests of softwood trees cut in thirty-year cycles and hardwood trees in sixty-year cycles, directed toward pulp, veneer, and lumber yields, but not more niche uses, such as instrument making. After private forestlands are cut, they are frequently leased out as hunting grounds for visiting hunters from more urban areas of the state and surrounding states.[39]

CONCEPTUALIZING CONNECTIONS AND CONTRADICTIONS

In making their lives and livelihoods, instrument makers navigate these policies and land tenure practices and witness the histories of the forest through the material of their craft. The place of their craft in the larger economy and ecology of the forest resounds through the everyday relationships and they make with instruments and musicians. For this reason, it is helpful to consider the complex relationships between humans, nonhuman beings, environmental conditions, and political economic systems and structures that give meaning to this work. These forces and actors become overlapping, entangled, and enmeshed in deeply meaningful ways that are not always easily apparent. Anthropologist Tim Ingold's concept of "meshworks" visualizes each person, being, and things as threads that enmesh like a textile or fabric.[40] As one thread pulls, it influences the rest of the social and environmental fabric and inflects changes throughout the system. Enacting different kinds of skills creates different kinds of changes throughout the system. For example, if a logger cuts a maple tree, she would be influencing her immediate meshwork connected to the forest community and economic system of logging. If, however, it is springtime and the loose maple bark is pulled off, as the logger loads her truck, she may realize that the log has "curly" grain and think to send it to a local instrument maker who told her how valuable that wood is to violin makers. Thus, both the tree that shed its bark and the instrument maker would be influencing the choices and actions of the logger.

This active process of connection and relationship building between unique properties of material, the skilled craft practice of humans, and meaningful environments is called "correspondence."[41] Makers, tools, wood, trees, and instruments "co-respond" to one another, "following the forces and flows that bring work to fruition," much in the same way as musicians move together through pieces of music in time and space.[42] The relationship between instrument maker, craft materials, musicians and other makers, and the forests in which they live in this continual process of correspondence does not simply produce "objects"; it creates things that are mutually influential over broad spaces of time and space. Instrument makers must express their craft skill beyond the making of instruments and even the larger context of their livelihood. Their work extends through understanding, negotiating, and navigating material meshworks and their political, economic, and ecological ramifications. Thus, the craft of musical instrument making emerges through relationships among skilled human actors, the qualities of materials, and navigating politicized landscapes and places.[43]

Recent studies of musical instrument making the world over also point to these connections and their impacts on the craft. From *saz* workshops in Turkey to those fitting drum heads to *tablas* in India and carving the bodies of Andean *charangos*, we find instrument crafters making meaning through their work as it extends from their shops into the larger social world.[44] The work of instrument making is much more than bringing song to quieted matter. It involves navigating global exchanges of instruments and materials, national policies and politics, and ever-changing aesthetics for the sound and image of instruments.

The aesthetics of an instrument are fundamentally tied to its sensorial relations with the maker and the person who will ultimately play or possess it. Visually, the colors and patterns of wood, the shapes and lines of the form, ornamental materials, and the polish of the finish draw in the eye and speak out across photographs and online profiles. The smell of the wood and varnish relay the natural chemical composition of the materials and the practices of making, concentrating into a wave of aroma that escapes every time a case is opened. The touch of the instrument shapes and is shaped by the body of the maker, manifesting as the perceived playability of the instrument.

Finally, and perhaps most importantly, musical aesthetics are judged by the instrument's *tone*—a term that encompasses the resonance, sustain, and quality of the instrument across all of the possible sounds it can produce. There are no certain universals in tone, as different kinds of music demand various kinds of musical tone to achieve their goals, and different instruments can only offer the range of their voice. Furthermore, there are not many agreed-upon words to describe the quality of tone, and they are frequently metaphors borrowed from other senses. A guitar may be warm, woody, bright, or sweet, for instance, and those terms may index drastically different qualities.

The aesthetics of musical instruments are thus negotiated across a broad field of desired sensory outcomes and experiences, which are further entangled in the history, governance, and transmission of tradition, the economic realities of making, and ecological conditions that give rise to craft materials. While I have frequently heard makers gloss this complex field with a simple "it looks right," the process through which something comes to look "right" is practiced and remade through making dozens of instruments, playing hundreds of instruments, and listening to thousands of songs. From such musical encounters, deciding on the correct look, sound, and feel of instruments is further refined by traversing meshworks of entangled environmental, economic, and political processes that all lead to a playable instrument.

MATERIALS IN PLACE

As the primary material used in producing acoustic musical instruments, the wood used in the craft greatly influences the tonal quality of the instrument. Rooted in the ground as trees that become musical tonewood, the wood forms sensory and experiential components of "place" that imbue forest and other social spaces with the meaning developed through the craft practice.[45] Unique "ways of knowing" the forest and trees arise from practicing the craft, as Roger Morillo suggested: "We treat the wood totally different than anyone treats it."[46] Through the craft relationship, makers come to know, see, hear, and experience the forest environment in novel ways and build a relationship with a changing forest landscape as a result.

This placed situation of craft production can be key to the success of a craft livelihood in competing with cheaper instruments produced by factory lines and long commodity chains that disassociate the meaning of the place from the final product. Evoking an "aura" of place and handmade process of craft, makers bring themselves, the landscape, and the productive flora and fauna into the final product to appeal to consumers' desire to have a connection to such places and processes through their ownership of a craft instrument.[47]

Global South are particularly vulnerable to overharvest to meet markets for so-called exotic woods. This overharvest is also linked to exploitative labor practices, leading to unsafe environments for both desired tree species and the workers who cut them for global export.[56] Though instrument makers are often quick to point out how little of the wood they require, the entrenched aesthetics of tradition in lutherie often keep makers returning to the same or similar species of their predecessors, feeding a cycle of desire and harvest of threatened trees. Makers can be complicit in the precarious and uneven global movement of craft materials, articulating alternative approaches to the forests at home while relying on damaging extractive forestry abroad. Demand for endangered and threatened species in musical instrument craft—for example, species of rosewood (*Dalberiga* spp.)—creates frictions between desires for materials that are said to be more effective at producing lively instruments and the sacrifice of forest environments in the Global South.[57]

Since the introduction of international regulations under the Convention on the International Trade in Endangered Species (CITES), makers must also navigate several hurdles to obtain such materials. Navigating the legal ramifications of global conventions and national regulations for small-scale makers, competition with large-scale corporate interests and private/public partnerships, and the networks that are mobilized around this resource can have costly impacts on makers' lives and livelihoods.[58] Makers' understandings of the policies, desires, and inequalities that influence international, national, and regional forest political ecologies are crucial to knowing how place and environment influence and give meaning to the work of the makers, as well as how such work may be predicated on the exploitation of workers and forest environments in other places.[59]

Roger's "beautiful phrase" revealed a central contradiction of making musical instruments: the necessity of taking life to make lively song. Yet, attention to the meshworks at play in the "placed" work and global circulation of craft materials shows another contradiction: instrument makers both engage in "ways of knowing" at odds with extractive forestry and must support such extractive practices to make their livelihoods. For many instrument makers in North America, this contradiction is less immediate, as long commodity chains separate them from the sites in which wood is harvested. However, in West Virginia, we find makers in the very forests from which their tonewood can spring, while they are also reliant on global trade of other tonewoods to make their projects come to life. They confront the historical legacy of extractive timber while engaging with its harvests, occasionally following the forms and aesthetics set by enterprises complicit in past devastation while navigating their own landscapes and economies. In the next three chapters, we join makers as they practice in these meshworks and seek to find meaning in the work they give their lives to. By following the processes by which instruments, tonewood, and makers themselves come to be, I explore how makers make sense of the contradictions, meaning, and beauty of their work to find music in material and to make a tree sing.

CHAPTER 3

A RED SPRUCE GUITAR

Christopher Zambelli, who has lived in the Allegheny Mountains of Randolph County all his life, had been making guitars since he was a teenager. Beginning with a guitar and little instruction in a high school wood technology class, he was later driven to try again when a friend gave him a few books on guitar craft in the early 1980s at Davis & Elkins College. While working for the local United States Forest Service (USFS) office and subsequently for the General Service Administration, he continued pursuing the craft as a side project. He kept careful record of the dozens of guitars he had made in a small leather notebook, recording small changes and the resultant tone of the finished instrument in pursuit of the ideal dreadnought-style, steel-string guitar. As he refined the tone of his instruments and explored physical and anatomical principles that guide sound production, he became particularly attached to red spruce tonewood for the soundboards of his instrument. Not only was there a local population of this spruce foresting the peaks of surrounding mountains, the wood had also once fed the C.F. Martin and Gibson companies during their golden years of production, and—as Chris discovered—it had cellular properties that manifested in unique volume and tone in instruments. As components of the mountain forests surrounding his home and the instruments that defined acoustic steel-string guitars and mandolins in the twentieth century, red spruce was an integral part of Chris's craft.

From selecting the tonewood to planning the instrument and through its construction, Chris saw the process of making a musical instrument as labor of personal expression, evoking a re-enchantment of labor through skill in a total process of religious self-expression informed by his Christian faith. He felt that he had been given skill as a woodworker and saw his work as a dutiful expression of that gift. This spiritual commitment was accompanied by en-meshing himself in the relationships with and among materials to realize the project. Each stage in the process reflected Chris's commitment to bringing out ideal tone in the instrument through his skill of working wood and recognizing musical qualities. Comparing this work to the waged labor he had previously done, he said,

> In a lot of jobs, you'll eventually peak out at whatever you are doing, and you are structured and dictated by that working environment. In this busi-ness, there's a huge difference in being able to control what you do, grow with your work, and evolve. There's an opportunity to expand your skills and grow your potential. And not be somewhat confined to limiting your potential. Once you complete your instrument, if it turns out at all success-ful, you'll grow from that, and you're more in unison with your own poten-tial. That becomes more of a personal attachment to your work. You are more associated with the outcome, and that is the motivating factor for me.

After I conducted an interview with Chris in 2015 in which we spoke about the importance of red spruce and his efforts to maintain the affective labor of instrument making, I asked him if I could return as an apprentice to work alongside him in the shop; he agreed, and our work began in August 2016. Since he had recently retired from work with the federal government, he was looking to his established work as guitar maker as a livelihood that would provide income for him and his wife. As his apprentice, I would assist him in making a steel-string acoustic guitar modeled off a 1934 C.F. Martin D-18, modified for the neck to join the body at the twelfth fret. It would be a close rendition of a guitar that Chris had made in consultation with famed American musician and songwriter, Norman Blake. We began work on the guitar in early August 2016, and the project began in earnest with selecting the wood that would be used to create it, as well as processing and sorting Chris's tonewood stock for sale as kits to other guitar makers. The client had a guitar of Chris's at another point but had regretted trading it, so he commissioned an-other. With a deposit for the instrument, he sent along recordings of Norman Blake playing a specific guitar whose tone he wished for Chris to emulate in the guitar.

Fig. 3.1. Chris Zambelli's workshop

Our work took place almost exclusively in Chris's workshop, a five-room structure that he had built on the same property as his house. He started his shop in what was originally a one-room outbuilding and expanded it to accommodate the needs of a guitar shop, such as ample space and ventilation for machinery, storage, and spraying finishes. The entry room had a table covered in finishing supplies, as well as a jig to cut the rosette into the top of a guitar, a rack with clamps of various shapes and sizes, and another table, which Chris generally used to plan out the instrument.

Dozens of guitar tops were leaned under a window on the exterior wall. When Chris sorted through them, he seemed to have a plan for them all. One top might be for a Herringbone D-28, another might be for a dobro, and there were always tops that Chris set aside for personal guitar projects, though he could never find the time to get to them. Frequently as we spoke about one guitar project or another, he would reach for one of the tops, tap it, and listen intently, judging the tone to see if it would be appropriate for the specific tonal requirements of a particular instrument project.

The other room contained some of the large machinery, as well as a table where we assembled the guitar. The third room had a couple of band saws, a bench with a vice, and storage space, holding fine tonewood components and instrument accessories that were not kept in the garage with the other tonewood. Working in this space for three and a half months, Chris taught me the basics of designing and constructing a guitar, often sparking conversations on the meaning of the work, the sound technology of the guitar, and current events and political changes. Sitting on the shop's stools at the end of the workdays or during a break, we occasionally played music on guitars as a reference for tone, and Chris adroitly demonstrated his flat-picking style through the catalog of gospel songs his band had been playing.

At the outset of our work, Chris wrote down each step of the process in a spiral-bound notebook and educated me in the basic principles of sound physics and plant biology that he had found delivered a higher-quality instrument. Reaching for a spruce guitar top blank, he tapped the wood with his knuckle and described the tones that would come out of it. The client wanted a warm tone, so he wanted a lot of overtones that would contribute a "diverse sound." He spoke of overlapping frequencies that gave the warm tone to the wood we would be using. He connected this to the cellular and anatomical structure of red spruce that was unique among the soft woods used for guitar tops. Frequently during our conversations, he would go into the assembly room to his bookshelf and pull books on wood science, engineering technologies, and instrument design. He stressed how sound changes as it travels through the material due to the physical qualities of the wood. Chris called the concept of medium of transfer "pretty amazing" when speaking of the diversity of tones that can be drawn from different woods, suggesting that the density, grain structure, and stability of the different woods used in the bridge and soundboard all drastically influence tone. Through the design and construction of the guitar, I would learn that this self-taught scientific approach to material and tone, spiritual beliefs, and the material relationship to the red spruce and other guitar components contributed to the re-enchantment of labor for Chris.

SELECTING

For Chris, the first step in planning the guitar is to select wood that will yield the tonal qualities that maker and player wish to draw from the instrument. When reproducing known models of guitars, it is a matter of selecting from a specific species wood that has the best material qualities—that is, straight, quarter-cut wood free from defects. However, in other cases, when designing with a more open ended project, Chris and other makers rely on their experience in working with a variety of woods to suggest what kinds of wood will deliver certain kinds of tones. For this project, he had selected mahogany (*Swietenia macrophylla*) for the neck, back, and sides that he had purchased years before from a local wood-processing company. That would leave us with the selection of a board of red spruce for the top or soundboard, which is considered the most crucial piece in creating a lively, singing instrument because it carries the vibrations of the strings through the entire instrument. Going through tops one by one, we pinched each board in the corner, held it up to our ears, and struck it with small felted mallets, listening to the tones and overtones reverberating through the wood. Through repetition of this technique of "tone-tapping," I learned to hold the wood at a node—a stationary point in the sound wave moving through the wood—to not dampen the waves and reveal the full range of tone emanating from the wood. When he tapped the board, Chris would excitedly ask me to listen to a range of tones that I was not able to hear until working in the shop for a couple of months. Though all the spruce guitar tops we went through were already worked up as "blanks," planed down into thin, flat boards, they had started in trees on a mountaintop about a forty-minute drive to the south.

Sorting through tops in the shop, Chris revealed that "it was a *job*" getting the wood out of the forest, inflecting the difficulty of moving the three-foot sections of log through the woods. In 1998, he had been approached by a forester from the USFS about the possibility of removing some old red spruce trees to improve habitat for West Virginia northern flying squirrels (*Glaucomys sabrinus fuscus*) that make their nests in high-elevation spruce forests. Chris was somewhat surprised that the Forest Service would let someone take logs out of what he called old-growth forest that had been overlooked by loggers due to surveyors' error. His surprise was rooted in the presence of such an opportunity in a time period he thought of as particularly restrictive in harvest for the USFS. Knowing that such an opportunity would not come up again, he quickly agreed. However, he found regulations on extracting logs much more difficult than he had expected. Forest regulations prohibited the removal of the logs by machinery to preserve the soil, and there was no road on the national forest land nearby the trees. He hired a logger to professionally cut down the tree to prevent damaging it as it fell, and they worked to slice it into sections that could be carried out by hand. Luckily for them, as Chris described, the land abutted a private tract, owned by what was at the time Plum Creek Timber Company, and it was still crossed with overgrown and rutted logging roads that would permit all-terrain vehicles to remove the logs.[1] Ultimately, they

Fig. 3.2. Chris standing next to a spruce tree

hand-carried the sections fifty yards to the private road, where they loaded it onto ATVs and then onto the truck bound for Chris's shop.

While working, Chris had talked to the forester about the use of the trees and how the project had been approved. The forester explained that the trees were coming to the age where fungus and pests would begin to drastically affect their health, so it was best to cut them for wood if possible. Chris said that while they worked, they heard the logger yell and, fearing he was hurt, rushed over to him. He had not been injured but told them that fungus had rotted much of a recently felled tree, and very little would be able to be cut out of it. As a result, the unused portions and the tree tops would be left on the forest floor, subject to human and nonhuman forces that would return them to the undergrowth.

At his home shop, Chris began work to delay the activity of the same non-human actors that would be breaking down the wood left in the forest. He split the wood up into large wedges known as billets, debarked it, waxed the end grain, and waited about three to four months for it to dry out in his garage. Afterward, he worked to get the wood into "board form" quickly before fungi began to process the cellulose and create blue "stains" in the wood. Such stains draw away from the agreed upon aesthetic clear-grained wood, devaluing the tonewood and any instrument that it is used in. Finally, he would "resaw" the wood into blanks and keep them in plastic bins to interrupt the life cycle of beetles that drill holes through the soft wood.

Parsing through the bins of stacked, book-matched sets, we looked at some of the spruce we would select from for the top of the guitar. The fact that his spruce comes from West Virginia and has a deep temporal connection to the human history of the place is of great importance to Chris. Not only does it sig-nify his personal connection to place and the trees that formed the backbone of the forest that he lived and worked in, but it is connected to the making traditions of the great North American stringed-instrument companies. While selecting wood, Chris acknowledged his personal preference, telling me that based on his averages, the ideal combination of red spruce and Brazilian rose-wood of the old Martins is the "holy grail" because it has a broad range of overtones and suits so many different styles. For Chris, it was "a difference of brightness versus warmness." He said that mahogany gives more bass clarity but has fewer overtones than rosewood, and the preference is perhaps a differ-ence of playing chordal rather than melodic music.

However, for Chris, red spruce was definitely not exaggerated, and perhaps it was not a matter of preference. "You really have to mess up a red spruce guitar to make it not turn out," he said. This is all despite the "fad now of people wanting red spruce" beginning in the 1980s and '90s with a "wave of folks that realized the value of red spruce." He then said that he had a part in the drive back toward Appalachian spruce when he contacted Gibson about using his spruce when they moved to Tennessee in the 1980s.[2] They accepted his offer to send some tops down, and they considered them for their F-5 mandolin production. Gibson, however, decided against buying from him because he could not meet their price point, but he speculated that other suppliers had sold them, because Gibson began to manufacture and market red spruce–topped mandolins once more.

Chris had recognized this shift take place in the larger community of craft instrument makers as well:

> But the people that I talk to—they didn't really know, you know, they just thought, well, you know, spruce in this area for many years was used primarily for housing industry construction. They just were not aware of the value that it was a very unique wood for instruments. But I'd say most of the makers, and especially in the past twenty years, you say this resurgence kicked in and now it's just not only in eastern United States, but it's across the United States, too. Most makers, you can pick up the phone and any really good maker, even on the West Coast, would say, "Yeah, I know red spruce. Yeah. I'm using it, too." Yeah, I guess [it] really caught on in a big way, like a big wave.

After selling red spruce to C.F. Martin, other cutters "started chains" and began marketing the wood to expand their sales. Soon others had started writing articles about the wood and suggesting its use to emulate the prewar guitars. This drive gave Chris concerns about market saturation, and he said that it doesn't seem to make a lot of sense to fully devote himself to the trade. This conversation led him to describe a Martin 1941 D-28 Herringbone that he had seen for sale on eBay with Brazilian rosewood, mahogany, ebony, and red spruce on sale for $65,000. He questioned whether the quality of the wood was much better than his, and he thought better of the quality of red spruce he had harvested.

As we sat at the planning table and chatted, Chris exclaimed, "Guess what they found out about red spruce?" He continued that his friend, an engineering professor at a nearby college, was researching the structure of red spruce and discovered that the "roofs" of the cell frequently collapse and create doughnut-shaped cells in the wood. This gives the wood unique material properties, as this phenomenon occurs more frequently in red spruce than any other type of spruce, Chris explained. However, he mentioned that there were similarities between red spruce and its European and Western American cousins, and that they also made good tonewood for guitars. Drawing these comparisons of local woods and woods situated in a broader international circuit of exchange was a near-daily conversation for us in the shop. We often discussed how local trees might be substituted for the imports demanded by the American steel-string aesthetic tradition due to continued international and national restrictions and a paucity of reliable resources.

Though Chris argued that suitable native alternatives such as white oak, walnut, and cherry existed, they were more often left stacked in the corner, while mahogany and East Indian rosewood were privileged for the projects we worked on while in the shop. Referencing a sale of boards of sassafras to another local maker, Chris said, "That sassafras rang like a bell. We've barely touched on [the use of] local species." Though he had found that customers expect the traditional tonewoods utilized by the trend-setting golden-age instruments, he was seeing a shift to makers accepting North American, sustainable alternatives.

The larger conversation concerning materials and sustainability in the world of guitar building promotes a discourse on the use and procurement of sustainable materials, yet it continues to push large production of instruments using threatened species and lumps together factory producers with small makers as allies, for better or worse.[3] In 2017, I was at a national-level conference with luthiers, and a representative from a large tonewood and instrument company discussed the possibilities for future wood buying. He steered the conversation toward the adoption of alternative woods, while also advising that makers buy as much ebony as possible now, as it would soon be listed on the Appendices of the Convention on the International Trade in Endangered Species (CITES). The Appendices to CITES establish which species should be controlled or outright prohibited in international trade, and they include many traditional guitar tonewoods, a source of great consternation for guitar makers in the United States.[4]

These traditional tonewoods are caught up in international regimes of legality and consumer and producer desire for both the material qualities of the wood and the symbolic gloss of craftsmanship they often carry. Kathryn Dudley suggests that the "ghosts of empire" persist in a market that requires makers to use certain desirable "exotic" woods, yet neoliberal ideologies emphasize holding individuals culpable for possession of woods that may have been acquired before international regulations prohibited their use and international trade.[5] In a craft trade that depends on international marketing, due to the primacy of the American steel-sting guitar in the global music scene and the high prices of these instruments, this can be detrimental to guitar makers who are regulated and fined in the same ways as large corporate producers. For example, when the Gibson Company was raided by the U.S. Fish and Wildlife

Service in 2009, Gibson launched a campaign to get individual craft makers to politically identify with the company as fellow makers and push back on governmental regulation.[6] I found that makers confront the uncertainties of changing policy by stocking up on this wood to resist price changes in the future, as well as to engage in "cannibalizing" other wooden objects made of tonewood-quality species.[7]

Chris frequently mentioned how lucky he was to buy extra materials from large instrument companies in previous decades where the wood was of higher quality or bore distinctive traits that are favored in the market for artisan guitars. We used many parts that had been made in the C.F. Martin Company Factory and sold through their "Guitarmaker's Connection," a retail store that sells used tools and downgraded tonewood, or directly to Chris. Tail blocks, neck blocks, sides, and fingerboards that had come from Martin were common in the shop, waiting to be custom fit to the projects Chris was working on, having been cast away from the uniform necessities of an assembly line. Sometimes, we marveled at how the sides had maintained their shape for over twenty years sitting in the shop, and other times their status as factory rejects was clear, bearing defects or being under the specifications for thickness or width. However, this did not mean that they could not be used.

Factory production requires mass materials at exact specifications, while the craft labor oriented toward a single instrument meant that Chris could use his skill to modify the factory parts to work. Referring to a stack of ebony fingerboards, he joked that "Martin might want these back." They had uniform black coloring that is increasingly hard to come by, but they had been sanded unevenly on the surface in the factory. Within thirty minutes' work on the belt sander, Chris was able to modify the fingerboard to fit his specifications and the customers' expectations.

For other needs, Chris looked to sources of tonewood to repurpose for guitars. While I worked in the shop, he often referenced a guitar he wanted to make with spruce from an old piano. He had stripped off the soundboards, shaped them, and rejoined them into guitar tops. He was looking forward to using tonewood that not only had been aging for so many years but that had musical vibrations and sound waves passing through it that might give it that extra material quality to produce a remarkable instrument. Though Chris was unsure if the piano had been made with red spruce from the region, the fact that it had a prior existence as a musical instrument and a connection to musical tone made it a meaningful addition to his personal guitar project.[8]

These stockpiles of materials collected over years of craft practice reflected a larger anxiety and concern for the future of certain tonewood for Chris and many other guitar makers. Makers are aware of the scarcity of these materials and seek to acquire them when they can, looking for good prices and quality wood through dealers, other makers, or on eBay or other online sources. No guitar shop is complete without shelves or even an entire room filled with stocks of various tonewoods, local and imported. Nevertheless, Chris said that he was looking to move a lot of the material, as he did not think he would end up using it all in his career. He thought that some of the wood might have appreciated about $100 in the fifteen years he had it and wanted to move it along if he was not going to use it himself. He was concerned about using the wood on guitar projects and told me about a friend of his who had died, leaving his tonewood to be undervalued and sold cheaply. He had a plan about what to do with all the wood, and he was working on selling it if he could to other makers, keeping its sonic qualities known through other makers in absence of its wooden voice. However, he also was always looking for a deal of his own and would reluctantly engage in the improvisational give-and-take of buying and selling tonewood, especially as certain materials became harder to come by.

Chris lamented that countries that source traditional exotic tonewoods had no sustainable forestry programs at the times of peak harvest that might have provided protections for the species and the instrument craftspeople who use them. Selecting and caring for the tonewood when beginning the guitar not only speaks to the temporal relationships at play in making an instrument but the greater political ecology of guitar craft and forest resources. Though craft guitar makers comprise a small percentage of woodworkers, critical issues of forest protection versus use of wood materials play out in the craft, where industry production is so tightly ideologically and economically tied into the local craft. Thus, makers like Chris are left to negotiate the localized livelihood practices taking place in their shops not far from their homes through global policy articulated in national laws. He felt that there was inadequate education for and unmeasured responses to regulation of the movement of controlled wood species for both small makers and large companies. Chris said, "You've got to have some level of discernment," expressing concern about the social consequences of heavy fines on small makers that could be potentially doled out by regulators.

While talking about local forest resources, Chris said that "locals want to use the resources of the forest," while "some people who live in urban areas do not understand this way of life and want [the forests] to be preserved." For him, it was an issue of local sovereignty and a failure of people not living within those environments to recognize a needed balance in resource regulation policy. He said that he didn't want to stereotype, but he continued to talk about how some people from some urban areas did not seem to understand how foresters can manage needed resources sustainably, suggesting that perhaps being away from those resources detached urban people from their use.

He pointed to the Amazon rain forest and explained, "They did not have reliable and sustainable forestry guidelines for years and years. Now cattle and agriculture are there, but how can you stop people from making a livelihood? What one person sees as a valuable resource another person may see as destruction of an ecosystem. So the key is to find a balance between the two." He referenced the CITES treaty as an example of an efficacious effort that allowed countries to enforce rules that worked best for them, using an international framework and national policies. However, within the United States, he was uneasy about how climate change regulations might affect materially productive livelihoods and suggested that some policy makers in Washington may not understand that "one shoe does not fit all feet."

Chris had been invited to speak at the World Wood Day Symposium in Washington, D.C., a few years earlier. He said his message was that "wood brings a lot of value into our lives," but some people don't want to see that. There's a special value to having a "personal connection with wood being furniture makers or in the arts," but the key question was "Can we have sustainable forests with our demands?" He said that we need a balance to accommodate overpopulation and overconsumption. When I asked what he thinks of his own consumption of wood products, he responded thoughtfully: "Maybe I overconsume, but the shop is just part of my existence." He saw the collection of wood as a necessary part of ensuring the material and financial circumstances of his craft and livelihood in the future. Having such a collection of wood was an investment in his ability to provide for future customers and diversify his business in selling tonewood if the need arose.

BUILDING

Although the general stockpile of wood had been selected, it still remained for us to find that specific piece of spruce that would be the top of the instrument to match the mahogany neck, backs, and sides Chris had already chosen. In each of the blanks that he had cut years before, we looked for "in-check," where evaporating water escapes too quickly and ruptures the fibers, creating cracks in the wood. Wax along the edges keeps the water in longer and makes the wood take longer to dry as the moisture is forced to evaporate from the face of the wood rather than the ends. Chris told me that the lines of the cells are "kind of like a pipeline," evoking an image in my mind of the pipeline in the works in the region and how residents were voicing their concerns about how liquid would move through that medium.

As we looked over the potential candidates, Chris talked about how the strength-to-weight ratio of red spruce was one of the characteristics that made it an ideal tonewood. Its relative lightness requires less energy to vibrate the top and project sound. As he flexed the wood between his hands, he also demonstrated how its relative cross-grain strength would handle the stress of the string tension that would pull on the thin wood. Drawing a finger across the minute ridges on the surface of the wood, he explained the difference between springwood and summerwood in the grain. Springwood (the lighter rings) has a larger diameter with thin cell walls, and summerwood has a smaller diameter with thick cell walls. A wider grain with more springwood will give you a better bass response, he explained, but customers often use the density of the summerwood as a gloss for the quality of the wood.

Regardless of grain density, all tonewood should be quarter-cut, Chris added. By cutting the log radially into "pie sections," the maker can best capitalize on the strength of the fibers by keeping them whole and in line. The wood must also have minimal runout, where the grain is not exactly straight and flush through the piece, he explained, as he demonstrated how the wood splits evenly when broken with a piece of scrap. Finally, we checked for "ripple," or lateral movement in the grain, to make sure that sides would be equal and straight.

From wood that met these properties, we planed a few tops to the approximate thickness to see which one would make the top of our D-18–style guitar.[9] Pushing them through the contractor's planer in his garage left us covered in downy spruce dust and revealed some dark stains inside the wood—a period of stress in the growth of the tree—and very dark brown lines in the rings of the grain where sap had been trapped. As Chris looked at the two pieces of wood, turning them over to evaluate which side would be better up, he reiterated the importance of the bookmatch to meet the expectations of what a guitar top should look like. He said, "I really enjoy this part, laying out the wood and seeing the relationships between the patterns." He flipped the pattern around and around on the wood, looking for the place that would avoid the major flaws in the visible part of the guitar top. The most important aspect was to keep the straight edge of the pattern in line with the grain. When Chris cut the wood, the straight edge followed the grain perfectly, demonstrating how straight the tree had grown.

Chris was pleased with this set of tonewood, which had been cut about twenty years before, saying that the aging had seasoned the fibers, stretched out the wood, and made better tone. "Older instruments have a peak," he told me, alluding to the "golden age" instruments that he said are peaking in tone right now at fifty to seventy years. Thinking through the "natural process of wood" developing and maturing as it ages, even once it is in a guitar, it is a crucial aspect of the planning for Chris. "Some people might not care about the state of their guitars in fifty or sixty years," he said. But he was concerned with how the tonewood would age beyond his shop and continue to season, reminding me of his conversations with the forester about the lifespan and harvest of a tree. If an instrument also has peak liveliness before a gradual decline like a tree, the process is opened once more for further material production of new guitars and guitar parts. As I would find looking through old guitars with Chris, many had tops that had been replaced or augmented over the years, though they still retained considerable monetary value.

Chris enjoyed this process of selection, though it also frustrated him as a guitar maker and occasionally seller of tonewood. He felt that the demands on visual aesthetics were too stringent and drove unrealistic expectations of the natural medium. He talked about the small variations in color on the surface of the wood and asserted that "people get too hung up on the wood" and that "as wood [has] dwindled away, you have less to choose from, [and] you have to accept slight cosmetic variation." Tops of guitars "are individual interpretations, like paintings," and different people will have different views. With red spruce, "it's the nature of the beast" to have small defects and discolorations, so in considering the aesthetics of perfect wood in guitars, it's "not realistic to look at it in that kind of way."

I asked him if he classifies his wood into different categories and, if so, which class this one would belong to, having seen labels of "economy" on some pieces of wood in the shop. He said yes, and that the classes are cosmetic. His range runs A, AA, AAA, AAAA, and Master Grade. He considered that the piece of wood we were working with would be Master Grade except for the fact that it had some compression where the wood had grown quickly, but that was purely a cosmetic issue. Wishing to demonstrate this, he then picked up the wood between his forefinger and thumb and began to tap it with a felt tone mallet, listening for "mid, low, high end tones" and trying to measure "how much energy it takes to get a response." He handed the tool and wood to me, and I tried to get a sound, blindly mimicking Chris's mallet strikes. After some adjustment, I started to hear a range of tones, and Chris asked which one I preferred. I found that I could not parse out the individual frequencies, but after several more strikes my ears settled on a midrange tone that seemed to be particularly resonant. Chris decided to use that piece and put it on the planning table where he had stacked a series of patterns for the instrument.

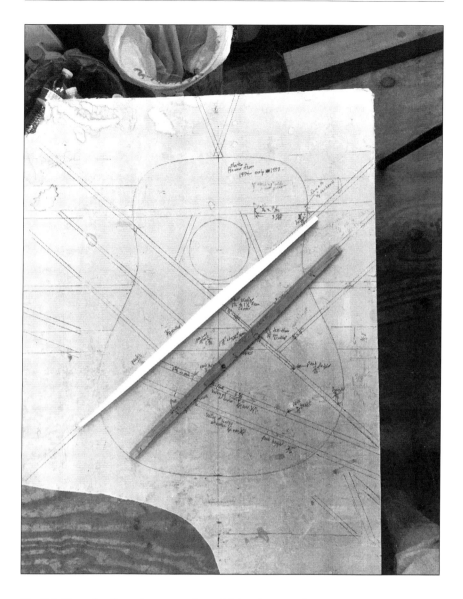

Fig. 3.3. Plans for the red spruce guitar with bracing templates

With a top selected along with its potential tonal properties, the next stage was to plan the instrument from a set of specifications that Chris had created, inspired by Martin's model with his own modifications. This was a process of assessing material correspondence: knowing how materials will work and respond to tooling and construction, checking, constantly transforming pieces to keep them fitting together, and ensuring the scaffolding of producing musical tone. Joining the two pieces of the top and back in a bookmatched joint would be a crucial measure of this correspondence and the future of the instrument, as the failure of these joints could be catastrophic for the future liveliness of the instrument. With this in mind, Chris had designed a clamping jig that would assure even pressure in the joint as the glue dried. However, before gluing, we had to make sure the edges of the joint that would run through the middle of the back and top were perfectly flat and flush to maximize surface contact and minimize the probability of wood moving in the joint.

In this process, Chris taught me to rely on materials and environment as indicators, or points of correspondence with the wood, through the task. He positioned the pieces on the table—placing one piece slightly offset beneath the other—and checked it with a long level to attempt to see if the line was straight and flat through its whole length. As the mahogany for the back was not flat, Chris showed me how to use the level with sandpaper glued to its flat edge and sand the mahogany joint flat. He assured me that checking the sandpaper for an unbroken line of sawdust and evenly piled dust on the edge of the wood would show me when it was done. I found it challenging to apply pressure evenly with two hands against the edge of the wood, but soon the red sawdust began to pile up in the peaks of the minimally undulating edge.

As I attempted to get the material level, I gave the pieces to Chris to get him to judge whether I had, and he showed me that light could be used as a secondary indicator for the flushness of the joint. Holding the two pieces together and up to the light, he told me if any passed through the joint, then it was not perfectly flush. As I awkwardly clattered the boards together in the attempt to hold the joint flush and up to the light, we could not fully decide whether one spot was flush. So, we turned to the third material test by placing the pieces in the gluing jig and tightening them with wedges and clamps that held the boards down and together. We could see the slightest of gaps, so I returned to the table and worked the level back and forth on the piece, beginning to feel the arduous nature of this task. I continued for another thirty or forty-five minutes until I felt that the joint was ready and it fit snugly with no light passing through. When Chris asked if was learning anything, I told him that I was surprised how long it can take to do the simple introductory tasks. He responded that the patience necessary in instrument craft was the quality that most creates an instrument maker.

With the spruce top, Chris first pushed it across the rotating blades of the shop jointer, which cut an almost perfect joint. I replicated the process of

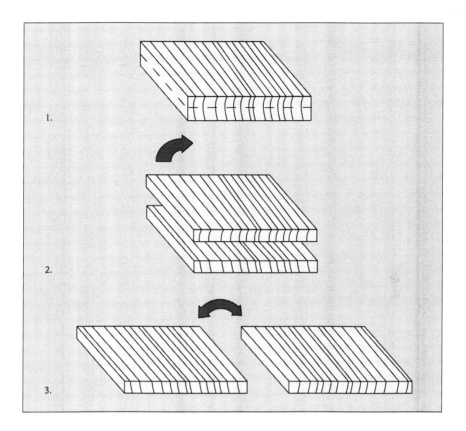

Fig. 3.4. The process of "bookmatching" a set of wood

clamping and checking with the level, but I had to do very little work with the sandpaper-covered level to get the joint right. When I held it up to the light, the joint was almost perfect. This contrasted to a rosewood back with which I had also practiced. After working on the matched rosewood planks over thirty minutes, it appeared that it was still not flush, and in fact it was becoming worse. The red dust piled up on the middle, but its pleasant fragrance was not a consolation for the tedium. Chris chided that I should keep up, as patience was required in guitar craft, but after my shoulders began to burn from the lateral motion and my back began to ache from bending over the card table, I asked Chris if it might be better to run it over the jointer again. He did it, and the joint came out almost perfect.

We then glued the center joints on both the mahogany back and the spruce top with a jig. Clamps pressed the center of the pieces down so they would not buckle as we tapped wedges into the edges to bring the joint tight. The relatively long working time of the wood glue we were using allowed us to adjust the wood and bring it perfectly together, as well as clean the joint with wet rags so that no glue would show dried onto the surface of the back or top. When we removed the pieces from the back, I worked to sand off any glue that we had missed in cleaning, and Chris tone-tapped the wood, producing a clear tone and a satisfactory result.

The sound-productive qualities of the top and back are greatly diminished without signature braces, which make the D-18 and carry its sound throughout the instrument. Turning to the task of roughing them out, Chris understood that they should all be made in comparison, so he pulled out a pattern for the D-18 top with all the braces and measurements traced out in ink. The pattern was written on heavy-gauge cardboard that was torn off in one corner, but the ink copy of a 1934–1939 modeled Martin dreadnought was neat and without errors. Neatly crossing the top with angular extensions recalling a Germanic rune, the braces are normally considered the most important design aspect of drawing out tone. Chris emphasized that they allow for strength and flexibility, and that they are crafted to enable desired sound waves to carry through the entire instrument. Having all the curvature in the braces smooth and flush would allow the "top to work as a complete unit."

While sighting down the thin strips of spruce that were going to be repurposed into the cross braces, he said that we would use the tight grain pieces for the treble side and the wider grain for the bass, as they would permit different kinds of sound waves through them. He tried tone-tapping both, and we both heard higher and lower pitched knocks reverberate through the wood. Chris said, "You can learn a lot by just tapping on your braces," and continued to knock on them to chase out the sounds he wanted. He was looking for the potential sound in it and how it would be shaped, as the braces have a slight curvature to them that pushes the top into a convex shape that keeps it stable and strong with the stress of the strings.

After tracing his patterns on the brace, he showed me how to sand down to the curvature and gave me the rest of the pieces to copy his method. Following his instruction, I rocked the piece back and forth on the belt sander, bringing the spruce down to the line and checking it for squareness and straightness as I went. Besides constantly sighting down the wood and checking it with the square, Chris showed me the other way to check the bout was to put it on a flat table and wobble it to feel whether it was running down the bout flat and even or twisted to one side or the other.[10] He prompted me to try, saying, "Feel that to see how it moves." I took the wood and rocked it back and forth, feeling the flat plane of the curved surface and imagining the contact it would have with the back when we glued it on.

Although machine work offers considerable expediency in some steps of the craft, the commitments of time to the machinery can sometimes offset their cost savings. To be an instrument maker, one must also be a mechanic to fix the machines. Belts and blades need to be changed regularly, and machines exposed to years of sawdust, oil, and heat inevitably fail. There were several times in making the constituent pieces that the belt sander or band saw would break down, giving a slight shudder or knock before requiring a repair that might take the better part of an afternoon. In reinstalling a blade or belt, knowledge of tuning mechanics is absolutely necessary to continue the process. However, maintaining and repairing machines also gives makers a corporeal knowledge of how the tool functions: feeling, hearing, and smelling the transforming material through the machine.

Once the curvature was established, we laid out all the braces and glued them into place with a series of clamps. Some had to be fitted into others snugly to allow them to work together as a unit, so they took some working with a small saw and chisel—as well as many pencil reference marks. The back braces also had a strip through the center to add strength to the center joint and give Chris a place to affix his brand on the center, in a similar fashion as the higher-end Martin guitars.

We constantly referred back to the other components that were clamped together inside an external mold: the sides and the neck and tail blocks. The tail block had come directly from Martin, and Chris had made the neck block and blank from mahogany based on a Martin design. Nearby our working table, a couple of patterns for neck profiles sat next to a large block of mahogany where he had stenciled out two necks to be cut from the one block, heel to head. Chris showed me how to cut the blocks and how we would sand them to fit into the curvature of the sides and back of the guitar. To dovetail the neck blank into the neck block, we attached angled patterns to the pieces with double-sided tape and pushed them through a table saw. These pieces created an angled cut as Chris pushed the blanks along the straight fence of the table saw, assuring that the dovetail joint would be the best fit.

Chris had sides that were already bent, but we practiced on two other sets for future projects on the heated brass pipe he had clamped to a work bench. As he bent, Chris said, "It's definitely an art of trying to bend wood. It's a specialty. Some people tend to have a knack with it. Other people struggle with it. Sometimes it's just experience." At about an hour in, it began to become clear how difficult this process can be, as "one place it bends and another place it changes" with the rosewood that he was trying to bring back to a serpentine curvature. Referring to his heated bending jigs, Chris said, "Now you can see why you build your bender, as it gets time consuming." We tried it in the mold and had to cut new shoes and use clamps to get it to fit into the mold. Ultimately, Chris used a wet rag, a heat gun, and his mantra of "one more time" many times to get the side to stay sure through the whole mold. I got a little frustrated with the process, and I thought maybe that's the part some people don't get about the work. Chris said, "I'll bet you never thought we were going to finish bending that wood," and he told me about how hard it is to work with the rosewood: "You're putting wood into another state," and it resists by going back into its "natural state."

We took an hour getting the sides of the guitar straight to get it ready to attach the neck block. Chris iterated, "It's being contrary," or "Wood is wood," or "When you bend it, it isn't always predictable," as we continually adjusted and flipped the mold onto its side to see if the "hills" or bouts of the sides were running parallel to one another. Once we found the spot with some ripple in it, he suggested that we should use an L-shaped piece to correct the ripple when the top is glued on. We then spent another hour flipping the mold over and over in order to get the neck block set into place like we had done with the tail block. After cleaning and brushing the glue on, we clamped it tightly onto the sides pushed against the mold.

With bracing attached to the top and back and the sides awaiting in the mold, the skill of working pieces down from their rough states to finished component laid before us. Working with hand tools and machines, this reductive process is a "meshwork" of skill, manipulating the material qualities of the wood with those of the tools and machines. This largely rests on embodied skill that is extended through machines and tools and a relational materiality rooted in continued practice and exercised through points of correspondence. In Chris's shop, I joked that pencils, pencil erasers, and blue masking tape were among the most important tools as they created the basis for the corresponding marks, effectively making the correspondence a material phenomenon. '

Success at quickly shaping and assembling the material components is reliant on the combination of embodied skill and measuring material correspondence. For example, finding midpoints is a crucial aspect of designing and building guitars, as the generally symmetrical guitar is largely based around a midpoint that runs through the length of the instrument. When preparing the curvature of the tail block of the guitar, Chris had asked me to find its center. I fumbled around with a micrometer, trying to do some mental math, and he interrupted me to ask if he could show me something. A skill that he learned from an old banjo maker, he told me, was to get good at eyeballing the center of things. He held the block near and far from his gaze and then made a quick strike with the pencil lead, saying, "That looks about halfway to me." Once he measured it, it was indeed halfway between. While I often would have to measure many times, Chris's "eyeballing" of measurements was often spot-on, a measure in itself of his long practice.

As we worked to finish the fine-tuning of the top by sanding the spruce board and scalloping the braces, he said, "You're probably getting pretty bored, aren't you?" Getting the spruce top and mahogany back down to the appropriate thickness and removing pencil marks and stubborn streaks of glue was tedious work, but seeing the pieces start to assemble produced a noticeable excitement in both of us. After we had cut them out to within an eighth of an inch of their outline and installed the rosette around the precut sound hole, we were ready to tune the bracing for the back and top. Taking the back, Chris tapped it a few times and commented, "Listen to that come to life." Pleased with the outcome, he would work on bringing the bars down a little with the finger plane in order to do the preliminary tuning. As the back braces are largely structural, the more intense and skilled effort goes into tuning the top braces.

With all the braces brought down to the dimensions documented in the plan, he used a chisel, a finger plane, and a small sanding block to "scallop" the braces and tune the top. This process removes weight from the braces, letting them vibrate more freely while not negatively affecting their structural strength. Chris asked me, "Did you ever take physics?" and then began speaking about how the sound waves move through the media of the guitar top and how the bracing impacts the possible range of overtones. The scalloped bracing contours provide strength yet "unstiffen" the braces to achieve flexibility that bass waves need in order to set wood into motion. Chris explained that "scalloping in theory provides more flexing for the wood," which gives a wider array of overtones. When I asked why it is more important to have more overtones, he suggested that it makes the sound more pleasant and "woodier," giving it a warmer tone.

He checked the dimensions against notes in a small leather-bound journal from 1984, his record of twenty years of guitar craft. While the models might be the same, he said, you have to think through every guitar top individually because its stiffness will change the resultant tone. He then tapped on the tone plate, a brace through the middle of the top and over the tone bars that run into the bass side of the instrument. Chris said that adding the bracing had pushed the tone up a "notch," as it typically does. Before gluing the bracing, the needle on the electronic tuner had read "A"—which Chris had written

Fig. 3.5. Chris fine-tuning the internal bracing of the guitar top

on the top—and then it moved to "B♭" when the bracing was put on. He tried different angles, different distances, and different tuners to try to assess the range of overtones that the top might produce. At first, I could hear only the principal tone, and I was skeptical that the overtones could be observed and manipulated. After about ten minutes of tone-tapping the top, however, I began to hear a very high pitched overtone that I had not noticed earlier. As I noted earlier, this was a turning point in my understanding of how the musical tone and knowledge of the materials relate to a specific bodily disposition that allows makers to clarify and refine musical tone.

With the braces attached and preliminarily tuned, we were ready to begin assembling the guitar box or body. We had the sides and blocks in place, dove-tailed the neck and neck block, planed down the sides and tops, sanded everything to thickness, cut the sound hole and inlaid a rosette around it, and we were ready to take it to the next stage. While maintaining material correspondence through measuring and marking pieces in this stage was crucial, errors were easily corrected by making new pieces or modifying the process slightly.

However, in the assembly, the composition of the adhesive demands practiced precision and control to bring the instrument into its recognizable form.

ASSEMBLING

Bringing together different types of materials into specific forms requires the mitigation of uncertainty and risk in the shop to bring the materials into the form of a musical instrument. It is at this point that many of the uncertainties of materiality manifest, as pieces are fixed into position and more or less guaranteed to be part of the form. Bringing together the different kinds of wood with hide glue requires that the maker have knowledge of how the materials respond to the environment of the shop, to each other, and to the movements and pressures of the maker and tools. The various types of wood that have been cut in myriad ways have qualities that respond differently depending on humidity, and the hide glue that Chris insisted on using has a short working time before it "gels up" and will not make a strong joint. The constructive phase, therefore, requires mitigating many uncertainties expressed through material agencies to produce the beginning of the three-dimensional form and the singing qualities of an instrument.

The repetition of these processes fixes makers to specific kinds of activities and practices to assure success in what is a very uncertain process. While I sanded the top, for example, Chris got the tail block in shape for gluing, and I joined him in the assembly room to put it all together. Working within the external mold of the guitar, we made sure that the sides were pressed evenly against the walls and did a "dry run" with the six clamps and to make sure that everything would fit in smoothly and squarely. Chris had cut a couple of pieces to specifically fit in the curvature, and the clamps each had its own place and purpose. We checked all the edges with a paint knife to make sure they were pulled in tight and began to prepare the wood for gluing. After scrubbing the block and sides with alcohol to ensure that no remaining sawdust could ruin the stability of the joint, we heated it, brushed it with hot hide glue, and fixed the clamps in the order we had taken them off. However, the bottom clamp was not tight enough, and the bottom came slightly undone. Afterwards, Chris blamed it on the humidity and assured himself that it would end up coming out alright, as we could reclamp it, and it was largely wood that would be cut away in a later step. After so much practice and planning, Chris found it slightly frustrating that the wood had come undone. He said that he had friends who had tried this kind of thing, but they would not have had the patience to persevere through so many hours of work. After we were sure the block would not come undone, we left it for the night to set and harden.

Though he had blamed the humidity, Chris did not seem to mind the atmosphere of the shop as much as managing the interrelationships between components up to this point. I noticed that even though there were temperature and humidity readings in the shop, Chris did not seem to pay much attention to them, opening doors and windows as he pleased or sometimes letting it get sweltering hot, to the point that he would drip sweat onto the guitar and have to spend time cleaning it off. However, one day as I was leaving, he made a point to tell me that the humidity would be just right—between 40 and 45 percent relative humidity—which would provide a good average to put together the body and minimize the impact of fluctuation in the future.

As summer gave way to autumn in the mountains, the weather became a cause of consternation. Outside the shop, the clouds and incoming rainstorms showed that the seasons and the weather were changing. Chris worried that fluctuations in humidity could drastically change the dimensions of the wood, which would make the guitar body unstable when put together. Chris told me that the lower humidity that came with fall weather would be better because guitar expansion is not as bad as contraction in stressing the joints. But he added, "I've had bad experiences when the weather began to shift," as the daily changes in precipitation and temperature greatly affected the atmosphere within the shop.

Managing the construction of an instrument also requires managing and existing within different scales of time, from years and seasons to seconds and minutes. Though the wood ages for years and changes with seasonal shifts, the hide glue that Chris insisted on using can be worked with for only a few quick minutes before it becomes ineffective. As a result, Chris showed some anxiety in doing the process quickly, and he always insisted on doing a few "dry runs" first. After the glue was applied, there were only a couple of minutes of "open time" where the pieces could be adjusted and clamped into place before it began to change chemically and "gel up." If it were to gel, it would make a very weak joint because the glue would not chemically bond with the wood properly. To avoid this, Chris used techniques to expand his working time to affect the material. He kept the glue warm and liquid in a hot pot, and he would also use a heat gun to warm the wood first to allow for more working time. We did this when gluing in the blocks, strips of spruce for additional support, and the kerfing that runs along the sides to provide a larger surface area to fix the back and top on.

Gluing in the strips with hide glue was a particularly salient example of Chris's attempts to manage the ultimately uncontrollable. He would keep the glue in the refrigerator to stymie the growth of bacteria before heating in the pot, attempting to control its material phase in the crucial instant of joining. Furthermore, the strips we glued in did not provide an intentional function of sound or support; instead, they served as stopgaps in the event of a crack in the side. If the side were to crack due to environmental change or mistreatment, it would be fixed by the small strip on the inside of the instrument, which would be chemically bonded through the glue to the side.

Named after the kerfs, or partial cuts along the lining that allow it to be bent, kerfing is generally made of Spanish cedar and is one element that guitar makers often elect to buy rather than make to save time. We installed it in lengths at a time, clamping our progress in place, to accommodate the short time frame of the hide glue. As with the gluing of the braces, we used a heat gun to heat the wood and quickly brushed the glue from a hot glue pot so that it would remain clear and liquid, ensuring a tight joint once clamped down. The scent of the Spanish cedar dominated the shop in these times, as the hot air lifted the distinctive smell out of the wood and into the shop air. Afterwards, I used a finger plane and a sanding block to bring the kerfing level to the sides, while accommodating the curvature of the back. The Spanish cedar came off easily, as I brought it down to the level of the mahogany sides and cleared the hardened drips of glue. Removing glue drips is a crucial aesthetic step, and it is a "sign of the quality craftsmanship to be clear of glue," as Chris told me. Although the material came off quickly, it also created a lot of dust that itched on my arms and made me sneeze, causing me to retrieve my respirator before I could finish the task.

The uncertainty of success was palpable when attaching the back and top to the sides, a process that would effectively "close" the box and make adjustments to the interior of the guitar much more difficult. Chris was definitely anxious about the process, which essentially could only be done once, so it required patience and precision. We mounted the body of the instrument into a large clamping jig and practiced screwing down the clamps several times before we could glue the top on. A wooden ring in the shape of the edge of the guitar body went between the clamps' jaws and the body, and we further added pressure by tapping edges into the spaces where the top was not closing completely. We placed the wedges along the mold, exactly where we would need them when we glued. Despite the heat of the end of the summer, Chris brought a gas heater into the shop to heat the room to 104 degrees Fahrenheit (40 degrees C) to give us more time to work with the hide glue.

Furthermore, as Chris described, this was the process by which Martin had made so many guitars in their glue room in the early twentieth century. Highly skilled workers would heat the wood pieces on the large radiators before assembling the guitars that would come to dominate the world's vision of acoustic guitars. With the gas heater blowing, the temperature rose along with the stress through the rest of the constructive process. While we ran the dry clamping, screwing down the jaws and tapping in wedges, Chris kept an eye the humidity; it never went above 49 percent during the day. Perhaps assuming that I thought the process was excessive, Chris warned, "You might try to predict what will happen, but this part is what makes the guitar." He explained that if you can keep the humidity constant when bringing all the components together in their fixed form, you can mitigate fluctuations that would damage the assembled instrument.

Sweat dripped down our faces in the increasingly hot room, and the smell of the gas heater mixed with the smell of the Spanish cedar and mahogany as we quickly heated the gluing surface on the sides. We each took a brush and quickly spread the glue into a thin layer across the surface. We lined the top up on the sides with small pins we had drilled into the neck block and worked hurriedly to bring the jaws of the clamps down and tap the wedges into place. Now, with the top and sides held into place in the clamping jig for a snug fit, glue squeezed out of the sides of guitar, and Chris and I used rags wrapped around flathead screwdrivers to scrape up the gelled glue. Once we finished, Chris was noticeably less stressed and pleased with the outcome of our work together. "You just did a highly specialized task," he complimented, adding that he thought only a few people in the Martin factory would be trusted with such a task.

As we left the guitar in the jig and waited for the glue to cure, I thought of how the time frames of success had changed so rapidly. From the crucial seconds of applying glue to leaving the form for days, the materiality of the process had caused a shift in attention to time and managing the scale of time to assure the success of the instrument. This was somewhat ironic, as I had encountered musical instrument craft shops as places where occasionally time seemed to stand still. Makers are dedicated to and engrossed in the craft, and they act more on the rhythms of the day and breaks in the process than time on the clock. For instance, in Chris's shop, there were two clocks whose arms did not move, and Chris neither carried a cell phone nor wore a watch in the shop. Rather, the day would start and stop with the beginning or end of tasks in making or if outside events intervened, such as lunch or personal tasks or appointments. He was always task oriented and projected those tasks throughout the days and weeks into the future. Being involved through the entire process of creation requires that the maker be able to switch between these different kinds of time, managing the hypercritical small scales of seconds in glue timing and the large scales of years in maintaining and looking after tonewood. At both the beginnings and ends of the instrument craft process, there is a lifetime commitment to the wood and the instrument. Chris was acutely aware of this, talking about what lives his instruments might have after they leave the shop and, importantly, what happens to the tonewood during makers' lives.

Many times, I heard makers speak about having a lifetime supply of wood. Chris told me that he had worked hard over the years to accumulate enough quality wood for his needs, now having enough that he might sell unused stock to other makers or as assembled kits online. Despite tonewood's sometimes-precarious materiality, if properly cared for, it can still last beyond the life of the maker. As noted earlier, Chris expressed concerns to me of what might happen to his cache should it outlast him. Some makers wrote into their wills what the wood was to be used for and what it was, so there would be no confusion.

As a result of these anxieties and a desire to make some extra income, Chris was buying and selling tonewood sets for future guitar projects and as a way to keep his business diverse and not too reliant on making. One day when I came into the shop, Chris was excited to show me a couple of sets of tonewood he had just purchased. "Chris," he posed to himself, "why would you get these sets if you were just selling other ones?" He admitted that "once you get into this wood stuff, it's kind of an addiction in a way." One of his friends described having a personal connection to Brazilian rosewood, buying it and checking in on it. Chris laughed as he remembered the friend referring to them as his "babies." Chris agreed, though, adding, "The wood is part of your history, what you are and what you do." However, the same friend was thinking of giving it all up owing to the changing regulations of the trade and use of such woods. Chris often repeated his observation that there seems to be a lack of clarity and that people were unsure of what the future held, extending the temporality into an uncertain future.

Our conversations about the time of craft abated when the glue dried, and we were ready to take the guitar out of the mold for the first time. At this point, we had to rout out the overhanging edge of the back—glued in the same process as the top—to get the guitar out of the mold. We flipped the mold over and attempted to push out the guitar body so that it had a little more space to rout out the back, but Chris cautioned, "It may not want to move." I asked what the difference would be in routing out the mahogany instead of the spruce, and Chris told me that the mahogany would be more brittle and a little harder to work. He said that you had to "feel how it pulls" through the wood in order to guide it, but he approached the mahogany much faster than he would the spruce top because of its more uniform grain structure.

We pulled the body out to "see what we got," as Chris often remarked in the shop, and inspected the edges to make sure the top and back had pulled in tightly around the entire perimeter of the instrument. We removed the exterior mold screws and saw the body of the guitar together by itself for the first time. Chris inspected it to make sure that the top and back had pulled on correctly, and I was amazed at the form that had emerged. It felt as if it had been born out of the mold, taking recognizable shape for the first time, and I felt compelled to study the edges and bouts of the box. As I felt we had completed a major accomplishment, I asked Chris what he thought of the process. "It's rewarding because of the labor," he said, but he cautioned that we still had a lot of work to do before we had a successful instrument.

The first work on the assembled body was to go inside and clean up glue and pencil marks from the inside. While looking inside the instrument, Chris remarked that we had "taken care of the interior work," as that is part of what makes a quality craft-made guitar. He tone-tapped the body and seemed happy about it being a G, as it had risen in tone in the assembly and he would have some room to tune it back down to F$^\sharp$ to accommodate the bass-forward tone requested by the customer. As we continued to refine the instrument, Chris said, "There's relationships you should start to see develop" in creating the ideal tone.

He took out a small square of carpet, set the guitar on it, and then had me work on sanding the sides for cleanup and to even out the bouts, which appeared to have a slight skew when we looked at it. I sanded out the small variations, checking against a square as well as the burn marks, pencil marks, and glue that were material signifiers of the correspondence of planning and construction in the earlier phases. I perceived an irony in the erasure of such marks that signified the connection of the maker to the materials. Chris continually told me that people look for such signs as glosses for quality craftsmanship, and I would learn that material signifiers of a maker's absence or presence are a major defining difference between guitar craft and violin craft.[11]

The next step was to rout out the spacing for the ornamental, inlaid purfling and binding that would run around the perimeter of back and top. We bent purfling in a similar technique as the sides, turning the thin, straight line of the laminated black and white wood strips into a serpentine curve that mirrored the guitar body. The binding, made from a mock tortoise shell plastic, then wraps over purfling and the corner where the sides meet the top or back and protects the wood from knocks and cracking. While some makers use knives or planes to cut the channel that the purfling and binding sit in, Chris uses a router and a special jig to work around the body of the instrument. The router saves considerable time, but it can also cause catastrophic cracks in the wood if the fibers are not taken into account. As we pushed the spinning blade around the edge of the instrument—first Chris and then myself controlling the throttle and movement—Chris made careful note of which way the router would need to move to work with the fibers. He sketched arrows on each bout denoting which way to move the router, so that we would not catch a wood fiber in the wrong direction and risk a crack through the length of the instrument. With his careful attention, we completed this step without incident.

In order to glue in the binding and purfling, we used acrylic glue, which offers a longer opening time than the hide glue. However, the binding resisted the curves of the bouts, so Chris and I had to work closely to hold them in place and use blue masking tape to hold it in until the glue dried. As we worked hand over hand around the instrument, I marveled at how Chris routinely does the task by himself, as it presented enough difficulty with both of us. The blue tape held it into place until it dried, and when we peeled it off piece by piece, the box of the guitar was almost completely constructed.

With the box completed, we moved to the next task that Chris had listed in his notebook: carving and attaching the neck. As with many stringed instruments, understanding the relationship between the neck and the body of the guitar is the fulcrum upon which an instrument's success hinges. As we worked at the small table in the front room, he started to fine-tune the joint that we had cut on the table saw. He first filed out the groove in the neck joint to fit the dovetail and tried the joint to see how it would fit. He wanted to take off some of the wood so that the back of the joint would fit well and snug and "not have a lot of play." The goal of this process is to bring the neck flush with the sides, keeping the dovetail tight across the body yet leaving some space for alterations in the future. Chris said, "You always need to be thinking about future repairs," as he pointed to the space around where the fingerboard would be placed; other luthiers might inject steam there to loosen the hide glue.

The alternative in many guitars to this time- and skill-intensive process is to run a bolt through the neck block and screw it into the neck. I asked Chris why he chooses to perfectly fix the dovetail rather than use the bolt-on neck, typical of inexpensive factory-produced instruments. He told me that the dovetail has more contact, more transmission or "conductance" of soundwaves between the neck and body. Though the bolt-on necks are pulled in tight, they are not working as a single unit as they are when the glue physically bonds the woods together.

Chris then removed wood that he found he wouldn't need near the front of the joint. He took the neck to the band saw and used a small angled block to cut off the angled edges of the neck heel. I asked why he did not just angle the table of the band saw, and Chris said he didn't know; that's just a way to do it. He came back to the table and took off small amounts of wood with the file from the front, so that the back could fit into place. He would check it by pressing the joint in and then seeing if there was any space for the neck to move around. However, he also had to simultaneously check to make sure that it was centered in the guitar. We would take a long straightedge aligned with the midpoint of the bottom of the body, pass it over the sound hole on the top of the body, and lay it across the top of the neck.

It was slow work, as any wood removed could not be replaced. If too much material was removed, a small shim could tighten the joint again. At one point, Chris used a spit-soaked oak shim to try and get the joint right, but he did not end up needing it. For these reasons, Chris said that setting up the neck is a crucial process, and he added that "some people don't like to fool with dovetail because of the specifics," unless they have the woodworking skill and patience to seat the neck correctly. In order to do so, the maker must keep in correspondence with five surfaces that impact the joint in four directions and the angle of the neck in relation to the body that determines the height of the bridge saddle.

We repeated the process of using a file or sanding block to remove a slight amount of material and fixing the neck into place. For each check, we would use a clamp to bring the wood in tightly to the joint to "see what we got." We repeated this process twenty to thirty times, checking each direction, the angle in relation to the body, and its trueness to the midpoint. He asked me throughout the day if I found what I was expecting in the craft process. I responded that precision seemed key, and I didn't mind taking a long time to do anything. Chris commented on the competition in the craft and industry and how important it was to do quality work. "You find yourself at the mercy of the competitiveness of the market," and so you need to be precise and do good work.

As we worked, I asked him more about his personal connection to the guitar: "The thing about the guitar is, if it's something to you, it continues to be used, and you have that personal connection, the ongoing effects of your work and labor." As we fit the neck, a visitor had come to the shop who had visited a couple of weeks prior. He was surprised that we were still working on the same guitar project. As we got back to work, Chris mentioned the comment the visitor had made and said, "Some folks just don't understand the nature of this work. They think it's a smaller thing, so it must go quickly in making it."

Once Chris was happy with the joint, we turned to finishing the neck, which included the headstock and carving the profile of the neck. As with many aspects of the finer work, it took making special tools and patterns to finish the task. For the neck profile, I took measurements from a Martin guitar Chris had and made three patterns to replicate the neck at three different points. For the headstock, I needed to make three pieces: a cradle to hold the neck while I worked on it, a dowel sanding block, and a long, square piece to take out the squared part of the end of the slot. While the carving of the neck went fairly quickly—using an angle grinder and then a rasp—the headstock was much more detail oriented and took finer work. We had laminated a piece of rosewood onto the squared headstock to match Martin's signature design, as well as a piece of paper with the design of the slots that would go through the headstock. At first, we used a router and a jig to get the slots through, but it took considerable work afterwards to get the angles square and matching. The three materials laminated on the headstock—the paper, the rosewood, and the mahogany—contrasted in durability and made the task more difficult, but with some planning and reference points, I shaped out the slots. From this point, we could install the tuners, and Chris could carve in his mother-of-pearl signature initials on the headstock.

As I worked, Chris came in and asked if I was getting a sense of how much work goes into one of these guitars, including the artistic elements. I had already been thinking about that as I shaped the slots and realized how specialized a piece of wood the neck is, with contours to fit a hand, a base joint to fit the body, strength to hold the strings, and evenly spaced holes to accommodate the tuning posts. He said that "some people just think these things grow on trees" and don't appreciate the time that goes into them, having their expectations governed by factory-produced instruments.

We then worked to install the truss rod, an aluminum and carbon rod that extends through the neck, which is crucial to maintain tension to resist the strings. We slotted it into the neck using a router and covered it with a veneer of mahogany. While some makers create a space in the headstock to access the nut that allows one to adjust the tension, Chris insisted on putting it inside the guitar. Putting the access through the neck block allows the maker to keep a solid veneer on the headstock, and, importantly, this is the way that Martin does it. We were then able to glue the fingerboard on using a couple of pins set into the neck, and we were ready to move onto the final step of construction: the fretwork.

Using a spool of fret wire from a small guitar company while doing a repair on one of their guitars, Chris showed me the process. With a series of small files and saws, he demonstrated how to open the fret slots up slightly, hammer the wires into the slots, and finish them by filing down the sharp edges and polishing the surfaces. There are two important material aspects to consider. The immediate aspect is that inserting the wire into the slots causes the fingerboard to cup, so you must cut the slots wider and wider as you progress down the board. As the space between the frets reduces with the scale of the instrument, the added material of the wire can cause the ebony board to cup, stressing the glued connection to the neck and body. The other aspect to consider is that other makers or repairers might eventually have to refret the instrument in the future. The slots need to have sufficient width so that the teeth that hold the fret wire in place do not tear out the wood fibers along the fingerboard. As I finished, just as my mind was dulled by the repetition, Chris came in and approved my work. He said that I could probably pursue fretwork as an occupation on its own, but that I might become a little weary of the repetition!

As I polished the last fret, Chris had been fitting a bridge onto the top by attaching a piece of sandpaper where it would sit and working it over the almost imperceptible curve of the top. As he scraped the ebony piece over the sandpaper, it left clear marks denoting the high points that still needed to come down so that the entire piece would be completely flush with the top. Once he had completed that and fit the small bone pieces that would function as the nut and saddle—the two pieces that suspend the string over the body—he announced that the constructive phase of building the guitar had come to a close.

FINE-TUNING

The fine-tuning of the instrument involves applying its protective finish, adjusting its final tone, and setting up the instrument to be playable. Chris used techniques that he had developed over years in a process of trial and error and intensive documentation. Unfortunately, I was not with him in the final steps, as my schedule and funding prohibited me from staying on with Chris. In adjusting the ideal tone of music in the instrument, Chris established the final aesthetics inspired by the golden age of the C.F. Martin Company and arrived at the final form that the instrument would take in his hands and the beginnings of the instrument's life beyond.

In Chris's adjudication of tone, he leans heavily on applying scientific principles to methods of his own design. At the intersections of sound physics and cellular biology, Chris referenced texts and terminology to measure and explain why certain materials interacted so well. He would negotiate these scientifically informed principles with his own process of figuring things out through reference points and different kinds of measuring correspondence. For instance, while we worked, Chris sometimes played the CD that the client had sent of his ideal guitar. This was an important part of communicating the ideal for Chris:

> I even say, "Provide some music for me, pick out your best guitar, like here on record or something or some type of CD or something and send it to me so I can listen to it for a while and begin to understand [what] you tell me versus actually what I'm hearing," because people can describe sound. But it's actually, you know, you can do that to a point. But actually, when you hear something, [it] clarifies exactly what they were saying, you know, that supports what you're saying. So for me, I'd rather hear something, or if I can't get that, you know, give me a supergood description of what you want, you know, in terms of balance of sound or what you wanted.

I figured this was mainly for inspiration until the body was complete. At that point, Chris held up the guitar to the speaker of the CD player and listened to how the tone of the music was reverberating through the instrument. He seemed pleased with the result and asked me to help him with another test to see how the box might turn out acoustically.

He said that the volume of sound a guitar was capable of producing could be measured by how much air it could displace from the cavity in the middle. While I first thought this would be a matter of measuring the spatial volume, Chris complicated my assumption by suggesting that the flexibility and vibration of the top acted as a bellow that pumped the air out. So he asked me to strike a match and hold the flame in front of the sound hole while he tapped the sound hole with a felt mallet. The air from the guitar moved the flame, though it did not put it out, as Chris had hoped. He admitted that the test was not too important, and that the real test was honing in on the correct tone for the instrument.

One day while working on setting up a factory guitar for a friend, Chris brought up the principles of how tone is cultivated in the guitar. When you pluck the E string, he said, you get a fundamental tone of about 82 hertz per second, and then as you move down the neck you can isolate those tones, getting half the overtone at the twelfth fret halfway down. The top must be designed to be responsive to these tones, keeping what he called "forced oscillation" of the top in correspondence with its resonant features. Sometimes, he said, makers will put fine salt on the top and pluck the strings to see where the top is going into motion to respond to the tones and fine-tune to make sure everything is oscillating without stressing the top. Chris said that other luthiers rely a little more on a tried-and-true mechanical process than he does. "I try to use a more quantitative process so that you can see the relationships better." Referencing other techniques, he said, "Why, back years ago before they had electronics, they probably had to do it that way," but now with the technology and the scientific knowledge he had in his books, he was able to have a different perspective.

While Chris applied these principles to the tone, he was also guided by the mechanical and aesthetics traditions and practices of the C.F. Martin Company, essentially replicating factory instruments from the 1930s and 1940s. From the placement of the label to the square edges of the headstock, design of the outline, and even fabric strips on the inside of the sides, he constantly referred to Martin techniques. More concretely, he was also getting parts and jigs from factory settings, such as factory rejects from Martin that could be adjusted for new instruments. Through each stage, Chris's collection of Martin guitars was also present, and they were used as references for tone and shape. We often used a 1969 twelve-string Martin as a reference for measurements. I had used the neck as a model for the shape of the neck on the guitar we were building, and earlier he had used it to measure the distance of the back braces. He was slightly thrown off because the guitar body was smaller than he had anticipated, and he played a few songs before realizing that the longer scale of the twelve-fret guitar would change the proportions. Finally, Chris used a 1940s D-18 as a model for tone in the shop. At certain points, he would bring the guitar into the shop and play it to the guitar-in-becoming as an inspiration for tone and finally as a reference.

The reliance on Martin parts, techniques, and instruments presented an interesting juxtaposition of attempting to create a craft instrument in the style and material shadow of an instrument principally produced in a factory setting. With some techniques, it appeared as if we were attempting to create factory line production for only one instrument. Chris relied on ideas and imaginaries of how the Martin shop had done things in order to replicate the company's success at making instruments renowned for their tone. He would use factory forms like jigs in order to reproduce a consistent form, if not the exact tone that went with it. However, he was acutely aware of how his work was different from that in a factory, in that he embodied the entire routine, from processing tonewood and design to the final instrument, including its sale and work. "People think that work progresses as it does in a factory," he said as we worked one day, in response to a visitor that had asked, "Are you finished? Is that another guitar?"

Chris told me that my questions and presence as an apprentice influenced

Fig. 3.6. Chris playing a "golden age" C.F. Martin guitar

him to think more deeply about his work. One day, he suggested that "your questions have made me realize personal connections and influences. It gives meaning, once it gets in your blood. People who really appreciate art and wood—especially people who play music—it really impacts. Then you are trying to use your own personality to make adjustments. There's a lot of wonderment and creative thinking. There's a lot of personal connection. The end product is a personal assessment of your personality and skills—the transferal of your personality to wood. It seems to be reflective of you as a maker."

A sociology class Chris had taken in college introduced him to the idea of alienation, about how an auto worker is trained to do parts of the process without a personal connection to see the project all the way through. He felt that doing the entire process gave him the satisfaction of knowing how it was done and done right, saying explicitly that his work was not alienated. He mentioned that the customer we were building for called him up and requested a guitar based on the one he had previously sold, and that he really appreciated the uniqueness of the instrument. He continued that this really made that work meaningful to him. He said that it was what pushes the work beyond the mechanical and technical to the social level.

As Chris had used the word *meaningful* several times, I asked him how he would define the word. He said it was difficult, but it was about achieving personality through craft. He felt that it is about achieving the destiny of what skills you are attuned to and have been endowed with by God and therefore are compelled to practice. He told me a story about an album that he had recorded that a nurse had listened to while recovering from a car wreck. She told Chris about how the album had helped her recover from the wreck, and it made him realize that the scope of his craft in making instruments and playing music extends much further than the shop.

Chris acknowledged his family history of music, which enabled him to explore these talents and his spiritual destiny. This got him into a theory about artistic people and how they don't always appreciate their talents and try to see how the "grass is greener in other pursuits." They can get into ruts of impatience and frustration and try to pursue other things. People "who can't play a radio" don't understand how people who can play might just put down their instruments. He said, "Artistic people tend to be more sensitive to their environments" and that it can positively impact the mentality of the maker to keep on producing.

While the work is rendered meaningful through handling the materials, the connections to the red spruce, and the extension of Chris's labor into social and spiritual realms, the talent of guitar making is still highly contingent on his ability to make a living from it. We would sometimes speak about the politics of developing diverse economies in Appalachia, and Chris normally brought it back to his own practice. He mentioned that he had once talked to another local business owner about how important it is for a business to keep diverse, and how he tried to keep his own economic activity as diverse as possible in order to make up for shortfalls in demand in certain areas—making guitars, selling wood, creating kits, and doing repairs. Having helped him with the sale of tonewood and kits and with repairs, I wondered if he thought of trying to increase the production of the shop. I asked if he ever made extra guitars to sell on consignment, or if he even had the desire to. Chris responded that he did not have the time, but he was going to really push to make guitar craft a full-time occupation. Though he was recently retired, he needed the added income for the obstacles that arise in health and home.

I left Chris's shop in this period of uncertainty, and in the last couple of weeks of the apprenticeship he spoke about how he was going to miss having the help around the shop and how he might need some other motivation to

Fig. 3.7. Chris fretting the finished guitar

work there. Right before I left, he joked that I would need to call him the next Monday to make sure that he was still working and not caught up in the other distractions life throws your way. However, when I returned to the shop a few months later, I found the guitar completed and two other instrument projects in progress.

I welcomed the smell of mahogany, rosewood, Spanish cedar, and spruce as I felt the plywood floor flex beneath my feet again. Along with two dobroes in progress, I saw our guitar, finish shining and ready to play. After many hours of sanding and coats of nitrocellulose finish, the guitar gleamed in the light and provided a tone equally brilliant. As I picked it up, Chris chided, "Like a factory guitar, isn't it?" His comment resounded with one of the great ironies of this kind of craft guitar production: factories attempt to produce and market guitars as individual hand-crafted artisanal objects, while hand-crafting artisans seek to replicate factory techniques and factory products, albeit of a different time.

I found it to sing a series of resonant overtones when played in the key of A, and I felt a pride of my own in handling the finished instrument before he shipped it to the customer. Chris later sent me a review from an online forum where the customer had reviewed it. The client told the story of how Chris had made a Martin-style guitar of his own design influenced by conversations with Norman Blake, and how he had wanted a new twelve-fret "prewar" D-18–style model after he traded one he had owned. He described the tone as crystalline and piano-like and expressed his great pleasure in the finish and detail of having a handmade instrument. Happy with wood from trees that had rooted and grown for hundreds of years in the forests of West Virginia, he complimented Chris's connection to the wood that he harvested himself and vowed to reacquire the other Zambelli guitar he had sold.

CHAPTER 4

BRINGING CREMONA VIOLINS TO LOBELIA

Lobelia Road runs off Droop Mountain in southern Pocahontas County and snakes its way through the small valley into the levels of Hillsboro like the water that eases through the limestone in this area. Perched on the side of Lobelia Road in the shadow of Droop is an American Foursquare farmhouse with a couple of outbuildings, a sunny porch, and a garden filled with tools of projects in process. The house is home to violin maker Paolo Marks, his family of five, and his instrument shop, as well as a frequent site of local get-togethers and music jams with neighbors up and down the valley.

I first met Paolo when visiting his home and workshop for an interview in 2015, following his careful instructions down the switchback road off the mountain inscribed on my field notebook. He welcomed me in from the porch, where he had been lightly plucking on one of his mandolins, and led me through the entry hall rayed with summer light and into the shop. Paolo's workspace took up a third of the ground floor of the house, consisting of two rooms that he had modified into a large workshop. About half of the place was occupied by large machinery needed for the woodwork, carpentry, and working on car mechanics—namely, a table saw, a large band saw, a small band saw, a large lathe, and a drill press, all fitted to an external dust-collection system. A large wood stove stood stoutly in the middle of the room, ready to burn wood for heat, boil maple syrup, or whatever seasonal task might emerge. A sink nearby the stove sourced the running water for the shop, instrumental for ensuring fine edges while sharpening tools. The sink, stove, and dust-collection system formed an elemental divide in the workspace, with fire, water, air, and dust flowing through the three systems.

On the other end of the room, large windows lit two workbenches garlanded by tools hanging from an array of magnets and hooks. The back wall hosted a bookshelf stacked with tonewood and a series of violins and other instruments in various states of construction and deconstruction. Lamps perched on booms above the benches, ready to augment the light streaming through the large windows. Everything was covered in a slight patina of sawdust, oils, glues, solvents, and children's scribblings, but it was kept nominally neat and orderly, with instrument and car parts and tools packed into milk crates or other improvised storage containers. We settled into the high stools at the opposing benches, as I removed the tools of my trade: a recorder, my notebook, and a folder full of consent forms approved by the Institutional Review Board. A year and a half later, I would be picking up Paolo's tools as we began working together in an apprenticeship.

In his measured, poised responses to my questions, Paolo brought levity to the conversation and explanations—as he would to our later work—through jokes, with a glint in the eye and an easy smile poking out from his bushy beard. As I was interested in how the work of an instrument maker fit into the local environment, I asked questions related to rural, forested spaces and the meaning of working with wood materials. Paolo acknowledged that the house and workshop's position in the rural valley was sometimes a challenge, but that it fit into his idea of a livelihood.

> It takes a long time for people to notice you. If I opened a shop right on the main street in Brooklyn, by the next month a thousand people would go through there. And you'd need a thousand customers just to pay the rent. But that's not specific to West Virginia, that's kind of a rural challenge. It takes some time, and you have to drive more to get things and show things. Other than that, I mean you can make a violin anywhere, and I much prefer to make it in a surrounding like this, and at home. That's the nice thing about violin making, you don't have to go to an office. You can be a father and take care of the kids and if you have twenty minutes you can go to the shop and work.

Paolo's innate curiosity was shown through our conversation, as he began asking questions back to me about how other West Virginia makers' livelihoods are entangled with their craft techniques:

How does it fit into your whole schema of living? Does it fit very function-ally, like I was saying with the kids? But do you also play? Do you talk to other makers? Do you really know your customers? It's not just making, it's making and getting it to people, playing music with them and getting feedback. The whole process is fascinating to me. Violin making—there's so many aspects of it. There's the craft of making it. There's the whole history of all the makers and the styles. There's the varnish, which is kind of a chem-istry and cooking. Then there's the whole acoustic aspect, the actual playing. Musicians and violin makers can be the same and they can be completely separate. You don't have to be a musician to be a violin maker, but it helps.

Paolo pointed to how the aesthetic choices and craft practices of instru-ment makers are involved in communities of all kinds: musical, work, material, economic, and social. As our relationship developed from an interview to col-laborating through apprenticeship, he showed me how his work was enmeshed within his family's household, which emphasizes sustainable practices and a close relationship with the forest surrounding the small valley.

While his work was less tied to the timber of the immediate forests than the other craftspeople I apprenticed with, the family was entrenched in forest knowledge and livelihoods. As I worked with Paolo, I experienced not only the different ways of seeing the wood but a holistic attention to craft practice and re-enchantment of connections through the work and household. Paolo cut wood to heat the fireplace from a nearby timber stand, the family frequently camped, hiked, and foraged in the forest, and Erica, his wife, was a seasoned forest forager and ran a nearby nonprofit that emphasized practical ecologi-cal and livelihood knowledge. Working from the house, Paolo could also take care of the children while Erica was working, and their youngest child was a frequent companion of ours during lunch breaks.

In this place over five months of apprenticeship, Paolo would teach me how the craft was embedded in a constantly unfolding field of practice, from the minutiae of craft actions to the history of form and aesthetics. His expres-sion of the Cremonese ideals of violin craft perfected in Renaissance Italy and handed down through the generations took a place-based inflection from his home and community in the Lobelia Valley in the shadow of Droop Mountain.

Paolo had been making instruments since 1998, having completed forty instruments and worked on countless others. Intrigued by the histories and stories, he replied with a measured tone that he did not really follow up with his instruments that well, adding that he thinks it better if he doesn't see

Fig. 4.1. Paolo Marks describing how sound travels through an instrument

them again, because that means that there were no errors or necessary repairs. Before I could follow up, his curiosity about my world of knowledge prompted him to ask about ethnographic explanations of how the world works. In short order, our conversation turned to how incidental or coincidental events can transform our expectations, leading us to search for explanations of seemingly unexplainable events. I told him about E. E. Evans-Pritchard's *Witchcraft, Oracles, and Magic among the Azande* (1976), and how anthropologists have talked about magic not necessarily as an intentional act—the kind of magic Paolo dismissed when denying any magic to the craft of lutherie—but rather as an explanation of events that we see purely as coincidental, such as a tragedy or accident befalling a friend or finding the perfect piece of tonewood.

This framing unlocked the narratives of past instruments made and sold by Paolo, and he began to rattle off their stories like a biographical dictionary of instrument tragedy. He told me a story of an instrument that he had made that was destroyed when its former owner died. Another had survived a house fire but retained the smell of burnt vinyl, bringing a noxious plastic smell to the shop when it came for repair. He also recalled a repair job he did after a violin was backed over by the family station wagon. He said that person still calls him to thank him for restoring the family instrument, even though Paolo did not think it was a great job given the severity of the damage. One of his first apprentices had actually come to him, along with a crushed violin, under similar circumstances, but then asked if he could do the repairs himself. Paolo gave him instructions to do the basic violin repairs on his totaled instrument.

As for his own instruments, Paolo said that he doesn't have a large collection of them. He owns and still plays his first violin, which shows the wear of years of playing and his growth as a maker during its life. The sagging wings of the f-holes and dark brown, dusty varnish contrasted with the sturdy yet elegant flowing volutes and clarity of the violin he was working on during my apprenticeship. Drawing on an old proverb, he said, "What is the old saying? The shoemaker's children go barefoot?" to describe his instrument that he sometimes lends out and is admittedly rough on, knowing that he can fix it if need be. He doesn't have a drive to collect instruments and own an array of tonal variation, seeking instead to concentrate on creating a diversity of tone through the production of his instruments before sending them out to their fates.

In the fall of 2016, as I finished work with Chris on the guitar project in Randolph County, I began to work with Paolo to structure out what my apprenticeship with him would look like. He approached the possible work with a laid-back attitude, emphasizing his flexibility and tacitly encouraging me to find the rhythms and routine of my work in the shop. As I had little experience playing violins, let alone working on them, Paolo recommended that I purchase an old violin to refurbish and learn the basics of violin anatomy before going through the process of making my own. I agreed to do so.

I spent lunch breaks while working with Chris submitting bids for online auction listings of violins to load on my phone and dreaming of receiving what the ads promised. "Vintage GIOVAN PAOLO MAGGINI," "Violin Vuillaume A Paris," "Incredible Old French by P. Gautié" excitedly called out to me from eBay listings before a perfunctory "OUTBID" appeared in my inbox. Finally, after a week of bidding and unfruitful local requests for a damaged violin, I won "ANTIQUE VIOLIN JACOBUS STAINER" from a Canadian attic. "Perhaps," I thought, "this will be more than a copy. A genuine Jacob Stainer violin that has weathered the years, waiting to be reawakened." It was not.

Paolo and I looked over the instrument upon receiving it: a crack had developed in the top, the fingerboard was worn and discolored, a lone string remained on the instrument holding the bridge in place, and the scroll listed to the side, as if it had sat too long in an errant sunbeam and had begun to melt.

While my naive hopes of my first repair job being the long-lost product of one the seventeenth-century's great makers, Paolo set quickly to work assessing the instrument's true provenance from what material clues remained.

He estimated that it was probably a factory instrument made in the early twentieth century in Central or Eastern Europe, despite its internal label proudly proclaiming "Jacobus Stainer in Absom prope Oenipontum 1736."[1] Without any other markings, we assumed it to be made prior to 1891, when the McKinley Tariff Act of 1890 came into effect requiring that all imports to the United States be marked with a country of origin. Looking into the violin for clues as to its origin, Paolo removed the endpin and peered inside the instrument as a ship's captain might look through a spyglass to gauge the sea. He reported that there were no corner blocks and that the bass bar was carved into the top, rather than being an individual piece that had been carved to fit the curvature, both indicators of a quick industrial craft production. As I glimpsed inside the instrument attempting to locate the clues that he had quickly identified, Paolo described how the factories in which these types of instruments were generally set up. Unlike in his shop, a single person would do only one specific job in the process, often taking any possible shortcuts. So the bass bar, instead of being carved from a separate piece of perfectly split wood and meticulously fitted to the top, would have been hurriedly carved from the top as part of the process of forming its signature arch. The scroll was likewise hurriedly produced, resulting in its uncanny cant. We spent some time thinking through what the process would have looked like and speculating how the workers must have considered the craft—a recurring theme in our conversations about violin craft in Paolo's shop.

Paolo also commented that the material and wear patterns could show what kind of players had played the instrument in the past. Based on his reckoning, they had been people who generally would have played melodic music in the first position—colloquially known as "fiddle tunes"—rather than symphonic music that might require the use of the many hand positions on the fingerboard.

Sensing my eagerness to begin the repairs, Paolo instructed me on the beginning assessment of the work that remained ahead. The first step would be to open the instrument and remove the top and back by breaking the bonds of the hide glue holding the instrument together. Despite the availability of other glues with easier application, hide glue has remained a mainstay in violin making due to its physical qualities.[2] Paolo described how the fundamental difference between hide glue and wood glues was a distinction between chemical and mechanical bonds with the wood. Unlike wood glues that wrap tightly around wood fibers to hold the joints together, hide glue forms a chemical bond with the wood itself. It creates a strong joint with very weak shearing proprieties, meaning that it can be broken easily with a tool if a repair is needed. Wood glue, on the other hand, will often require steaming to remove the components without ripping away wood fibers and damaging the wood components of a violin. While makers debate about when and where to use hide glue in guitar making, every joint of a violin is bound with hide glue except the permanent joints of the bookmatched top and back plates. Violin makers, Paolo explained, build their instruments with a long future in mind. They understand that their instrument will need to be repaired for some reason or another inevitably, and using hide glue ensures that the instrument can quickly and easily be disassembled for repair. He added that hide glue is also superior acoustically, because it has no elasticity to deaden sound in its final state.

Grasping the violin body in one hand while holding the waist of the instrument between his knees, he stuck a palette knife into the joint of the top and ribs of the violin. The instrument began to make a sharp cracking sound, which he assured me was the sound of the glue beginning to break and not the wood. He began to work the paper-thin knife around the perimeter of the instrument, shearing the bond of the glue and opening the joint. With the knife still stuck in the instrument, he handed the violin to me to finish the job. I replicated his measured pose and squeezed the instrument between my legs. I struggled to pull the knife through the joint with the ease and steady motion he had applied. The knife jumped and stopped as the glue cracked and I pushed my thumb against the thin edge of the tool. Finally, it began to wiggle and open, and the interior space of the instrument was revealed.

Inspection of its inner workings in the full light of the workshop revealed the hurried work of its nineteenth-century factory makers. The top was still coarse with the strokes of the tools used to rough out the arching, and a C-shaped micrometer revealed that it was too thin in some areas. Seeking sandpaper to smooth out these coarse fibers, Paolo counseled that I apply my efforts with a scraper, a thin piece of steel with a burnished edge that pulls away the wood fibers. Handing me the half-moon–shaped tool, he revealed that scrapers keep the fibers smooth, rather than roughing them down to a soft texture, as sandpaper does. The scrapers cut at fibers as they smooth out the material, while sandpaper abrades the fibers until they are sufficiently soft. This keeps the wood fibers as complete as possible to conduct sound more efficiently. I placed the violin in a small cradle and set to work with the scraper, applying pressure with my thumbs to the middle of the flexible tool to create a small working edge and smooth out the spruce and maple.

The end and neck blocks, which provide surfaces to hold the instrument together, were splitting and in need of replacement. With a chisel, I began carving out the neck block and noticed a pin knot running through the whole piece of spruce that was making it harder to carve. When I drew Paolo's attention to this, he said, "Why would they do that? I mean, it's such a small piece of wood," questioning the lack of attention to detail and the economy of production for the factory instrument. Nevertheless, the chisel made short work of the pieces, and they went into the waste bin to be burned in the wood stove.

Over the next two weeks, Paolo coached me through the basics of violin repair. I cut and set new blocks for the neck and tail of the instrument, reset the neck of the instrument in its mortise, added cleats to strengthen the joint between the maple pieces of the back, refinished the fingerboard and fittings, installed a new bridge and soundpost, and strung the instrument up. The finished product was playable, even if a bit crude, and the notes I drew with a borrowed bow seemed to list out of the instrument just as the scroll did from its neck. Nevertheless, I was grateful for it and quickly began to practice short fiddle tunes in the evenings back at my house in preparation for the instrument to follow.

PLANNING A NEW INSTRUMENT

Having learned the basics of the violin and practiced the woodworking elements of the craft, I turned my focus to the main task of the apprenticeship: building a violin from wooden blanks. While many violin makers meticulously copy famous violins by exactly replicating their dimensions and characteristics—going as far as including pock marks and blemishes on the instrument—Paolo generally builds his instruments based on the established proportions of known instruments. He takes measurements of famous instruments from posters or schematics and, rather than using the measurements exactly, uses them to establish the proportions of the instrument. However, he does not antique instruments to make them look old; instead, he relies on "time and usage to impart an authentic character." He emphasized that "Strad made *new* instruments." He found that the process brought more satisfaction when discovering and expressing the relationship of the proportions of the instruments, especially in replicating the "golden mean" proportion found throughout nature.[3] In our initial interview he explained as follows:

> Anytime you are in nature, these forms that we're making, these violins are based on proportions that you see all the time in nature unconsciously.

Like if you see a beautiful horse, you don't see a leg, a tail, a head, a back. You see a horse. It's one thing. It looks perfect. It's a horse. It's beautiful; it's proportionate. It's correct, and it's exciting to look at. It looks like it has motion even if it's standing still. The same thing with the violin. If the proportions are right, you don't say, "Oh, there's a f-hole, there's a purfling, there's the edge." You see a violin and it looks right. Proportions are right and it looks like a single object instead of . . . it's more than the sum of its parts. It becomes alive. It becomes like a horse, you know? And that's difficult to do because if you make something that's not proportionally correct, your eye will see it immediately and it'll stand out and so look like the f-hole is too big or the scroll is crooked. [There is something] about the scroll that's kind of interesting. I once asked a violin maker, "Why do they put a scroll on the top?" Aesthetically, it looks nice, but acoustically [it] has no purpose. You could put anything up there. And he said, "Because it's the hardest thing to make." And what he meant was, you know, that the scroll, that shape, that spiral, which you see in plants and in shells and in that proportion, [it's] the golden mean. The way that plants grow. The way that plants grow is all proportional. And that proportion, if it's a little bit off, you see it immediately. If you saw a shell that was kind of lumpy on one side, it would look unnatural. So to make a scroll that is proportionally perfect is very difficult, and if there's a little mistake, you see it right away.

He had established the proportions needed to fit the generally accepted dimensions of the instrument and gave me one of his designs to base my mold on. He unraveled a sheet of drafting paper and gave me a piece of plywood that would serve as the interior mold. Paolo used a method of proportional units in a common ratio to plan the dimensions of the instruments. Likening it to the division of a string into lengths that vibrate at different frequencies, he said, "Everything is based proportionally, so that's why it looks nice, but that's [also] why it sounds nice. You know if you took a string and divided it exactly in half, you'd have an octave. The ratio 2 to 3 gets you the perfect fifth and 3 to 4 reveals the perfect fourth, which are the building blocks of all Western music."

Walking a compass through the length and width of the planned instrument, I would then use the compass to trace patterns of overlapping circles on the piece of three-quarter-inch plywood. Tracing a finger across his pattern, Paolo said, "You can find all of the lines of the violin in these overlapping circles, you just need to follow them." Indeed, as I inscribed the circles across the surface of the wood, I began to see the outline of the instrument. I traced in

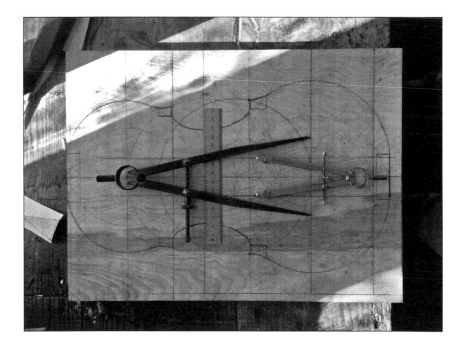

Fig. 4.2. The proportions of a violin

the lines of the instrument, drawing in the corners of the bouts and the spaces where the blocks of the interior would fit into the mold.

The interior mold is the hallmark of making in the Cremonese tradition.[4] The components are secured to the mold on the inside of the instrument-in-progress rather than the exterior, as Chris and I had done in making the guitar. While some makers do use exterior molds, Paolo told me that the interior mold variety was more typical of the Cremonese makers and gave each instrument their "individual charm," as one's personality emerges through the little changes that happen as the pieces are attached to the forms. Exterior forms are more typical of factory-produced instruments like the violin that I had recently finished refurbishing.

After "finding" the violin's forms in the series of concentric circles on the plywood, I cut out the shape, as well as the spaces where the corner, neck, and tail blocks would be glued in to begin the construction process. I then established a square edge along the mold's perimeter with a plane or chisel where necessary, because small inaccuracies in the mold would compound as more and more parts were added. The relatively stable material of the plywood did its best to resist my attempts to make small alterations. Once I had negotiated the laminated form and everything was square, I cut the blocks from spruce that would serve as the scaffolding upon which every other component was secured and used a small amount of glue to "spot glue" them in.

Paolo then took me to the other side of the shop and laid the mold complete with blocks on a large slab of granite with fine grit sandpaper glued to its cool, even surface. This "surfacing plate" was perfectly flat and would ensure that all of the blocks would be flat and even in relation to each other. Holding the mold by its circular central cutouts, he pushed the mold over the plate. With each pass over the large, perfectly flat stone, the blocks screeched over the sandpaper adhered to the plate's surface. Paolo handed the mold back to me and left me to the task. As sawdust began to accompany sound, one line of spruce dust turned into four on the black paper, and my constant checking revealed the surfaces of the blocks had become smooth, appearing almost like shell worn by the tide. The sound of the blocks' friction, their white traces on the matte-black paper, and their smooth flatness all served as indices that the blocks were in line and the cornerstones of construction in place.

A MAPLE'S LAST JOURNEY

Now that the scaffolding had been raised, the task fell upon us to select the wood for the back, top, neck, and ribs of the instrument. Following near ubiquitous practice in the use of violin woods, we would procure maple and spruce for most of the structure of the instrument. Tough, resilient, and strikingly patterned maple would form the back, sides, and neck, while the soft yet strong fibers of spruce would amplify musical tone through the top of the instrument. While these trees grew in abundance in the Lobelia Valley and on the surrounding mountaintops, the material necessities required by the craft would mean a trip to nearby Lewisburg, West Virginia, to the shop of a local tonewood dealer and instrument maker, John Preston. After negotiating a day when we could make the drive to John's shop, Paolo agreed to accompany me to select wood, in combination with his visit to a local double bass player in need of a repair. We loaded his daughter's car seat into the cab of my truck, and the three of us headed over Droop Mountain to the small regional center in the next county over.

About an hour later, bundled in our winter coats against the gray winter sky, we pulled into the gravel driveway of the Old World Tonewood shop. We were greeted by the easy hospitality of John Preston, who stepped out of the shop, welcomed us, and told us that Travis Holley, the shop's sawyer, had just stepped out to pick up lunch from the drive-in down the road. Travis arrived soon after our pleasantries, and we fell into conversation about the tonewood business and local happenings in the musical instrument world. With his daughter cradled in one arm, Paolo gently chatted with John about cutting tonewood.

John described to Paolo the basics of his supply chain, either buying logs from local timber operations to cut down into blanks or importing blanks from tonewood cutters in Romania. As we perused the shelves stacked with blanks and hanging slabs of poplar and maple, John talked about using the local species of red maple versus the European maple and how their densities and depth of the figure (grain) affected the ability to carve the signature arches and volutes of the violin. Paolo's interest was piqued, and the two began to exchange statistics on the densities of their preferred maple, how each material might best fit the aesthetic and acoustic structural demands of the violin, and which material was best in the hands of a novice such as myself.

Paolo noted his preference for the red maple, which is softer on the arms and hands when carving, but John suggested that the European maple would be better for a first violin project. The deep swells of the curls in the red maple could easily pull unwanted fibers out of the wood with an unpracticed chisel stroke, while the European maple might provide a more uniform substrate for my beginner's skill. Paolo asserted that I should buy the best possible wood I could afford, and John said that plainer, less-figured wood would be better for my first instrument. Between the two, they negotiated what they thought would be the best starting material, and Paolo seemed to have faith in my skill as a wood carver from his limited view in the shop.

I erred on the side of caution (and my student wallet), and John selected a few options of backs, necks, and sides that seemed to match in color and figure from his stock of European maple. He suggested a top with a small pitch pocket and the neck that had a bit of bark inclusion, noting that these do not sell online well. He furnished a pattern and lightly drew out the outlines, illustrating that both "imperfections" would carve out and not impact the final product. John mentioned that these are issues he likes to work around in his projects, as they speak to the character of the wood, but they are quickly dismissed by prospective buyers with only a JPEG for reference. He bundled the set of wood up with cellophane and a receipt, but he mentioned with a joking smile that I could work off the cost when I would be apprenticing with him.

Paolo was also interested in wood for his own projects, and he perused the shelves of ordered and numbered blanks with the intent of one who knows exactly what he is looking for and in no hurry to find it. Still with his daughter in one arm, he knocked on a series of slabs of maple that were hanging by wire loops in the wood shed. As he pondered their woody responses, he told John that he had been working off of the same large piece of maple for the past few years but was interested in buying some new stock, particularly the kind of one-piece maple backs seasoning in front of us. However, given his propensity to work off of one large piece of wood for an extended period of time, I wondered if these two- to three-foot lengths would meet his demand, as they might furnish only two or three instruments.

As Paolo looked through John's stock of tonewood, they talked about their material preferences in working with different species of maple. John preferred the lighter color and weight of European maple that made it easier to carve, whereas Paolo was more interested in the red maple, as he was finding a greater desire for local wood from his clients, and he appreciated the deep ribboning effect of the red maple's curl. John had one-piece mandolin and violin red maple backs to sell, and Paolo was interested, but he qualified that he would need wood that had aged at least ten years. John's had not; the longest was about seven years from the early days of his business, and most pieces had been seasoned for only about two to three years.

While he had been using the red maple in his projects, Paolo had told me that he didn't sell or market his instruments using language of local woods common with the region's woodworkers and crafters. With a confident air, he said he would use any wood if it has the qualities he was looking for. "A good violin maker adapts to work with and bring the most out of any material they are working with." If a customer came to him looking for local wood, he would find it, but he would ultimately stress the primacy of the tone in creating the instrument.

Maple and spruce had been the settled-upon norm for a reason. He said that 99 percent of violins are made with the same kinds of wood because they have been proven to produce the best sound. He speculated that this probably had to do with the differences of the plucked and bowed instruments and how the quality of the wood and replicability of tone might be more difficult to capture. He explained that when bowing an instrument, the vibrations are constantly feeding into the instrument rather than resonating at intervals like plucked instruments. He likened it to the instrument speaking and trying to achieve a humanlike voice. If the tone is off slightly, instruments can sound uncanny, so makers look to the replicability of materials. The spruce and maple used by old Italian masters could be relied upon for these qualities, so they have made for reliable partners in replicating sought-after tones. The fact that the trees are fairly common and thus not subject to international treaties on threatened species—as the traditional tonewoods of guitars are—makes for an even stronger case for their use.

Despite his waning interest in the maple, he was interested in the spruce as he was running out of tonewood that he had bought piecemeal from a violin supply company. When he mentioned this, John seemed to know the exact company and speculated that since it was European spruce, it may have come from the same Carpathian forests as his own stock, though German or Polish forests may have been equally likely. Since the wood is sold primarily by grade, he explained, its provenance is often lost on warehouse shelves under labels like "European Spruce 3A Grade." John, however, could often speak to the biography of the wood, from its purchase on the log yard to the tonewood factory in Romania and finally to his shop. Nevertheless, Paolo was not tempted by anything in John's stock, but he promised to return when he was in need.

As we were driving away from the shop, Paolo told me that the tonewood I had bought was a good deal, but whether you spend $75 or $500, it doesn't really matter when you have such a drastic transformation in value through the creation of the instrument. "If you are able to sell an instrument for $7,000, for example," he said, "it's almost all in the labor." He suggested that I would be able to sell my first instrument for about $1,500 if I executed it well, so the input of the cost of the wood was not as important as the processes that would come to transform it. Thus, the costs of material had to be considered with the costs of the labor in transforming wooden blanks into their final forms.

Paolo, years before, had been making all the wooden components of the violin, including all the fittings, such as the chin rest and the tuning pegs. In his shop, he had a basket of old fittings made mostly of hard, imported woods such as cocobolo and rosewood, which are now regulated by CITES appendices. He had some chin rests that were in the shape of leaves that he made for people who were allergic to plastic. He said that now he often uses a nonallergenic chin rest, before adding that the "the environment is allergic to the plastic." However, the intricacy of the fittings created a tension of productive time and earning money, so he had to decide to use only purchased fittings rather than ones he had made. "Fittings are not seen as integral to the value of the violin," he added; "over the life of the instrument, they will likely be replaced many times." In this case, he had decided that the extra labor time and value added by handmade fittings was not worth the modest cost of manufactured fittings. Decisions of time and labor figure heavily into the craftwork of livelihood, when makers must fine-tune their processes in addition to the instrument in order to work with the enjoined expediency and skill that satisfy the maker's exigent standards and the client's pressing desires. Mastery over tools and improvising with technological interventions become not only a way of knowing the wood but also of achieving the facility demanded by a craft livelihood.

LEARNING AT THE EDGE

As the mediator of the skill and labor of the crafter's body and the qualities expressed by the material, tools are another element in the equation of successful, singing instruments. A skilled maker knows how to translate their intent through the qualities of the edge of a chisel or knife blade onto the material at hand. When cutting the internal blocks, for instance, Paolo had produced a worn-down butcher knife, whose sole function was to split small pieces of spruce for blocks. He lined up a piece of quartersawn spruce from a scrap basket—repurposed waste from a previous project—on the bench, lined up the worn steel edge between two growth rings, and tapped the back with a fretting hammer. With a sudden snap, the wood split evenly along the growth ring, showing a shining, sheer face that contrasted the rough, sawn edges. "It wants to split that way," Paolo said, handing the tools to me to try on the next piece. The blunt edge provides a focus for the energy and takes advantage of the soft wood between layers. The result, in a straight-grained piece of wood, is a flat surface from which to begin work and uninterrupted wood fibers for sound waves to flow smoothly through. The next step of installing the end blocks involved something that the wood very much does not want to do but is, nevertheless, essential to making a successful instrument: making it completely flat. To do so, I would need a tool with a perfectly flat and razor-sharp edge.

Before I left that day, Paolo told me I should get a tool set of my own to learn the practices of sharpening, honing, and maintaining tools, stressing the necessity of having tools that personally fit the crafter. I found a couple of my great-grandfather's rusty block planes in his workshop—the basement of the house that my great-grandparents had built and sheltered me in during my time apprenticing—and tossed them in my backpack, along with a few jagged-edged chisels my uncle had recently given me. I returned the next day with these sturdy yet neglected steels, and Paolo put me straight to work rehabilitating them. Gazing through the rust to adjudicate the steel with the same measured look with which he gazes past the surface of wood into its grain, he determined that they would make fine companions at my workbench.

Next to the shop's sink, Paolo turned on the switch to the turning waterwheel sharpener. The grinding wheel smoothly dipped into a trough of water underneath, creating a soothing sound, as he demonstrated how to hold a block plane's removable blade to its porous surface in order to get a flat and sharp edge. He worked the blade across the surface of the wheel, creating a chorus of grinding sounds that indicated the worn and chipped edge of the steel was wearing away. After a few minutes, he showed how a small arc was now established in the cutting edge of the blade that would be more finely honed by a series of sharpening stones known as Japanese water stones.[5]

Sitting submerged in water in a nearby tub, the water stones would put the final cutting edge on the blade. Paolo removed one of the dripping wet, rectangular stones and pressed the blade against the sharpening stone. "You can feel where the bevel wants to be," he said, before clicking his tongue in emulation of the blade settling into position perfectly flush with stone. He began to rhythmically push the blade in figure-eight motions around the stone, creating a red slurry from the abraded stone working against the steel in combination with the water. He handed the chisel back to me and encouraged me to try it myself.

Empowered by the ease with which he had transformed this dull steel into a shining and sharp tool, I made best efforts to replicate his actions with the blades of my chisels. As Paolo had mentioned, the cooling of the water took material away quickly from the edge of the broken chisels without generating heat that might change their delicate chemical composition. However, its cool touch also made me oblivious to the fact that I had begun to sharpen my finger while I worked, exposing the subcutaneous tissue in my finger as well as a new cutting edge for the chisel. This would not be the first cut on my hands in the shop, as Paolo's scar-flecked hands had already indicated is common for a violin maker.

After I had worked the blades on the finer sharpening stones, he checked the sharpness of the blade on his fingernail. He ran the edge of the tool over his thumbnail, taking off a hair-thin shaving to see how smoothly it cut, and he said approvingly that I could continue. He stressed the importance of sharp tools, noting that when the wood feels like it is resisting your work, it's almost always a matter of sharpening your tools. He reflected on how Japanese makers and craft woodworkers practice a relationship to their craft through their tools that are designed in such a way that emphasizes their sharpness. He described watching videos of contests in Japan where the goal was to cut the longest and thinnest ribbon with a block plane from a plank of wood. The planes, he added, are also designed to pull toward the crafter, which he attributed to a self-reflective ethic in the craft process.[6] I was intrigued.

"Do you have an aesthetic or philosophy that is expressed through your relationship to the craft?" I asked. He responded by framing the craft in his usual manner, as a series of simple processes built upon one another to a successful conclusion. "There's no magic to it, it's a craft that anyone can learn. There's no secrets among violin makers." He balked when I asked about how some people consider it to be magical, rebutting, "It's about knowing the materials, working with the same tree for fifty instruments." As I spent the rest of the afternoon grinding the sole of the plane perfectly flat on a granite-surface plate, I contemplated getting to know the material of the tools through continually reworking their edges and bodies and how favorite tools are known by their wear, from the pocked and beaten butcher-knife splitter to the polished rows of sharp chisels in the shop.

CONSTRUCTION OF THE INSTRUMENT

On the bench that I regularly used in Paolo's shop, the wood lay wrapped in a piece of plastic, as it had since we had brought it from John's place. I looked over the mold and began to daydream about what the instrument might look like once completed and how this form reflected the generations of violin makers who had brought me to this place at this time. As Paolo and I worked side by side in the shop, mainly using hand tools, I thought of how this arrangement might reflect workshops of the vaunted Italian makers whose forms we were attempting to recreate. We frequently discussed those makers in the shop, whether through a discussion of a particular technique or an occasional bit of trivia that Paolo had picked up over the years. Thinking

Fig. 4.3. All of the constituent tonewood of the violin

through the process of acquiring the wood and "roughing out" of the instrument that I was about to undertake, I asked Paolo if he would be able to tell where Stradivari's work started and his workers' or suppliers' work stopped.

Antonio Stradivari and the other Cremonese makers would have had to employ a crew of apprentices, journeymen, and tonewood suppliers to produce the sheer volume of instruments they did.[7] He wasn't sure, but he did talk about how Strad's—as he is often known colloquially—work got noticeably worse as he got older. Paolo speculated that he himself did the finer work—that is, scraping the final arching and the final scrollwork—while his assistants probably did all the roughing out and the more physically demanding work. Paolo described how the shop became a family trade, but the sons did not deliver on the quality of Antonio and took other paths, such as dealing the instruments of Cremonese makers throughout Europe. He added that Strad would likely have had a relationship with his contemporaries in Cremona but suggested that understanding what actually happened in his shop is probably conjecture.

Even though many contemporary makers of violins seek to replicate the instruments and techniques of makers like Strad, I was curious if anyone was still maintaining the political and labor organization side of the craft. I told Paolo I understood that guitar makers in the United States initially came from the cabinetmakers guild in Europe and sought to escape the restrictions of the guild system in the United States.[8] Paolo suggested that the violin makers would have been a luthier guild, starting by making lutes and, as they went out of style, focusing their attentions on the viol family of instruments. However, he acknowledged that a lot of luthiers probably did some other woodwork: "You had to do what you had to do to make a living," adding with a smile, "Maybe some of them even repaired diesel engines," as a nod to his own side project of rebuilding a Volkswagen diesel engine on the other side of the room.

I asked him how he identifies himself as a worker, and he said that he is a luthier but will introduce himself as a violin maker if he thinks people may not know what a luthier is. Around the region, he normally just says he is a violin maker or fiddle maker, which often prompts people to describe a member of their family that had made a violin or two. He hears that comment a lot and it is often followed up by a request to do some repairs on old, homemade instruments.

Our conversation steered back toward the guilds, and I asked Paolo if he belonged to any professional organization that might act in the absence of a guild in the United States. He had bought a membership to the Violin Society of America in order to enter their violin competition a few years ago.

The competition was mainly about earning status that could elevate a maker into financial success, as the winner could get a ten-year back order from the renown of placing in the event. He figured he was around the middle of the pack but added that it was a valuable experience, as he got good feedback on his instruments and their quality at that point in his career.

The judges had declared that his instrument's finish was too glossy, reflecting too much light and preventing the viewer from seeing "into" the grain of the instrument. To do well in the competition, he had also learned, the violin must be based on a known design from a famous instrument maker. If the design is too unique, it becomes hard to adjudicate because it becomes too subjective, he explained to me. Some people in the competition will attempt to recreate instruments by makers such as Guarneri, who include small scraper marks and other asymmetries associated with that maker. Paolo said that "at the time [of the competition] my instruments were kind of my own," so he worked to conform a little more to Strad's design and metrics in later instruments. However, he added, the Cremonese were not trying to win competitions; "It was about an honest way of doing it."

On the same day, I received a comment from a colleague on a Smithsonian Magazine article that added fresh fuel to the debates about the singularity of Stradivari's instruments.[9] The article explained recent research that suggested that Strad had dipped his tonewood in mineral baths prior to its use and speculated that this could have been one secret of his singular craft. My colleague, who had led an effort to scan Cremonese instruments in 3-D, articulated that while this is true, materials scientists often overlook the mastery of the maker in attempting to find an answer.[10] In other words, I asked, Why can't it be that Strad (and his workers) were exceptional craftspeople who were attuned to the relationship of wood and the skill of craft?

Paolo agreed with the premise of the question, adding that individual pieces of wood are always different. It was up to the maker to use their skill of working with a specific piece of wood within the given metrics of violin building to create a successful instrument. He had stopped his work on his own violin project to engage in the conversation, and I could see that he had roughed out the top (without the aid of an apprentice) and was now using only a scraper—a thin piece of steel sharpened along its edge—to work down the arching. Extending our conversation to this process, he said that some people use a template to establish the curvature of the arching, but he never does. "The great Cremonese makers rarely used templates for the arching," he said. Paolo's teacher had told him, "If you begin to use them, then you can only ever use them, and you will never have a feel for the nature of the instrument." The piece of maple had a smooth curve, like the gentle undulations of the pond in the field behind the house, and I marveled at how he had really captured the look of natural curvature. He said that he seeks to capture an appearance that resembles fabric in the color and form of curly maple draped across an object, likening the idealized curve to a catenary that captured the imagination of the Enlightenment architects and designers.[11]

THE RIBS

As soon as I began the first process of construction the next morning, the aura of Renaissance and Enlightenment ideals ran quickly out of the workshop. The gentle hum of a spindle sander—one of the few power tools I would use in the construction of the violin—precluded any conversation, and I was eager to begin building up the body of the instrument. Though generally overlooked in the final instrument, forming and bending the ribs of the violin comprise the next step in building the instrument along the interior mold. The thin strips of maple are bent into the iconic bouts of the violin with water and heat, and the wood's stability keeps the form upon which to build the rest of the instrument. From blocks of maple matching the neck and back of the instrument, violin ribs are cut in thin blanks to be brought down to the makers' final dimensions. Luckily, John had provided a set for me to use, so I would need only to make them thinner to facilitate bending. Paolo showed me how to clamp a block close to the sandpaper-covered spindle to form a "fence" and run the rib blanks through, incrementally bringing the block closer and closer to the spindle. I ran the ribs through the spindle sander to bring them down to the rough thickness, about 1.3 millimeters, ending with the six pieces I would need for the violin. Paolo also handed me a set of red maple ribs for his violin project, asking me to dimension them for him while I was at the task. As I fed the pieces through the makeshift sander, I reflected on the plasticity of the thin strips of maple. They were very uniform and felt almost manufactured to specification in how well they were quartered and processed. However, once I began to bend them to fit the mold, the fragility of the fibers of the wood and the skill embedded in the process became apparent.

Through the afternoon, I attempted to bend the ribs to their correct curvatures across the six bouts of the instrument. Paolo had set his bending iron in one of his bench's vises. The steel tool evoked a cross-section of an airplane wing as it protruded out of the bench, connected to the wall by a cord spliced with a dimmer light switch. Paolo explained that he had to modify the tool in order to achieve the right temperature in its heating element. Nevertheless, he tested the heat after about thirty minutes, and water skipped off the hot iron in sign of its readiness. Though he normally wets the wood with a spray bottle, he told me, he couldn't find it on this occasion. In this case, he handed me a large half-gallon mason jar of water in which to dip the wood pieces.

Laying a handled brass strap across one surface of the wettened maple, I followed Paolo's instruction and pulled the thin plank toward me across the hot surface of the iron. Ideally, the middle would gently arc and the ends would wrap around the iron, giving the piece the iconic C-shape of the middle bouts. Remembering my training to allow the wood to release on guitar sides, I bent it slowly across the surface, hearing the sound of the water bubbling out of the wood. The hiss of stream was accompanied by a subtle crack as the fibers ruptured across one of the curls of the grain. I tried again with another piece, and Paolo watched expectantly this time. As I began to pull the wood against the iron this time, he advised me that I was not holding it tight enough. "The wood needs to be held tightly against the iron," he told me. There should be no space between the wood, the iron, and the strap, effectively leaving no gaps for the wood fibers to break into. He took the material and tool in his hands and demonstrated the technique. Paolo held onto the strap, with his thumbs on the inside holding the piece of wood straight and his two forefingers holding onto the small leather-covered wood blocks on the end. He then leaned back, putting his entire body into the motion, and pulled the small piece of wood around the hot iron as the water hissed out of it. He joked that I needed to be harder with it. "Violin making is violent work." On my next attempt, I carefully lined the wood up with the brass strap and put my body into the action. My hands drew the arcs of the C in the air, as I pulled the wood hard against the hot iron. I felt the wood release and then heard a small crack. With frustration, I looked at my diminishing pile of rib blanks and saw that I would need to make some more.

While matching the ribs to the design earlier in the day, Paolo had suggested having the angles of the curls of the maple all following a certain direction to provide continuity in the form, as is the standard practice for violin makers. He likes them to run toward the neck, but he ultimately left this small aesthetic choice to me. At the time, I had joked about using the red maple ribs I had worked up for him to make the instrument stand out. However, with several broken ribs, I was now in the position where I would have to use other wood to make new C-bouts. He pulled a couple pieces of red maple and we discussed how it would look, ultimately agreeing that the difference in size and shape of the figure would appear too patchy. He suggested that I cut a little off the neck blank and use those pieces, so I found an area outside the pattern of the neck and sawed and sanded the new ribs to size. The resulting blanks matched the originals John had given me, and I learned an important lesson in violin repair. Improvisation with materials can be the lifeblood of the craft, particularly in our setting with my limited resources.

With a fresh disposition the next morning, I found that Paolo's direction in bending technique served me well. I successfully bent the ribs of the C-bouts, with little adjustment needed. Paolo showed me how a system of dowels and rubber bands attached to the mold would pull the ribs into position so that when dried fully, they would accommodate the curves of the interior mold. Small dowels stuck through the mold and served as anchoring posts for another larger diameter dowel on the outside of the rib. Holding the large dowel in one hand, I crisscrossed a rubber band quickly between its end and the smaller dowel protruding from the mold and fumbled for another rubber band. It shot off onto the floor of the shop. On my second attempt, I held the free dowl firmly and managed to secure it in place. After all eight were in place, the mold looked ready for the hair dryer at a salon, curls held in place by small cylinders. One by one, I removed them, glued the completed ribs into position on the corner blocks, and replaced them to allow the glue to cure. As Paolo warned, the glue gelled quickly in the winter cold of the shop, so I had to return several times to reheat or reapply the glue. Small gaps appeared between the blocks and the ribs where the maple resisted the sharp curves of the corner blocks. In Paolo's instrument, they had been completely flush, but knowing that I might never approach that level of perfection, I applied a little more glue to close the gap and continued on.

THE NECK AND THE SCROLL

While the glue cured, I laid out the neck of the violin following measurements from a poster of a Stradivari violin and cut off the excess. John had cut the neck blank with a right angle along one of the edges, which Paolo appreciated, as it allows you to cut out the outline of the neck straight through the block of the wood. As I cut with the small band saw, I thought of how John considers his experience as a maker as an addition to the tonewood he supplies. In this case, his decision to make a ninety-degree angle in the block saved me the effort of squaring off a side of the block. It was not only the decisions of a single maker that influenced the success and process of the instrument-in-becoming but also all those who had laid hands upon it before.

Paolo told me to go ahead and drill the holes for the tuning pegs in the peg box at this time, though some other makers do not. He had learned in one of his apprenticeships that this method would save time in the long run, as I could better drill the holes perpendicularly through the block in its rough state. As the holes would need to travel perfectly straight through the center of what would become the peg box, I would use the drill press to auger through the tough maple. However, the surface of the drill press table was adjustable and readily slipped from a flat position. Paolo handed me a digital level and pointed me to a pile of shims and clamps, instructing me to ensure that the neck was level on both axes before drilling. With incrementally thin shavings of spruce, I was finally able to achieve digital flatness, and I quickly sprung on the task. Each spin of the handle brought the spinning blade through the wood and into the sacrificial piece of wood below it with a satisfying scratch, bringing the shape and form of the neck further into reality.

Blowing away chips of maple, I asked Paolo what to do next, as I did after every stage. He advised to keep working on the neck by shaping the scroll and hollowing out the peg box to make space for the strings on the completed instrument. Again, as he seemed to do at every stage, he instinctively reached for that part of his bench that had the necessary tool for the next process. He handed me the rest of the patterns based on the same Strad design I had used earlier. They were in the shape of the various two-dimensional profiles of the scroll, with small holes delineating the shape of the curling volutes and negative space of the peg box. With the point of a drafting compass, I followed the spiral of the pattern around, pricking the surface of the wood and wondering how I could possibly carve something so delicate and fine.

Handing me a saw with a long handle wrapped in bamboo, Paolo advised that I use this Japanese-style saw to begin making angled cuts to established depths that would allow me to rough out the ascendant plane of the surface of the scroll. Unlike so-called Western-style saws whose teeth are sharpened to cut when pushed, Japanese saws cut when pulled and have a smaller blade kerf, allowing for a more controlled cut. I laid out the angled lines and depths and began to cut lines across the top of the neck. They crossed one over another, like a geometry quiz designed to test one's knowledge of complementary angles.

He also gave me large gouge with a wooden handle wrapped with duct tape to begin removing the waste material. Warning me that the wood tends to break along the waves of the curl, he cautioned to take it slowly and "feel the material" through the chisel. The sharp edge of the gouge cut into the maple, resting once it passed through to the next cut. One stroke at a time, the tool peeled away at the lined surface of wood, revealing the shining, fibrous curls beneath that had not been shaped by saw teeth. As I progressed around the inclined spiral of the scroll, I found what I assumed to be a shape I was incapable of carving beginning to take form. I expressed my astonishment, and

Paolo—now working on the diesel engine on the other side of the shop—remarked that refurbishing an engine was like making a violin in that it was not complicated but involved a series of thousands of small steps. Paolo's assurance that violin craft was not magical but rather a commitment to following a series of steps was materially manifesting before my eyes. However, keeping the order and technique of the myriad steps in physical practice was no easy task. I feared that if my mind began to wander, the edge of the gouge—gleaming like a crescent moon—would cut too deep and take off a portion of my spiral.

Throughout the day, I slowly worked my way up and around the volute of the scroll, ending with a rough but recognizable and proportional spiral shape. Paolo encouraged me to begin to carve in the fluting that gradually runs along the dorsal surface, dipping from a ridge in the center like the underside of a leaf. However, at this point he instructed me to begin to think of all the tasks left in the scroll simultaneously and make the piece of wood "flow." I became overwhelmed, thinking of the three dimensions, textures, and curved lines that I would have to not only perfect but carve in perfect correspondence on both sides. With the calm of one who has done this work many times, Paolo told me that I should already carve the *smuso*—a slight bevel on the edge—as it forms a good reference point as you work down the spiral. "There are some makers that only put it on as the final touch, but I find it so helpful to visualize how the scroll flows," he added.

As I sat on the bench with the sun warming my back and my hands working the details of the scroll with increasingly small hand tools, Paolo said, "It's impossible to do one thing completely." It was clear that he was referencing the infinitesimal detail one could achieve in craft, as he looked at me cutting smaller and smaller shavings away from the *smuso* and toward the center of the scroll. Even though the function of the scroll is debated among makers, it is often used as a gloss for the craft skill of makers, a quick check of their woodcarving skills. It seemed to me that a spiral was an appropriate shape, as one could consume infinite time into perfecting the edges, depths, and contours of the scroll. When I finished with the gouge, I turned to a small, specialized scraper and rotated the scroll round and round as I scraped off minuscule shavings of wood for the sake of symmetry and form. The sharp burr of the small piece of steel cut away the dappled marks of the gouge and left the curls and fibers of the maple shining flat beneath it—the spiral shape and ivory undulations evoking a marine shell, which may have been its inspiration.

Noticing the emerging form of the scroll captivated me. Paolo said, "It's all about the flowing line. It can be applied to anything," even as a life philosophy. He talked about how music was a flowing line of notes from one to the other

Fig. 4.4. The emerging scroll of the violin

and projected his idea about flowing lines out the window of the shop and into the physical world around us. The violin in itself is a collection of flowing lines, not circles, as he previously had suggested—spirals flowing into themselves; a circle moving through time. That is what gives the violin its energy and motion: "It's a spiral that gives energy to that flowing line."

I connected this back to the ideals of proportions that Paolo had talked about when discussing the golden mean, which he said is reflected in the volute of the scroll. We discussed why the spiral of the scroll was the chosen symbol for violin makers. Was it a connection to the "natural" spirals of snail shells and growing plants?[12] Or was it perhaps an evocation of the Ionian capitals of Greek columns? Paolo answered that "maybe people are seeking proportions and order to see a little light in the darkness." He speculated that when Giuseppe Guarneri in 1731 became Giuseppe Guarneri del Gesú and dedicated all of his instruments to Jesus Christ, perhaps he was looking to bring some order to the restless nature of his work. Paolo conditionally added that any violin maker who has been creating instruments for years is in doing it for the sense of self-fulfillment. "The satisfaction comes from a job well done as a maker." But maybe Guarneri was searching for something beyond the work to give his labor to.

Struck by the emergence of this philosophical conversation in the midst of a quiet, contemplative task, I asked Paolo if he thought that being engaged in craft practice made him more philosophical. He said that the work is solitary and there is a lot of time to think, but the best work that he does is when he is "in the zone." When he is only in the craft, fully engaged with the material, and not really thinking is when he does his best work. He might look up minutes later and realize that he has been doing really good work without philosophizing about it. I had also been "in the zone" in the asymptotic carving of the scroll, yet the empirical part of me felt the need to quantify the time that was being invested in the work.

I asked him how long he takes to make a scroll, and Paolo responded by telling me about a master's school for violin craft, where the entrance exam was a scroll that the applicant had seven days to finish. He said his first probably took about seven days but now he could do it in two or three eight-hour days, and his completed scroll stood on the bench as a testament. But he warned me that I should not be too concerned about time in making. "There are only two times that violin makers rush through their work," he told me; "when they are about to make a mistake or when they have just made a mistake." When he makes a mistake that seems really difficult to remedy, he'll often walk away from it. A couple of hours later after telling me this, he sprung up out of his seat and exclaimed that he needed a break. He had not made a mistake but was tired of looking at the same spot on the arching on the back. His realization that he was no longer in the zone and not sure what he was doing had fatigued him. A violin maker he had apprenticed for in Holland had said, "If you don't enjoy it, why do it?" He said he tries to keep this ideal going in his craft: "You still have to make a livelihood but do the work that you enjoy." With that statement, he walked out of the shop and began working on fitting a refurbished starter motor into his rebuilt engine.

THE BELLY AND THE BACK

While I was working on the scroll, Paolo had begun arching out the interior of the back of his violin. Though "Strad didn't have a drill press," Paolo was using the large machine to serve as a guide for the process of removing material from what would be the interior of the back of the violin. He had set up a small piece of board with a piece of hot glue stick protruding from it that would be used to drill holes to a relative depth in the back. This is the same technique, he described, that Strad's workers would have used to save time in carving out the back of the violin, albeit with a mechanized tool. As he dipped the spinning bit of the drill, he positioned the maple back of the violin over the point of the glue stick. Each plunge of the spinning blade would cut into the maple to a predetermined depth, leaving about three millimeters between the arched exterior of the back and the depth to which the drill bit had sunk. The result was the so-called Swiss cheese method of removing material, as it had left the interior of the back plate covered in half-inch holes that bored down into the maple and would serve as indicators of the proper depth.

After drilling, he used a series of curved planes, gouges, and scrapers to bring the inside arching to the correct depth and made it perfectly smooth, again previewing a task that I would be involved with shortly. While he worked with the back in the violin cradle, I noticed how flexible the wood was becoming, as I could see the wood bending and flexing as he carved into it with a gouge. He lifted it out and twisted and torqued the maple back in his hands to show me how flexible it had become.

I was very surprised to see the wood known for its durability behaving in this way; the thin, arched shape and rounded bouts now gave way to a parabolic bend as he finished the inside with a fine scraper. As he worked, Paolo talked about how he gets a sense of the material by working it with the chisels. Through the chisel, he can sense the irregularities of the material and how it will work. With two hands pushing away from his chest in concerted strokes, he gesticulated the crafting motion of planing wood while he reiterated that knowing the wood is a crucial aspect to making a successful instrument. He said that people are also looking to buy instruments with a human connection that manifests through this relationship. "People like knowing the maker and where it comes from. They are paying for 'this,'" he said as he widely gestured around the shop to its aesthetic assemblage of tools and materials. "People could know machines," he speculated, adding with a wry smile. "This is *my* CNC [Computer and Numerical Control Router] 2000. I'm kind of torn," he said, "because I like gadgets and machines, and I would like to make a machine, but for the subtle stylistic differences, it's not the way to go."

Moving forward, he jokingly asked me if I wanted to see the birth of the instrument. He had lightly glued the back onto the ribs, still attached to the mold, and was beginning the process of removing the mold and "closing the box." He laid a sturdy rasp across the tops of the exposed ribs and extracted the mold by gradually tightening clamps that pulled it up and out of the instrument. He quipped that it was a natural birth and told me how he had broken ribs in this process before by attempting it too fast or by not spreading the pressure across the blocks with the suspended rasp. With surprising speed, he glued on the finished top. By the end of the day, he was able to tone-tap the instrument body for the first time to access what it might sound like. As he tapped, I heard the high tone of the instrument speaking out for the first time, and he tried to keep the tone alive in his mind by singing the same note. Holding the note with his voice, he reached for a tuning fork, struck it on the edge of the bench, compared it to his own sustained note, and figured that the note was in the acceptable range for this stage of the instrument. Once quieted, the tuning fork was also a quick way to measure the potential projection of the instrument. Paolo struck the tines of the fork against the edge of the bench again and placed the ball of its handle on the top of the violin where the bridge would sit. The vibrations passed through the fork to the top and amplified the tone, ringing the note through the shop. Paolo passed it around the surface of the violin, and we listened carefully as it diminished in volume around the edges before being restored around the center. Watching this process unfold excited me to begin carving out the back and top, which still sat on my bench in their squared-off and bookmatched blank forms. Surveying the pieces and the processes that would come next, Paolo explained,

> Ninety-nine percent of violin tops are two pieces, and the reason for that is structural and acoustical. Most trees start out growing fast to try and reach the sun as quickly as they can, and there's not that much mass, so they can put on a big growth ring every year. So at the beginning, when tree starts growing, it has wider growth rings. Then on the outside they get thinner and thinner. And so, where the bridge is you want tight growth rings, because that's a little stiffer, and you want [them] equal on both sides, slowly getting wider towards the outside. The only way to do that is to take two pieces of wood and bookmatch them.

With the last sentence, he unfolded his hands facing the ceiling and knocked the heels of his large palms together with a click of his tongue. To rejoin what had been cut apart on a sawmill in Romania, I worked on making what would be the inside of the top and the back perfectly flat in order to join them. With one bookmatched piece below the other, I used a long-footed jointer plane to make each piece perfectly flat. Watching me push the two-handed tool across the surface of the piece of maple, he said that he really likes this stage of the process—making the board perfectly flat—and I remembered his rhythmic cadence when planing the boards for own instrument. Noticing the occasional skitter and stop in my novice technique, he instructed me to not push the plane but to "let it flow across the board and let it find the high spots."

The spruce top went fast, and the sharp edge of the plane, having just been stropped by Paolo, slid across the surface, cutting away ribbons of spruce with a smooth scraping sound. It moved quickly, and I soon had the spruce ready for gluing. The maple did not go so easily, and though I felt that I would have it flat when "Old World Tonewoods" brand was cut out with the planer, I found the piece to be bowing. Paolo told me that this can happen if you do not apply even pressure through the tool. As it begins to leave the board, it will begin to cut off a slope at the edges of the board. Ultimately, he said that my troubles were due to the plane's blade simply not being sharp enough anymore. As I sharpened it on the ceramic whetstones, he reminded me once more that there is no magic in violin making—only sharp tools. Once the steel was sharpened and replaced in the plane, I once again found the flow of the craft action, let the tool find the high spots, and the flattened board was ready for joining.

In preparation for the next step, Paolo set up a large piece of glass on his bench and clamped a large wooden joining plane on its side along the edge of the glass, forming what is known as a "shooting board." He adjusted the blade of the plane and instructed me to scrawl some hard paraffin wax on the boards and on the glass so that it would run smoothly. Running the wood against the plane this time, I followed his advice to let the tool take away high spots. With each pass of the wood making a satisfying scrape, the plane's blade made quick work of it, ribbons of spruce and maple collected behind the plane. After several passes, I would check the squareness of the wood against a steel scale, checking for gaps between the wood and the straightedge.

Paolo asked if I knew about the light test, and I responded by holding the bookmatched pieces of the top up to the window's light as I had learned from Chris. A warm glow appeared around the edges where I held it, but the joint was perfectly flush and no light peeked through. I was glad to see no light, but I also felt another joy in the clack of the wood as the complementary surfaces pushed out the air between them. We took stock of the sound, bringing the wood together a few times, and Paolo agreed that the specific clunk of the wood also meant that the corresponding edges were ready to be joined.

I was getting ready to glue the back and top, but a quick check with the mold showed that the body of the violin was a little big for the back and top I had worked up. Tracing over the pattern with a finger, I saw that I had followed a wrong line in my pattern when cutting it out, so the instrument was much larger than it should have been. Paolo was surprised that he had not noticed this, but he chalked it up to the ratio and proportion still looking correct—perhaps due to the method of design. Ultimately, I had to remove the blocks and mold, bring the body of the mold down a few millimeters, and recarve the mold to accommodate the blocks. This was an excellent example of how small errors in the craft process compound as you progress through the series of steps. I worked hurriedly (and admittedly sloppily) so that I might return to the top and back plates.

Errors corrected, for the time being, I cut out and glued on tabs on the edges and surfaces of the back and top to create clamping surfaces to bring the center joints together. During a "dry run," Paolo showed me how he holds two clamps at a time and puts them on in unison when clamping the tabs on the end. I struggled at first with the coordination required to open and close the spring clamps simultaneously. But after a few attempts, he proclaimed me ready to join the pieces. Following his instructions, I used a hair dryer to warm up the surfaces, applied a thick amount of glue, rubbed the glue surfaces together until they basically stuck, then applied the hand clamps at the same time. Hide glue squeezed out of the joint in the middle, and it looked like it came together well. While Paolo uses the clamping method, many violin makers simply rub the joint together until it sticks. The qualities of the hide glue and the perfectly flat surface combine to create a tension that will hold the pieces together until the glue has cured. I was not so sure of my ability to join the wood, so I opted to continue with the clamping method for the back.

After the glue had sat to cure overnight, I used the bench plane to bring the plates down to an approximate thickness. With a pencil stuck through a washer, I traced the outline of the mold on the plates, the washer's thickness an index of the overhang on the completed instrument. After following that line with the continuous cut of a band saw, I could see all the blank pieces of wood starting to take shape as components of a violin. I told Paolo that it felt good to have made that much progress in a short period of time, after working on the scroll for so long. He said that's why he got into violin making, as it allows a much shorter time period before being able to see the progress of your work. In his previous pursuit of a career as a concert cellist, he felt that he could practice and practice and not really feel that he had made progress between one day and another. Making a violin allowed him to see that giving the practiced skill and labor a material form can be visualized in the greater scope of his work.

This ethic appeared to develop in his appreciation for the work of all violin makers, including those whose work had been destroyed or were anonymous. While working on setting up a plate for arching, I dropped a tool behind the bench. I found it nested in a basket below the bench that had pieces of old violins in various states of disrepair and outright destruction. One neck had the ribs curiously set into the neck and the fingerboard pinned on instead of simply glued. As I picked through the instrument pieces, many of which had arrived in a trash bag from a friend, I found many of them bore signatures or stamps beyond the label of the maker. One top had three different names with subsequent dates, along with a small portrait of Jesus that someone had pasted on the inside. Paolo told me that this was common practice for repairers to sign and date the changes that they had made to the instrument, leaving a record of the work that they had done. Gazing on the pile of orchestral flotsam, Paolo lamented, "Somewhere, sometime, somebody spent a lot of time on that instrument, so I can't throw it away even though it will never play again." I thought of my own violin in this context, and a deep sense of time washed over me. Would the scroll end up in a basket in some unborn violin maker's workshop? Would a crack develop in a decade and be fixed with an interior cleat and a quick signature by the repairer?

In carving the arching of the top and back, the first step is "hogging out" as much material as possible. The plate is bolted to a board to keep it station-ary, and the thickness is marked along the edges to establish the high and low points of the plate. Paolo instructed me to chisel out the basic, easing curvature on the long axis, then establish a flat edge around the plate before returning with a series of small planes to work the rough arching into shape. The hard maple resisted the large gouge that I used and required the use of a wooden mallet to remove large chunks of the material. I found it easier to work into the grain up the arching rather than with it, as it split off in larger pieces. The work was slow going and hard on the hands, wrists, and elbows. The maple tore out along its figure with each gouge stroke, threatening to take more than anticipated if I worked too fast or greedily.

He offered little in the way of how to establish the exact curvature, prefer-ring to check in on my progress and tell me whether I was close or not. As with many of the tasks, I had to return to Paolo's central aesthetic. Did it look right? Did the curve of the arch follow a proportion or line one would see in natural

Fig. 4.5. An old violin top bearing the signatures of previous repairs and a small icon

forms? Did it *flow*? He said that the one thing that really set the Cremonese makers apart was their mastery of arching—even if there were tool marks or other little things off, the arching would always be perfectly blended into a continuous curve. I expressed some reservations over my ability to achieve that level of competency. But with a wave of his hands emulating the arching's easy fade, he stressed that once you establish the high point for the bridge, everything simply blends to the edges that you have established.

He recommended using shadow as an indicator to see how the arching blended and determine if there are any spots that need to be taken down. Using a scraper with a flat edge, he demonstrated how I could use the shadow that it projected onto the instrument's surface to identify flat spots in the gradual curvature. Ideally, the shadow would bow away from the scraper's edge along the surface of the instrument. Any place where it lingered along the tool's edge indicated a flat spot that would need to be removed. I had to return to this technique several times, especially in the long arch of the lower bout. However, with work—and blistered thumbs from pushing a small plane through the tough maple—the tool-marked and splintered rough wood gave way to a smooth, arched, curly maple surface that Paolo deemed acceptable.

Following Paolo's technique of using the drill press to establish references on the interior, I quickly removed material from the corresponding arching on the inside. I found that the holes provided a reference of depth for "hogging out" the interior as well as negative space into which the wood could shift and break as I pushed the large gouge through it, feeling the fatigue and bruises in my palms. I worked eagerly and quickly, aided by a toothed plane with a rounded foot that seemed to eat the wood fibers as I pushed it through the maple. Paolo advised that I check the thickness with a micrometer and pencil in the relative thickness in each area as I continued. It was easy to take too much out, he said, and once you remove it, you cannot put it back. The wood flexed in the cradle as I worked it, and I proceeded much faster than I had expected.

I established the rough depths and began working with a scraper to make the interior surface as smooth as I had seen Paolo's about a month earlier. Again, Paolo instructed me to use the sunlight streaming through the south window as a reference. When holding the back up to the light, the wood warmed with a gentle, orange translucence. The warmth of the orange color is an index of the relative thickness and a guide indicating which areas to avoid while scraping. Paolo was a little surprised by how warm the orange light at the back of the maple was and marked an X with a pencil in one area, instructing me to avoid that area. When I checked it with a micrometer, it was indeed too thin, and I had to leave it with some rough tool marks. Unfortunately, this close attention, and perhaps the hurried work that had preceded it, revealed a near-fatal mistake. A stream of light had betrayed a slight opening about the thickness of a piece of paper in the joint of the back.

Following Paolo's advice, I massaged glue into the joint and attempted to stick it back together. But it appeared that the wood was no longer flush, and it would not come back together despite my best efforts. The joint was not simply broken; the wood had moved altogether in the arching process. Paolo said that it was hard to know what was happening in any given piece of wood, and carving out the arching could change the ways the fibers behave. The work had released a hidden tension in the wood, causing it to resist what I had assumed to be a static state. Knowing a tree by making dozens of instruments as Paolo does, I thought, reveals not only its qualities in tone and workability but also its capacity for change.

As a result of this change, I spent the rest of the day replaning and joining the back. Paolo encouraged me to simply break the back open with my hands, and I found that the glue snapped as I pushed open the seam, popping the piece open into its constituent pieces. I reset the shooting board, cut a new joint, and got ready to glue the back again. However, as the pieces were no longer solid blocks with centimeters of joining area but irregular forms with a very small surface area to join, the gluing presented a new problem. Throughout my apprenticeship, Paolo had coached me through problem solving, finding ways to adapt to my mistakes with proven techniques. But in this case, we worked together to find a solution.

We would need to figure out how to apply transverse pressure across the plate, while keeping it from buckling in the center. I tried and failed to make several setups work before suggesting that I just hold the pieces together. Paolo laughed and doubted that I could hold it for the long period. But he added, while clasping his hands together, a violin maker his brother had apprenticed with claimed that hands were the best clamps. Without the strength or patience to hold the wood, I opted to find some clamping method that might work. Ultimately, I found that a system of large table clamps and wood wedges held the pieces in place and demonstrated its effectiveness to Paolo in a dry run. I replicated the dry run several times for speed and accuracy, worrying about the outcome, and finally glued it back together. It appeared to hold, but Paolo advised that I put cleats through the entire joint to assuage any future anxieties.

With the back more or less finished, I ran through the same arching process with the spruce top. I found the material much easier to work and sped through the process, with the gouge making a ripping sound as it peeled through the soft wood. Paolo told me that in his experience, it feels like carving butter after the hard maple and goes much quicker. The softer density of the spruce, however, drew the tool into the wood much easier than the maple. I caught myself having to back out several times, feeling the tool cutting the wood fibers too deeply into the plate. I completed the top over the next two days, following the same patterns and processes of arching as used on the back. As I cleaned up my workbench after the final scraping, I noticed that the different tools and processes created a wide range of waste—all of which ended up heating us from the winter cold in the large cast-iron wood stove. The gouge ripped out large curls; the drill press punched holes in ragged scraps that split easily; the planes cut paper-thin shavings; and the scrapers left fine, downy fibers. I sorted each into piles, and we thought of how they were indices of the processes of creating the instrument as much as the pieces that were about to come together into the form of the violin.

JOINING THE PIECES

After arching the top and back plates, Paolo told me to move to the next phase of finishing the interior structure of the instrument by installing a bass bar. The bass bar is typically a separate piece of wood that is carved to the exact profile of the interior arching of the top. It is responsible for transferring vibrations from the bridge throughout the whole of the top of the instrument, one of the two hidden movers of sound in the instrument, together with the sound post. It also strengthens the top arching to resist the tension of the strings. As it is crucial to have full lengths of wood fibers to transmit the sound, the bass bar would be made from a piece of spruce that John had split out for this purpose. Splitting, rather than cutting or sawing, ensures that the fibers stay complete throughout the length of the bar, instead of "running out" of the edges.

I planed the bass bar down to a smooth blank and cut it out to follow a rough pattern of the interior arching. What followed was an intense period of fitting the piece exactly to the interior so that it might distribute the vibrations of the bridge evenly throughout the entire top. I rubbed blue chalk across the top and placed the bar blank on top of it, moving the bar only slightly to pick up chalk from the top. When removed, the chalk registered the high spots, showing me where to bring the spruce down, first with a chisel and then with a scraper. Repeating this process dozens of times, I finally came away with a bass bar surface completely covered in chalk about five hours later. Paolo checked its contact with the top. The bar made a thick clunk as it rested into position, a sonic index of its connection to the rest of the instrument. I then glued the bass bar in with sharp C-shaped clamps that were held in place only by friction, as was the process of Strad according to Paolo, and left the bar to glue. When it was dry, Paolo instructed me to round it along the top and bring the ends down a gentle slope to a feathered end with a chisel. He said that the "flexibility would help keep the bar from being knocked loose if the violin ever sustained an unwanted blow," demonstrating once again the foresight required by the craft.

Paolo said he was impressed with the speed with which I had fit the bar. He typically does it in about four hours, though he remembered classmates struggling through the process for days in violin school. It reminded him of the two different methods of learning the practice of violin making: speed or detail. One of his last apprentices had worked very slowly, meticulously poring over the minute details. With the mistakes that I had made through the process, I had opted for the speed method. Paolo said either path could take you to the combination of speed and detail that you need to produce instruments for a livelihood that must be made timely and with high quality. If you worked quickly, you would be more prone to mistakes at first, but you would eventually learn the measured practice of detail needed to produce a finer looking and sounding instrument. If you began with more attention to detail and worked more slowly, you would learn how to execute that attention with greater confidence and speed in time. In both cases, you would be adjusting your technique through practice to better control the exactness of the relationship between your corporeal movements and the qualities of the wood.

Managing this relationship would be tested in the last major task I had to complete before "closing the box" of the violin: the installation of the purfling. Set into the edge of the top and back, Paolo explained, the purfling serves both as an aesthetic accent and a means to mitigate the spread of an edge crack due to a blow or humidity. Made of stable laminated strips of pear wood, it runs around the perimeter of the instrument and slightly constricts the ability of the top and back to swell and shrink. Since pear is also denser than spruce, he described, the whole outline of the top becomes denser, which is acoustically beneficial. Paolo joked that Strad had a pear tree in his yard and that set the trend, though people have historically used a range of other materials. Nineteenth-century Dutch makers used whale baleen, some contemporary makers use a synthetic that does not need to be bent, and Paolo speculated that locally grown persimmon would make a suitable replacement.

Digging through his tool chest filled with specialized tools underneath his bench, he produced a purfling scorer. The tool has two parallel blades set to score two lines that then can be carved out to accommodate the inlayed purfling. I carved out the purfling channels, having to take three passes to make it wide and deep enough to accommodate the purfling. The toughness of the maple once again presented a challenge, and I looked forward to working

Fig. 4.6. Blue chalk marks the place where the bass bar is fitted to the interior of the top

the spruce top. However, I found that the difference between the spring and summer growth created an unexpected hurdle. The relative rigidity of the summer growth as compared to the soft spring growth effectively created channels for the blades to ride in.[13] Despite my efforts to keep the blades running parallel to the edge of the top, the lines of the grain pulled the blades out of line, causing a wider channel than I needed.

Paolo had a specialized chisel that he had made for removing the material for the inlay. I used it in addition to a sharp knife to clear the channel and fit the bent strip of pear into the slot as I worked. When I glued the purfling in, Paolo showed me how to keep it directly above the slot as I progressed around the instrument. The wood quickly swells with the glue and will refuse the purfling if you do not install it immediately. I did the C-bouts and cut the extra space for the "sting" of the purfling. At the corner, the two strips meet at an acute angle and extend into a thin strip shaped like a bee stinger. Like the scroll, the stings are sometimes used as a quick gloss for the quality of craftwork of the instrument. Once I had installed the purfling, a comparison to Paolo's "stings" demonstrated the difference between a master violin maker and an apprentice. All his stings symmetrically extended evenly into almost imperceptible points; mine did not. With the purfling in place, I placed the top in position above the back and sides, and I felt the instrument becoming something more than individual pieces of wood for the first time.

I applied a thin wash of glue to the interior of the violin in order to mitigate the passage of humidity and then glued the top on to close the box. Feeling like some small piece of ceremony was missing, I asked Paolo if it is common practice to include anything when closing the violin. He replied that Jean-Baptiste Vuillaume (1798–1875) had inserted portraits of himself in certain violins that could be seen through the end pin. He also mentioned the old tradition of inserting a rattlesnake rattle into the body of the violin. Many violins that he had fixed up for local people had these inside, and we speculated about the purpose. I had heard it was a magical charm meant to drive away negative spiritual connotations—a vestige of Puritan beliefs about music or West African material traditions that accompanied the vast tradition of African American violin players in the American South. Paolo responded that he had thought the rattle would deter any rodents or pests from seeking shelter inside the instrument, as he had worked on a few attic instruments that had signs of past tenants. With no rattlesnake tail, I opted for a small drawing on the neck block, applied the glue and clamps to close the box, and found that the pieces of wood were now an instrument-in-becoming, a violin "in the white."

The last major phase of putting the instrument together was to fit the neck into a mortise joint in the neck block. Paolo instructed me to use a chisel to clean up the heel of the neck and to be careful to let the chisel do the work of keeping the surface flat. "The chisel wants to take out the high points," he told me, alluding this time to the agency of the cutting edge. However, I struggled to hold the blade of the chisel down with one hand while cutting across the surface, and as a result, the material was difficult to manage. Wherever I would get it in one dimension, the other dimension would go out when a bump or bow might appear. After some time carving and checking the dimensions with a flat edge of a millimeter scale to check the surface, I finally achieved flat surfaces in all dimensions.

The complementary part of the joint would be the mortise in the body of the instrument, and Paolo illustrated how to cut out the slot that the neck would fit into. He took the body of the instrument between his legs and held it against the edge of the workbench to provide stability as he carved. I took over, and the chisel cut fast through the spruce to empty out the cavity of the mortise. As the neck is slightly angled to make it easier for players to access the treble strings, the neck joint's position must be conceptualized in three dimensions. Paolo explained, "There's the left to right, which centers the fingerboard over the top, the front to back, which controls the neck projection, and the rotation clockwise/counterclockwise, which creates the slightly higher 'overstand' on the treble side for ease of playability."

Once the dimensions of the mortise fit closer to the heel of the neck, Paolo instructed me to rub chalk onto the heel and then carefully place it into the joint. After removing the heel, the chalk indicated which areas of the heel were touching the neck block. After each fitting, a light pass with the chisel took away the high spots marked with chalk. Feeling too confident in the progress, I lost concentration and cut too much away. In another instance of learning violin repair as I was taught the construction of the instrument, Paolo demonstrated how I could find a matching piece of maple and glue it into place on the heel as a patch. It served the purpose, and within the next two days I was able to fit the neck into the mortise perfectly.

It was time to glue the neck into the body, and Paolo recommended that I use a hair dryer to heat up the joint to extend the working time of the hide glue. As he looked around the tall shelves of the shop, he was unable to find the appliance and suggested that I use the same method as did Stradivari—since *he* didn't have a hair dryer. He took a small lamp down from a shelf that had a crystal font and a small chrome top holding a wick. It was a "spirit" lamp, Paolo noted, adding that its denatured alcohol fuel would not leave any soot.[14] He showed me how to heat up the wood of the heel over the flame of the lamp, moving the body and heel in figure eights above the clean-burning, bright flame. I joked that he had repeatedly told me there was no magic in the process, yet there we were moving things in hypnotic patterns above the "spirit" lamp to make sure the joint held.[15] I heated up the pieces of wood and glued them into place, and Paolo jokingly asked if I had said the correct magic incantation to make sure the neck would not break out of its new seat.

We had ordered the fingerboards for both of our instruments from a luthier's supply catalog, but the fingerboard would need finishing before I could spot glue it on. There is a slight concavity in the middle of the fingerboard that must be created in order to create clearance beyond the fingered note in which the string can vibrate freely. The part of the fingerboard that extends over the body is also lightened to adjust the tone of the instrument. Taking a gouge and scrapers, I removed the extra ebony along the bottom. Paolo gave me an option of "tuning" the fingerboard by placing it on table as it would rest on the neck of the violin and thumbing the end to produce a tone. I worked to tune it to the closest note, unsure of what total effect it would have on the final instrument.

While the ebony was tough to cut, it was regular and responded well to the sharp edge of the gouge. I was surprised at the dark color and consistency of the wood for the price from the catalog, recalling the stack of fingerboards at Chris's guitar shop. I found it contrasted in color and quality to the piece of cello neck Paolo gave me from which to cut the nut and saddle of the violin. When I cut into that piece, I noticed that it had been painted black to cover brown streaks and occasional swirls in the wood. Paolo assured me that the ebony would be tough enough to handle the strings and "gut" of the tailpiece. It was a matter of aesthetic choice, Paolo described, and many of the original Cremonese instruments had not even used ebony in the fingerboards. This resounded with the issues of a modern aesthetic based in expectation of material perfection that played part in the overexploitation of certain tree species—in this case, ebony.[16]

As I carved the space where the saddle would fit, I remembered that Paolo had advised me to cut a small space on either side of the ebony. He said that factories, where instruments are produced to exact specification, often do not consider how the spruce moves with changing heat and humidity and will fit the ebony piece exactly to the spruce. When the spruce expands, the ebony stays stable and pushes back against the spruce, which can cause cracks.[17] While only a small space is needed, this kind of attention to the changing qualities of the wood can provide some assurance that the instrument will continue to be operable outside the shop.

The last step before applying finish would be to carve the neck and the button, where the back is glued against the heel. Using Paolo's handmade knife and instruction, I carved the button until it appeared to be like a setting sun above the plane created by two small notches on the bottom. He told me the area of the semicircle should reflect the golden ratio to "look right." In carving out the neck, I worked with rasps after it was clear that the wood was going to chip out around the curls in the maple, following the basic contours of a pattern Paolo had given me. I scraped the pieces into a smooth contour, revealing the stripes of curl in the wood, and I had then completed the construction of the violin.

FINISHING

Though Paolo had told me that there were no secrets among violin makers, I found that applying the varnish to the surface of the instrument was one of the areas where makers were likely to withhold the results of their experimentation. Along with the origins and treatments of the Cremonese makers' tonewood, the methods of making and applying the varnish are one of the most debated and tested aspects of violin craft. Paolo made his own varnish by boiling colophony in linseed oil to a colored viscous substance that dries onto the wood. Colophony, also used for the rosin of violin bows, is the complementary by-product of producing turpentine from pine resin. The resultant varnish is applied in coats, thinned out by turpentine—an unexpected recombination of the separated parts of the resin. While some makers include additives to influence the color of the varnish or its influence on tone, Paolo used only the linseed and colophony. As he normally boils the mixture for a couple of days, and he had just used the rest of his stock on his violin, he offered a varnish made of amber (fossilized tree pitch) and linseed oil for me to use.

This process is one that violin makers obsess over, recognizing the varnish's ability to elevate the instrument into different categories of aesthetic beauty and liveliness. Speaking of the Cremonse makers, Paolo told me,

> That's something they could really breathe life into it, make it look like it was alive, like it had blood in it. And that's something. You know, you put a violin in anywhere and it looks right. You can put it in the woods, you can put it in the seat of car, and you can put it in a restaurant. It just looks right. A stop sign, it stands out. And that's why it looks like that, so it stands out. But a violin, it blends in and it looks natural. The varnish was a big part of it. They knew their materials so well and how to apply them that it just brought out—it just kind of went into the wood and brought out more of the wood, but it didn't cover anything. It didn't make it look anything that it wasn't supposed to look like. Totally natural, but enhanced it. That's something that's difficult to do.

The violin is prepared for the finish by first applying a wash of hide glue to the inside of the instrument, which provides a protective layer to slow the movement of moisture in and out of the wood. Paolo will also "burnish" the surface of the instrument with the stems of the local horsetail plant (*Equisetum hyemale*), whose cells have a high concentration of silicates, to smooth out the wood fibers on the plates.

Spring had arrived timely, as applying the varnish is typically outside work for Paolo; the fumes of the turpentine bothered him, and the linseed oil base of the varnish can only dry in direct ultraviolet light. While he had set up UV lamps in a closet of the shop to cure the violin finish, he preferred to string it up by a wire outside to give it direct sunlight. I worked to apply the first coat with brush, smelling the sharp sting of the turpentine and watching the solution soak into the grain. With each layer, the added richness of the amber color stood in increasing contrast to the blue March sky, a complementary tone that set the violin in contrast and concert with the natural surroundings at once. Brushing each layer on, I would then hang it by a tree branch to dance in the sun, taking the occasional break to fly kites with Paolo and his kids in the March wind.

I asked him how I would know when I was finished applying the varnish, and he said that he applied six coats to his last instrument. But he added that it is mainly about getting a balance of texture. It's important for the varnish to soak into the wood to give the impression that you are seeing into the wood while still maintaining the three-dimensionality of the grain's surface. Paolo said that you need to let the varnish emphasize the wood's material qualities rather than cover it up under a thick layer. He bemoaned instruments that have "bowling ball" finishes that allow you to see into the grain but cover up its surface texture.

Over the next week, I added six layers of varnish, applying the solution at my house, Paolo's workshop, and even John Preston's shop, where I had begun work with him. With the layers accumulated on the surface, giving the instrument a unique pale-blonde color, Paolo had me rub down the finish with very fine sandpaper and linseed oil and then rottenstone or tripoli powder to smooth out the finish.

With the neck installed, the violin needed only finishing touches and setup in order to be restored back to a singing state. I would need to fit the bridge, set the soundpost inside the instrument, clean up the fingerboard, and fit the tuning pegs. The placement of the removable bridge is crucial to the instrument. Even the highest quality instruments can be undone by a bridge that has not been properly positioned and fitted. Bridges are typically not made by luthiers but by companies that specialize in producing the perfectly quartersawn pieces with distinctive cutouts, known as the "heart," "kidneys," and "feet" of the instrument.

Fig. 4.7. Paolo's violin curing in the early spring sunlight

Responsible for the direct transfer of the sound waves from the bowed strings to the body for resonance, the bridges, Paolo explained, rock back and forth on a microscopic level as they transfer sound from the bowed strings through the instrument. Full contact and correct placement are necessary to transfer sound on both the uneven surface of the top and through the bass bar inside the instrument. Using a business card slit down the middle and a flexible scale to measure through the f-hole, we located the bass bar within the instrument. One arm of the business card pushed against the bass bar inside the instrument, while the other laid on top, showing the location where the bridge foot should fit. With a pin, we pricked a dot marking the placement of the bridge foot and a corresponding mark on the other side.

Laying a piece of improvised graphite paper—typing paper with pencil lead rubbed liberally on one side—on the place where the bridge would fit exactly, Paolo moved the bridge slightly back and forth. When he lifted it, we could see the graphite as a measure of the contact with the uneven surface of the wood. As I had practiced in fitting the bass bar and the neck mortise, I knew the job would be done when the feet were completely covered in slick, dark-gray dust.

Paolo handed me his homemade bridge knife to cut away those barely perceptible high points. Following my Boy Scout instruction to always cut away from my body, I couldn't be precise enough with the blade to remove the gray points. Paolo watched patiently before correcting my grip and approach to the cutting. He told me to cradle the knife handle in my fingers with the blade facing toward me and curl the fingers into my palm to cut with the blade. This was a much more exact way of cutting and allowed me to control the knife's movement through the resistance of the wood. I worked for hours afterward, taking bit by bit, but I eventually had it perfectly flush with the uneven surface. Afterward, he showed me how to remove material from spots on the bridge, chamfering or beveling around the "heart," "feet," and "kidneys" of the piece of wood to direct soundwaves and make the wood more flexible, ultimately improving the tone.

While the names of these parts of the bridge are taken from their likeness in shape to anatomical forms, we joked about what role they might perform in transmission of sound. The heart obviously pumps the sound through the bridge, and the kidneys purify the tone, giving clarity to the instrument's voice. This tradition of naming parts after human or animal body parts extends through the entire instrument. On the scroll, the high points are often known as the eyes, while the protruding edges are known as ears. The edges of the scroll box are referred as cheeks. The bottom of the neck curls around to form the heel. The upper bout is also known as the shoulder, the C-bouts are known as the waist, the sides of the instrument are the ribs, and the top and back plates are also known as the belly and back, respectively. These terms are used interchangeably among English-speaking violin makers—extending through translation into German, French, and Italian—and speak to a personification of the instrument, whereas its tone speaks to its actual liveliness.

The ebony tuning pegs we had ordered from a luthier's catalog would also need to be custom fit to the instrument. I cut off the extra length and then used the peg shaver, a tool similar to a pencil sharpener, which removed ebony in thin, brittle sheets as I rotated the peg inside it. After dozens of rounds of turns, my thumb and forefinger began to ache, but I continued on, motivated by the prospect of a finished instrument. My thumb blistered against the durability of the ebony, but I soon had the four pegs roughly fit. The final fitting, Paolo noted, would be more sensitive. He instructed me to place the pegs in the holes that I had cleaned up with a reamer and spin them around. After withdrawing the peg, he placed it to his lips to measure the heat that was created through friction in the two contact points. He instructed me to follow this method and lightly sand down the areas that were hottest, until the pegs fit well but were not too tight on one side or the other. I followed course, checking the pegs for heat in this manner, and before too long they evenly fit through the holes of the peg box.

Finally, I installed the sound post, which was cut from a dowel of spruce. Paolo joked that the English word was inadequate as compared to the French âme, or soul, that violin makers often use to describe the piece. Sitting underneath the opposite foot of the bridge as the bass bar in the instrument, the sound post conducts sound from the top and the bridge through to the back of the instrument. It is held into position by only friction, and care must be taken to assure that it does not dig into or pressure the back or top. As a result, it is perfectly fitted inside the instrument, making its installation difficult.

After I finished measuring the inside space, cutting the dowel to size, and correcting the angles, Paolo showed me how to spear the instrument on a sound post setter, feed it through the f-hole, and position it with the other end of the tool. I worked the better part of the day feeding the sound post into the f-hole, positioning it, hearing a woody clink as it fell, and trying again. With a little guidance from Paolo on how to use the tool in concert with the body of the instrument, I found it was easier to brace the tool against the inside of the back to apply variable pressure in a similar fashion as holding the knife when carving the bridge. Once the sound post was in position, the final test was to make sure that it was not too fixed in place. Paolo took off the end pin that holds the tail piece, peered through it, and squeezed the sides of the violin. This caused the top and back to slightly separate and the sound post to fall with a clink. Paolo said that this meant that it was not too tight, but he worried that it might be too small or not fit properly. He explained, "A properly fit sound post should not fall when the sides are squeezed; instead, a small gap opens between the top of the post and the belly, and the post remains standing. It will only fall if the angle of the bottom of the post does not match that of the back arching or if the violin is not laying vertically. If no gap appears when the sides are squeezed, you know the post is too tight." After recutting a new length of spruce, checking its angled ends against the arching of the back and top, and hearing dozens of frustrating "clinks," I had the soul in the instrument and a violin ready to be strung.

The strings ironically did not touch any of the pieces of the violin I had most labored over on their journey from the pegbox to the tailpiece. From the pegs, they stretched over the small nut across the fingerboard to the bridge, after which they were anchored into the tailpiece, itself connected to the end pin of the instrument (also purchased ready-made). Gleaming in the spring sunlight on the bench, the violin sat completed and ready to make music. I felt

Fig. 4.8. The finished violin ready for assessment

a rush as both Paolo and I played the instrument, first pulling simple notes before more complex melodies started to breathe out of it. We began to compare it to the other violins in the shop, testing its response and clarity at various frequencies and speculating as to how its large size might affect its tone and playability. Finally, Paolo suggested that we test its projection at a distance. Erica, Paolo's wife, and his three daughters joined us on the porch for the final stage. Paolo took several measured paces away from us into the front yard and gestured broadly around with the bow in his hand. "This is the concert hall," he joked, before drawing a scale and then a test melody from the instrument. He seemed pleased with the outcome, and its test signaled the informal end of my apprenticeship.

The work had succeeded in what Paolo had suggested was the primary task of the maker. In our first interview two years earlier, he had suggested that "the violin is like the voice. You can really emulate the voice, which is what a lot of music is. It's up to the violin maker to breathe life into this inanimate object." As he pulled a melody that danced across the spring violets in the grass, I couldn't help but think that the violin was breathing the music.

CHAPTER 5

TONEWOOD
FROM THE OLD WORLD
AND THE NEW

Five thousand miles to the east of the Appalachians, the Carpathian Mountains stretch sickle-like across Central and Eastern Europe, retaining large stretches of old-growth forest. A walk in the forest of the southern Carpathians evokes the dazzling diversity of Appalachian forests, giving the uncanny sense of visiting a lost cousin whose features you recognize, yet whom you are encountering for the first time. Analogous species of trees to Appalachian cousins grow in familiar patterns across the mountain landscape, giving way to the seasonal cycles that change the forest visage, waterways, and human livelihoods that play across them. Given the size and quality of trees that come out of these forests—like the Appalachian forests of the early twentieth century—they are a landscape of desire for wood products, including a large tonewood industry based primarily in the extraction of spruce (*Picea abies*) and maple (*Acer pseudoplatanus*). While rumored to have supplied European violin makers since the days of Stradivari, Carpathian tonewood has become a mainstay for instrument makers of various scales of production in the twenty-first century due to its high quality and reliable availability.

Despite the heavily forested landscape of much of West Virginia, the lack of reliable and quality spruce and maple trees—coupled with a desire to replicate to the material specifications—drives many Appalachian makers to use Carpathian tonewoods in pursuit of lively, singing instruments. In the early 2000s, John Preston of Lewisburg, West Virginia, had returned fully to making violins after his retirement as an ecologist for the Army Corps of Engineers in Huntington, West Virginia. As many makers do, he began to accumulate wood for prospective violin family instruments and guitars, eventually deciding to source his own tonewood as an extension of his craft. He traveled to Romania for the first time, looking to establish a connection for importing European tonewoods for violin family instruments for his personal use. However, once he had established a strong, trustworthy connection with Catalin Murgoci, a relative newcomer to the business himself at the time, his stock quickly became larger than he and his house could manage. He moved the tonewood into an old auto/sign shop that had been converted from a motel in Lewisburg and opened it as a tonewood business.

He offered primarily European varieties of spruce and maple and niche tonewoods, marketing these to individual makers as well as large suppliers of tonewood and instrument parts. Travis, a colleague from his former job, also had an interest in woodworking, and having grown tired of "working in tall buildings," as they frequently put it, he began to work as the shop sawyer.[1] John also began to reach out to local foresters and timber companies to find local varieties of trees that would be suitable for tonewood. So it was that during my fieldwork, the Old World Tonewood Company operated with John and Travis working together out of this shop in Lewisburg, cutting West Virginia logs and importing Romanian tonewood for the global market of instrument makers.

As John was beginning to contemplate going to Romania for the first time, five thousand miles to the east, Catalin Murgoci was searching for tonewood in the Carpathian Mountains of the country. Catalin had been interested in the import and export of wood as Romania transitioned to a postsocialist state by first lifting export restrictions for private companies in the 1990s and then joining the European Union in 2007. He experimented with shipping lumber to Greece in the early 2000s before meeting a Spanish guitar maker who gave him a piece of master-grade cedar as a reference to find high-quality Romanian spruce. Catalin looked for two years, finally encountering spruce logs that could be used for instruments, though they were assigned a lower-quality "B" grade when "worked up" and assessed for quality. Nevertheless, this was the beginning of his trade and the Carpathian Tonewood Company, which continued to grow over the next decade, changing to meet requirements of the state and increasingly accessible global consumers. Catalin cut and subsequently aged logs for a variety of consumers, from individual luthiers to factories, and in quantities from "one piece to one container," as he explains. For instance, while we worked together, he still supplied the Spanish guitar maker's luthier shop as well as the Chinese company that subcontracted part of their production.

Meeting with John, they grew together as tonewood cutters in learning the process of the trade, namely the skills needed to locate trees from logging operations and to locate instruments coming out of the wood. Their strong interpersonal relationship undergirds the movement of the tonewood as surely as their regular visits back and forth across the Atlantic Ocean. Though they have no explicit business partnership, they refer to each other as partners, each recognizing the importance of the other in their journeys of learning the trade and becoming tonewood producers.

Describing how he learned, John said, "I think almost everyone out there in [the United States] that's doing tonewood is a first generation. There might be someone out there that's got his son or daughter, I don't know about that. The difference in Europe is that most of them go back some generations. There's a way of life with it if you pass it on." John contrasted that generational history with the mode of learning he and Catalin had experienced. Unlike those European family dealers, they have learned the process of cutting tonewood together as they developed the craft and business.

This mutual understanding of the wood and drive to continue the process connect the two tonewood producers, continuing the supply of Romanian tonewood into West Virginia. Echoing John's and Travis's escape from work in tall buildings, Catalin also grew tired of working in an office and sought a change through the tonewood. He told me, "This job allows me to go into the forest like you've seen and to go to the mountains, and also allows me to see people and visit people, so it's what I like." John added, "If I had not met Catalin, I wouldn't be doing this. I looked around, and he was the honest person doing it correctly, and it wasn't a year or two before I started talking about [how] I was just going to work with [Catalin]. We don't have any financial ties, but I call him a partner, because without him, I couldn't do the European wood. More of a friend now than a partner."

Working with John and Catalin through various periods from 2015 to 2018, I participated in this friendship and exchange of tonewood through an informal apprenticeship in both West Virginia and Romania. In this time, I experienced and participated in the processes by which wood is retrieved, selected, processed, marketed, and shipped through networks connecting global forests to instrument makers. Weaving meshworks of Appalachian and Carpathian human and forest communities, my apprenticeship in the industrial craft of cutting musical tonewood was a process of learning the role of the forest environment, the global trade in timber resources, environmental correspondence, the variety of labor in these enterprises, and the temporal relationships cultivated between tonewood and cutters.

Fig. 5.1. John Preston and Catalin Murgoci assessing logs outside a factory in Râșnov, Romania

Unlike my work with other makers, which followed a more or less progressive trajectory of unfinished materials to a playable instrument, working tonewood was a process of becoming interrupted by fits and starts of human input at different stages of progress. Trees are cut and demand input from human workers before nonhuman actors like insects and fungi begin to transform the wood to their needs. Orders arrive with little notice, requiring final workup to changing specifications. Meanwhile, the wood must be maintained through seasonal cycles of drying and aging over a period of years. Thus the work is done in stages rather than in a smooth process from tree to finished tonewood. Luckily, the extent of time involved in this project allowed me to see wood that was harvested in 2015 ready for shipment by the time I finished work in 2018. In this chapter, I follow the process sequentially, though the craft rarely does.

This work reveals how transnational movement of tonewood is enabled by affective meshworks between tonewood producers and the forest environments in which they work and live. Makers of tonewood search global forests for the sought-after tonewood species, building bonds between other makers and seemingly disparate forest environments. Yet the process of finding and producing tonewood opens the possibilities for the resource to be made and understood in various ways. Tonewood makers understand that the trees with the qualities to make singing instruments exist, but such qualities can only be found through the productive process of making tonewood.

Logs purchased for tonewood are uncertain candidates even when on the sawmill, having invariably passed to producers through commodity chains.[2] Near-finished tonewood must also age and contend with competing agencies of other nonhumans, such as the aforementioned fungi and insects. As a result, the status of tonewood as an affective material resource and a commodity is in constant flux. Logs purchased as commodities can quickly become gifts if found unsuitable in the selection process, while the small scale of production invariably turns "waste" into gifts for friends and other craftspeople. And even as a commodity, for sale on websites or to luthier supply companies, the material's relationship to the position of the producer, as a maker or an entrepreneur, casts a different meaning onto the wood. Nevertheless, the materialities of making this resource connect the mountain regions and sustain meaningful labor for the producers of tonewood in both West Virginia and Romania with whom I apprenticed.

A TONEWOOD COMPANY

The principal tonewoods of John's tonewood company and the affiliated Carpathian Tonewood Company were species of maple and spruce, the basis of the violin family instruments. The European spruce (*Picea abies*), or *molid* in Romanian, and the sycamore maple (*Acer psuedoplatanus*), or *paltin* in Romanian, compare to North American varieties of red spruce (*Picea rubens*), red maple (*Acer rubrum*), and the less frequently used sugar maple (*Acer saccharum*). In an interview, John pointed to the differences in the material qualities of the wood they cut and how that influences human action upon the wood:

> The woods are slightly different, but the quality—what you're looking for—is pretty much the same, generally, in the maple. What we're looking for is just nice figure, nice flame, if you will, whatever you want to call it. The whiter the maple is generally nicer or more desirable. Our maples here in this region if you get far north, it's not so bad. We get little brown streaks under the bark caused by an insect. Some people call it mineral streaking. But it's actually an insect, but then that's not so desirable to some people. Uh, the mandolin makers tend to not mind so much because that's always been used, but some of the violin makers don't like it. It doesn't occur in Europe, in the maple there. So that's a pretty readily distinguishable characteristic between our maple that we have here locally and the maple we get in Romania. Romanian maple is a little bit lighter. Generally lower density.

It's easier to carve generally, and I'm frankly quite fond [of] the European maple and spruce. Spruce is the same thing. In spruce, we're looking for trees with virtually no twist, a straight grain, no knots, no resin, and none of those are absolutely something you can achieve. There's issues in every log, and it's the same there as here.

The presence of tree species fulfilling similar cultural niches for tonewood production constitutes only one instance of the ecological similarity between Appalachian and Carpathian forests that influences human lifeways and livelihoods. Both Catalin and John describe feeling at home in their complementary mountain environments when they visit, referencing the familiarity of the landscape and spotting similar activities and lifeways.[3] The ecological and geological similarities between the mountain forests echo in similar industrial impacts and consequences of extractive industries, as smaller communities in both regions have confronted the role of extractive timber and mineral resources in the market and stress the importance of mountain tourism to their future economic livelihoods. Yet, the political ecologies and histories of these regions have resulted in much different impacts on the landscapes and species. Different regimes of property rights and protections of the Carpathian forests in the early twentieth century—namely through presocialist forest commons, socialist collectivization, and strict control by state forces through the socialist and postsocialist era—have left many larger extant stands of timber. This contrasts with the totalizing extraction of forests witnessed throughout Appalachia in the early twentieth century. Yet forest-related work was also the predominant field of paid labor in early to mid-twentieth century Romania, where small forest communities were also dominated by the extraction and processing of timber.[4] Exploitation in Romanian forests has taken different routes, with corruption and increasing privatization despite protections a serious endemic issue. Increasing privatization of forest land, land purchase by logging companies, and open borders as a result of free trade in the European Union have all resulted in overexploitation of Romania's forests.

Nevertheless, different tracts of forest development have resulted in tonewood trees in Romania that are usually larger and subject to greater scrutiny in quality as compared to those available in West Virginia, making them more suitable for high-end instrument craft. John explained that the value placed on spruce by the forestry industry also makes it difficult to pull logs from extractive flow timber products:

Spruce, the red spruce, there's just not much of it. . . . There used to be red spruce in West Virginia; it was a huge amount, and now there's like 50,000 acres or something and only grows 4,000 feet or above here at this latitude. And you know, it's a cull tree virtually for the forest companies. They can't get anything for it. There's a fence plant, a fence manufacturer, and they use spruce. But otherwise it's, they don't want it, you know, there's no market for it. So there's a lot of really nice red spruce gets cut that just goes to [paper] pulp mills.

Additionally, for many violin makers, the perceived traditions of instrument craft weigh heavily on the selection of instrument wood. The symbolic weight of using the same species of trees as the praised European makers of violin family instruments is important to violin makers, who often prefer those woods. Taken with the fact that Romania is said to have the largest stands of "old-growth" or "virgin" stands of timber in Europe, Romanian forests remain a significant source of the global market for musical instrument tonewood.[5] As a result, Romanian foresters have monitored and studied the potential economic impact and viability of these tonewood trees in ways that are not considered in the United States.[6]

Despite this demand and entrenchment in perceived tradition, the history of all great instruments being made with European wood may not be totally accurate. When John and I attended the Violin Society of America meetings in 2017, we were surprised to hear from musician and violin collector David Bromberg that some French makers of the nineteenth century preferred American maple varieties, inverting the expectations of tonewood provenance and continental desires. In a cursory examination of part of Bromberg's collection of American-made violins at that conference, John and I found the brown mineral streaks indicating red maple in the majority of the eighteenth-century violins, illustrating that American violins were also made with American varieties of maple.

While instrument makers require that both spruce and maple have straight, close grain, makers also look for maple that is figured with undulating curls of varying size, depth, and orientation caused by the grain growing in waves up the length of the tree. Depending on the instrument, the size, depth, and orientation of the curl can increase the value of the wood and perhaps the instrument. Though there is little evidence to suggest that the figure influences the tone of the final instrument, it is considered an essential aspect of the tonewood and one of the basic qualities considered when selecting logs for tonewood. This figure is also known as flame, and other patterns of figure in tonewood such as quilting, bee's wing, and bird's-eye are also valued, albeit in different ways for different instruments.

However, finding the trees with this figure adds another element of chance to a process that John described as uncertain at best. In West Virginia, the curly logs are best found in the spring, when the bark comes off loose while the logs are cut and moved. In this way, for curly maple logs, the first step is often taken when the logs reveal themselves in this manner, rather than tonewood dealers or instrument makers heading into the forest to select standing trees. Even if a tree appears to be curly on its outermost layer, or phloem, this is not an indication that the curl will extend into the xylem, or interior of the tree, or up the length of the log.

While there are environmental conditions that create larger, more uniform logs, it is difficult to pinpoint an exact condition or method of harvest that results in an optimal tonewood tree. Materials sciences and other quantitative-driven scientific investigations have pondered the effects of variables from trace minerals present in tonewood to the effect of solar flares on the growth of forest.[7] Violin makers and tonewood producers mythologize around the practices of the Italian makers to attempt to explain their mastery. Cutting wood during specific times of the lunar cycle, processing wood at a specific elevation, and aging wood in water are a few different techniques that I encountered during trade shows and conferences in my fieldwork. During our work, John gave credence to the idea that environmental conditions do influence the growth of tonewood-suitable trees, but he also questioned the romance of tonewood, frequently recalling the image of Stradivari searching forests for tonewood trees by striking them with a stick:

> Well, I mean there's things that are just the way it grows it will be the same. In this hemisphere, on the north slopes, you're going to find better trees generally because of the less direct sun, so you're going to have tighter grain, but I don't know. There's a whole lot of unsubstantiated wisdom. People have ideas about, well, you know, there's some minerals in the ground or how hard life is for the tree, the wind, or even the moon, there's all kinds of stuff that people think have a big marked effect on it. The old tale about Stradivari walking through the woods and whacking on trees until he found one he wanted. He didn't have time to do that. He made twelve hundred instruments. He didn't have time to walk in the woods and whack on trees. I don't think so. [Laughs] There's a lot of romance. I mean, it would probably be to my benefit to spread that, but I just don't like it. It's

not based on science. It just doesn't interest me. When people have these romantic thoughts about how wood should be harvested or grown, plus they probably don't have any basis for even thinking that way other than they've read it.

Instead, he speculated that Stradivari and the Cremonese makers likely relied on networks of knowledgeable loggers and dealers to supply his material, similar to his own network. In Romania and West Virginia, logging contractors and subcontractors are the first to cut the trees that eventually become musical tonewood. In both forests, John and Catalin relied on contacts and networks of foresters whom they have taught to recognize tonewood-suitable logs and benefit from higher prices than what might be gained from timber or pulpwood. Logging and timber enterprises that deal in logs run a range of different sizes and structures, from single workers with their own equipment to massive multinational timber corporations to state-operated agencies and companies. In West Virginia, loggers largely cut on parcels of private land, while in Romania they may be from a patchwork of private, municipal, or federally owned land.

For example, one "monster spruce log," in John's words, that was sawn while we visited in the shop in Romania in 2018 was cut by logging monks on monastery land in the Carpathians, while the others had come from commercial loggers. The regulations on harvest and trade are more stringent in Romania, where the cutting season is restricted to winter months to mitigate damage to forest soils and floor composition, and logs are required to be centrally registered through their harvest and transport. A serial number is stamped on the log and on the stump, the log must be registered in a central database, and the specific log must be ready for inspection at any time.

John drew the contrast between working in the two places, highlighting that a better understanding of what tonewood is might exist in Romania:

In Romania, one of the things they recognize [is] the value of instrument wood and that's because even under Ceaușescu, the violin industry is strong. I think it pretty much started in the fifties; it's not a terribly old industry there like it is in Western Europe. But they understand the value of it now. There's still timber theft and all [the] other problems, but I'm hoping that their regulations are promoting more of a sustainability, and if they do cut down a really nice figured maple, it goes to the highest use, which in my mind is for instrument wood. You know, there's so much of this really beautiful wood around here [in West Virginia] that's ground up into pulpwood. It's just the way it is. I hate to say it, there's more knowledge about the value of it [in Romania].

Additionally, he felt that it is important to keep the work of doing the main processing of the wood in Romania:

> I started out working when I was going to get wood from Romania, and my goal was to do as much of the labor I could over there because it's their resource and it should be done that way. So I don't take raw material. People often ask, maybe you bring the whole log in. And I said no; that would be a waste to do it that way. 'Cause [there is] a tremendous amount of waste in the processing [of] any given log in the instrument wood. But I would also take away the five or six people sometimes we periodically get to help cut the wood. So I think it's a good thing to do it this way. So what I do here is the final preparation, more detailed work.

This contrasted with the work that large instrument and tonewood companies were doing at the time, working to establish satellite, secondary facilities in countries in the Global South, where they could export semifinished products in line with national export policy.[8] Furthermore, it also contrasted with large international timber companies' extraction practices in West Virginia, as they would ship whole logs of valuable hardwood in containers directly from the United States without the finished product protections that other countries require.

The material aspects of the tonewood extended through John and Travis's work at the shop, producing placed differences between the work of processing the Romanian tonewood and the local tonewood. Though John also began to cut local tonewood years after he had already been importing the wood from Romania, separating the two parallel and tangled streams of work in his mind, the wood ultimately ended up at the Old World Tonewood shop, entangled in transnational meshworks of environment, human relationships, nonhuman actors, and demands of tradition and aesthetics. To explore these entanglements, the rest of this chapter follows the lines traced by logs from forest to tonewood through West Virginian and Romanian forests, respectively.

CUTTING IN WEST VIRGINIA

The shop that houses the Old World Tonewood Company, as noted earlier, was originally a four-room motel on U.S. Route 60 out of Lewisburg, West

Virginia. The former motel rooms of the building were painted white and gray and housed a large woodworking machinery room, a room for making instruments, and a small office occasionally converted into an apartment for Catalin's visits from Romania. Outside, there was an enclosed porch attached to the main building to accommodate the stock of tonewood in the shop while exposing the wood to seasonal fluctuations in temperature and humidity necessary for the aging process. There were four structures outside the building on the lot: a partly covered concrete pad that housed the sawmill, an adjoining Quonset hut where large pieces and the rough stock were aged, and two other outbuildings where wood was aged. The built environment of the shop established unique spaces for specific tasks: places to cut logs, to age wood, to "work up" blanks, to make instruments, and to do office work. While I worked there, John and Travis cut necks, tops, backs, and sides for violin family instruments, acoustic guitars, and mandolins, as well as bodies and necks for electric guitars and banjos from the local maple and spruce logs.

Trees arrived in the front yard of the shop from nearby forest cuts and from log yards in the surrounding, heavily forested counties, often from clear-cut operations. In West Virginia, where most logging is done on private land, the major regulations primarily exist to protect water quality. Companies exercise great flexibility in cutting trees on their property according to their management plans, often relying on clear-cutting as a method, as long as they do not cause a certain amount of sediment to get into streams and waterways. The system of subcontracting and quotas employed by timber companies can leave many disjunctures between workers and work at each stage and complicates how decisions are made regarding trees. One arborist working in the Alleghenies explained this system as follows:

> They [state regulators] don't give a stitch about if you leave an entire crappy beech stand or all invasive species or whatever. They don't care at all. You can never get fined or [written] up or get closed down because you know you're leaving nothing but rose bushes. But if you start, . . . [and] it rains too much, and sediment goes into the stream, they'll shut down in a heartbeat. So that's probably my biggest disconnect, because I have buddies that are loggers, you know, you don't need any educational requirements to be a timber harvester in the state, none whatsoever, which is fine, and all you need is a business license, and you need to have a certified logger on your crew, and you need to submit a notification to the Division of Forestry that

you are going to log this tract. You need to put your ID number at the log landing, and that's it.

Loggers cut and trim the trees in the forest and transport logs out of the forest on large trucks, a common sight on the region's two-lane roads that link the small municipalities of West Virginia. The trucks are unloaded at large centralized log yards where the size, species, and quality of the tree may determine its future, in accordance with political and economic influences, as well as the changing tastes and aesthetics of buyers. The biggest trees are often cut in the forest but can be too large for the infrastructure of sawmills for the milling or pulping operations, which are built to process high volumes of trees. Big trees are also likely to have internal issues such as cracks or rots, so they may be left to rot on the forest floor. Eddie Fletcher, a woodworker from Greenbrier County and frequent visitor to the tonewood shop, took advantage of this waste with a portable sawmill, buying logs that might otherwise be left to rot and sawing them into large slabs for countertops, tables, and a range of popular styles. Tree tops and large limbs are often trimmed and left in large piles, presenting tempting sources of firewood for locals, as well as shelter for animals.

At the time of my work, many walnut or ash trees were being shipped immediately as veneer logs for the furniture industry in China due to their high price and the increasing scarcity of the ash, increasingly threatened by the emerald ash borer (*Agrilus planipennis*). Smaller trees could be sent to be split as rails, ground for paper pulp, or chipped for mulch or to be turned into charcoal briquettes.

Because of this arduous triage, the foresters trained in managing forests are less likely to apply their knowledge to forest ecosystems than to their opportunity to manage sales on log yards. For larger timber companies, quotas are made "in board rooms," according to one forester working in West Virginia. These quotas are dependent on measurements made in board feet of timber for logs, excluding pulpwood, rather than total tonnage. As a result, estimations of production are not a good indication of what is being cut in the forest, so forests are cut at a higher rate than projected, which the forester described as "working ourselves out of jobs."

The majority of John's local tonewood logs were sourced from this assemblage of logs. He had worked with local foresters to teach them the kinds of things that he looks for in a tonewood log, such as the clarity of the grain and the depth of the curl in the maple throughout its entire length. Sometimes, after hearing a recommendation from a forester, he would drive up to the local log yards and peek under the tarps to look at logs, looking for indicators of the curl, the straightness of the tree, the fewest knots and branches, and an appropriate size for his sawmill. During our work, he also bought several logs sight unseen, trusting the judgment of the foresters, or buying unsuitable logs for another purpose, such as building shelves in the shop, in order to keep the relationship going.

I accompanied John on trips to log yards to assess wood and as he worked through splitting "cookies" to assess how they might work as tonewood logs. To assess a tree, examining "cookies"—slices cut off the end of the log—is the first step of deciding whether the tree will become tonewood. Slices are taken from the top and butt, or bottom, ends of the log with a chainsaw, and the resulting cross-section is split to look into the grain of the log, with both pieces helping project what the inside of the log will look like.

This was often done at log yards, breaking the cookie open on the spot, but occasionally foresters would send cookies to the shop for convenience. On one such occasion, upon receiving a batch of cookies of eight maple logs from a local forester, Travis and I split them on the edge of a concrete stoop to look at the grain inside the wood. As we worked through the pairs matched with spray-painted numbers, we tried to visualize the unknown length of the log between. We looked at the figure, the depth of the sapwood, the straightness and tightness of the grain, the clarity and color of the wood, the shape of the heartwood, and other indicators, such as bug holes.

Working from the small samples is difficult, as it is hard to predict how these indicators will run through the length of a log, where the grain may cease to be curly or the heartwood may move around, turning the log away from a trajectory of tonewood and toward some other purpose. Travis reiterated that this was tonewood, and you never knew what you were going to be able to get out of it. Splitting one cookie that looked by all measures to be what Travis called "a no-brainer," we then discovered the telltale brown streaks of the ambrosia beetle. Though other woodworkers prize so-called ambrosia maple, it would not likely sell to an instrument maker, and the solitary streak was not enough to entice another type of woodworker.[9] One beetle's sojourn through a log, and the resultant stained gallery from its fungal symbiote, can thus move a log from consideration for a violin to the firewood pile.

After deciding which logs John and Travis would take—only one out of eight was a sure buy, and the rest John wanted to offer to a local cabinet-maker—we sat on the porch with Eddie Fletcher, who had delivered the cookies from the forest, and talked politics. As we often did, we quickly turned to the environment. We talked about the choices communities are forced to make in the state and their experiences with environmental degradation, and they bemoaned the national and state leadership that appeared to be embracing policies that sacrificed environmental protections for economic development.

I seized the opportunity to ask John and Travis what they made of their role in the commodity chain of the extractive industry and how they squared their political beliefs with their business practices of buying logs often cut with little regard for the environmental impact. Echoing his response from our initial interview, John answered that it was all about transforming the wood into its highest possible use: a musical instrument. Travis agreed that the worst thing wood could be transformed into is paper pulp, a lower use even than firewood. Eddie chipped in that if curly logs don't get picked up for tonewood, "they will probably end up as McDonald's wrappers or Charmin [toilet paper]." Plucking curly maple logs from a commodity chain that might otherwise turn them into highly processed, single-use consumables to turn them into tonewood interrupts the process of disposal. I found it interesting that their language, mirroring as it does the "highest and best use" doctrine that often governs natural resource management of land, was reflective of a niche craft that depends on the sustainable exploitation of natural resources.

On the path toward the "highest use" of tonewood, as already noted, trucks haul the logs from logging sites and log yards to the shop on large trailers that are ubiquitous on the two-lane highway arteries of the region. Their coordination can be formal through contracts and subcontracts, or it can rest on informal connections as favors from passing friends and neighbors who have the means and route to pick up the large logs. When delivered, John and Travis unload them near the shed that houses the sawmill, where they wait a short period until they are cut. When the logs are taken off the truck beds and trailers, their size and grandeur give an impression of stout permanence. However, at that point they have already begun changing, as the ecological communities of which they are a part continue to act upon them.

Sunlight heats the logs and dries the ends, causing "end check" that can crack deep into the log. The heat, along with rain and other moisture, promote the growth of fungi that will "stain" the wood blue and brown as they begin decomposing cellulose and sugars in the tree. Small beetles and other insects also can begin to colonize the wood, though they might have already been beaten to it by others in the tree's life, like the ambrosia beetles that leave their tracks and holes in many maple logs. This is a crucial stage, with about two weeks to get them from the forest and cut before their path toward musical materiality is irreparably damaged by decomposition and organic renewal. This stage is the first in a process of years-long correspondence that requires shaping and monitoring the wood to produce the raw materials for successful instruments.

Maneuvering the logs with wedges and hooked levers known as cants to the bed of the sawmill requires negotiating the weight and size of the log as well as its imperfections in its slightly conical shape. Rolling the log across the grass yard and onto rails that run to the sawmill bed, John and Travis constantly checked the progress of the log by alternately applying force on one side while holding the log on the other to rotate it into position, and then they applied equal force to roll it across to the bed. Once on the bed, Travis debarked the logs with a bark spud, a long-handled tool with a head shaped and sharpened to accommodate the curvature of the tree trunk and remove bark without damaging the wood below. Because the logs are generally brought while the bark is loose, it typically comes off in sheets without damaging the logs. They then cut it down to length with a chain saw while keeping the sections within the parameters of the lengths of various instruments they might be cutting for.

Their mill was custom-made by a specialist for the purpose of cutting tonewood. It consists of a large, horizontal band saw mounted on a carriage that Travis pushed by walking it forward through the log on the bed. A series of "dogs" hold the log steady on the bed while cutting by digging into "sacrifice" pieces of wood placed on the surface. John and Travis's roles as craftspeople in the area also made the sawmill one of the more accessible ones for other craftspeople, who often brought wood of their own to cut on the mill as a favor. As a result, work on the sawmill frequently included cutting a piece of a tree limb or a log for another person to clear out the work area for a tonewood log.

Once the tree was debarked (and the sawmill cleared), Travis and John worked together to determine how to cut the log to maximize their yield of tonewood for a variety of instruments. Looking down the length of a log, John would measure the depth of the prospective cut and the width of the log at any given point to determine what kinds of instruments might be possible to cut for. They then centered the heartwood by adjusting the angle of the log on the bed and measured down to where the cut of the first board would be at least five inches wide, the minimum width for the wood they cut.

Before the cut, Travis adjusted the height of the blade to match the five-inch width of the cut and adjusted the tension of the blade with a pneumatic pump so that it would cut straight yet have the flexibility to move as needed. Travis walked the blade mechanism slowly forward, looking at where the blade was going to be and feeling its movement through the handles. He took a first skim of the outside of the tree where the bark had been stripped off, and I pulled off the skimmed surface of the curly log, which laid like a piece of a

Fig. 5.2. Travis Holley debarking a maple log before beginning to process it for tonewood

giant rippled snakeskin on the mill. The sawdust from the cut stuck to the damp surface of the wood, and as John swept it away, it revealed a bit of green stain on the first half inch in the sapwood, indicating that we were not the only organisms working upon the wood.

While Travis kept the log and saw in concert with his bodily movements, walking the blade along the carriage, John simultaneously anticipated aesthetic and structural desires for certain kinds of tonewood, recognizing specific kinds of tree qualities that manifest during the milling. After each cut, John subtracted the millimeters of height for the parts that were to be cut from the remainder of the log—calculated to include how the wood would shrink in drying. He relayed that message to Travis in several ways: by hand signals, yelling, or by writing on the face of the log. He also circled defects and scrawled large X's on lengths of boards that had too much stain, ambrosia lines, other insect marks, or were otherwise marred in some way.

The first cuts were "slab-cut" across the grain for one-piece violin backs, before John told Travis to cut for electric guitar necks that are thinner and sawn slightly flatter. Wood that is flat-sawn has the grain running flat through the piece, meaning that it is much less rigid. This quality is perfect for electric guitar players who prefer some flexibility in the necks of their guitars.

Fig. 5.3. Travis and John discussing how to cut the log

Recognizing both the necessary qualities of the final instrument and the limitations of space in the log before reaching the unusable heartwood, John and Travis were able to maximize the productive yield of the tonewood while working quickly. After each board or two, John would get out the electric chain saw and saw the boards into smaller pieces, measuring the proper lengths of the pieces. I then stacked them and waxed the ends of the wet boards to prevent checking on the end of the boards.

They then turned the log ninety degrees, resecured it, and cut pieces for mandolin backs. Though violin makers prefer perfectly quartersawn two-piece backs, John said mandolin makers "will use anything" and tend to like how the figure is broken up and flared when it is not quite quarter-cut, as it is reminiscent of the factory-made Gibson mandolins of the early twentieth century. They then made a cut for guitar backs, although John lamented, "Not that we could ever sell it as guitars," pointing to how North American steel-string guitar makers seem to be constrained by exotic tonewoods. When there was a question about what to cut next, Travis said, "That's what we always do, cut 'em for what's best. What are we going to do otherwise?"

They then cut for electric guitar tops that makers would model after the Gibson Les Paul guitar, which has a curly maple face. Unlike mandolins, acoustic guitars, and violin family instruments, which are bookmatched, these can be slip-matched, meaning that they can be mismatched from other parts of the log. Makers look for this placement, and John suggested that this was because Gibson was probably pulling from scrap piles of their mandolin manufacture to make their instruments, "slip-matching" pieces from different lengths of the same log.

As we worked toward the center and the unusable heart—which quickly splits and warps as it dries—they kept the skimmed surface pieces for a friend to carve into spoons and cut boards where the dark heartwood started running in for another woodworker. For the last few boards we cut off the log, Travis cut from the bottom rather from the top so we could stop doing the subtraction and get a more accurate cut, with the weight of the heartwood keeping the board steady. When only the heartwood was left, we loaded the green blanks into the truck and took them down to the shed to dry out for a few years.

Tonewood is also split rather than sawn in order to produce pieces that mitigate runout, when the wood's fibers "run out" of the face of the piece of wood. When split with wedges, the long strands of wood fiber remain complete and capable of carrying sound waves uninterrupted through the piece of wood. This is more often done with spruce, as it is especially valued for bracewood and tops of instruments as the main media for sound waves in the instrument. One rainy day, a friend brought a small red spruce log to the shop that had been salvaged from a roadside cut where other people were scavenging spruce for firewood. From the outside, it appeared that the log was straight and large enough to split out bracewood for guitars and the bass bars of violins. Travis looked it over on the trailer, remarking that it had some growth issues: it had rather large growth rings on one side, perhaps indicating that it had grown on a hillside. After some discussion, they decided to split it rather than cut it on the sawmill.[10]

A few days before, I had been up at Paolo's house and workshop, splitting apart chunks of a silver maple for firewood in exchange for a violin bow. I thought about how imprecisely I had been swinging the splitting maul, and I questioned how Travis would split it evenly. He and John looked at the log, bisected it with a chain saw, and divided its face into equal pie-shaped sections with a red lumber crayon. Travis began pounding metal wedges into the log with a sledgehammer along the diameter of the tree traced with the crayon. When the wedges had begun to create a crack that divided the log, he took an L-shaped froe, put the blade inside the crack, and turned the haft as a lever to open the crack down the length of the log. As Travis worked the froe down the log at his feet, the log creaked and cracked open, straight down the log.

Fig. 5.4. Tonewood yield of a typical maple log

Seeing how straight the log had grown, John remarked, "It's a nice split, isn't it?" However, other organisms had already appreciated the clarity of the log. "Look at those bugs though—God!" John added. "Those bugs got it. They're all the way in it."

"Aww, shoot!" Travis lamented. "There you go. There's the heartache." With a few forceful blows, he opened the split through the rest of the wood and used the sledgehammer to bust apart the last holdout fibers, leaving two equal halves.

Travis pivoted the half-log around toward the light and pointed out how fast the tree had closed up around the young limbs poking out of the heartwood, as if a smaller tree made of darker wood had been enclosed within this one. John praised the beauty of the wood, but upon measuring it, he lamented that insects had burrowed into the first two inches of the sapwood. This ruined its prospects as bracewood, as the most suitable wood comes from around the bark of the log. Travis stooped over again with the froe and tapped it into the half-log, trying to pry it open. He struggled for a moment before it split open, revealing a large knot in addition to the bug holes on this side.

We worked together to split up the rest of the wood, looking for something usable in the wood that had come to the shop for free, ultimately coming up short. "That's part of the work," Travis sighed, "trying to get something out of nothing." The more strenuous work of splitting wood seemed to be wasted work and wasted wood in this case, as it had only resulted in firewood for a summer bonfire. Yet, in the shop, the uncertainty of tonewood cast a questionable future for the wood that could have been considered waste.

I heard over and again from John, Travis, and Catalin that the uncertainty in the logs was the trademark of the craft. Tonewood producers attempt to find wood that not only has grown to have the characteristics vaunted by makers and musicians but also without the defining internal issues that are everyday occurrences in trees. Other organisms make their mark on trees inside and out, and the turbulent life of even a stationary organism is evident in the trees' internal scars and healing responses. "Windshake" leaves cracks visible only inside the tree, sap pockets form where the tree has had to heal itself, and limbs swallowed by a tree's growth persist as knots "shadowing" the wood around them with curved grain to accommodate the outgrowth.[11] This results in logs that may be perfect from the outside but, when opened up, are revealed to be unsuitable tonewood, but nevertheless they are not wasted.

The "waste" of the process is repurposed to one end or another. Like industrial sawmills, whose large volume of processing allows them to sell sawdust to farmers as bedding or to be chipped for paper mills or charcoal, by-products of the tonewood are quickly converted for other uses, though not necessarily commoditized. After cutting logs on the mill, we would shovel the sawdust into large sacks for a chicken farmer to pick up for his chickens. Other wood was taken for firewood or given to local woodworkers. I joked that the shop was

Fig. 5.5. Travis splitting the log and discovering the "heartbreak" of bug holes within

being turned into curly maple, as many of the wooden elements of the shop, architectural and otherwise, had been replaced by curly maple counterparts. After one morning of cutting logs, as we sat and ate lunch in a small restaurant, I looked to see that the doorway was framed in curly maple. John told me that he had given wood that could not be used to the owner as he renovated the space.

However, these gift networks do not extend only to friends and social networks but also to other craftspeople in the community who may not even know John or Travis. In the course of cutting and processing wood, scraps and large pieces unsuitable for tonewood would accumulate, and John and Travis would use them to fill a wooden bin in front of the shop. As I was bringing blanks into the shop to work up one day, a man pulled into the parking lot and began searching through the bin, picking up small scraps of wood. Though he did not know John or Travis, he knew that he could find scraps of quality wood in there and had stopped by to pick up some good pieces for turning pens and to make a toy box for his grandson. I did not see him again but ran into others who stopped by the shop for similar reasons during my time. This practice recalls the ethic of the highest purpose of the wood that reverberates through wood-craft, emphasizing the use value on even the smallest pieces of wood over the exchange value that could be gained by collecting and selling the waste wood.

The relatively quick process of turning the log into boards that will fit differ-ent instruments' specifications is just the first step in the series of years-long curing and drying of the wood that must take place before it is ready to become an instrument. While Travis guided the revolving saw blade through the wood and John calculated which instruments they might become, I often began the subsequent part of the process, "stickering" the wood for its first stage of drying next to the sawmill. Stacking the long planks of wood and placing small sticks, or stickers, between to separate the boards allows air to pass over the surface of the boards and mitigates the microscopic cultures that might damage the wood. I also sealed off the ends of the wood with a wax compound that prevents water from evaporating out the ends, allowing for the wood to dry slowly through the faces to mitigate cracks, checks, and warping in the blanks. After the tree is stacked and kept by the mill, it is normally kept in the shelter with the saw as a convenience. We would then move it into a covered space to either air-dry or be dried in a small kiln, after which it would be stored in a rough state until an order or need in the stock of the workshop required that they be worked up into finished blanks. For the occasional tangentially cut, one-piece violin, viola, or cello backs, Travis and John would drill holes in the corners and suspend them in the air with wire to give full air exposure to the valuable piece.

The period of aging wood is of utmost importance, as it imparts stability to the material as it loses water content and, potentially, gives superior musi-cal tone to the wood the longer it ages. Makers will usually not consider using tonewood until it has sat for at least two years, and tonewood normally has a premium placed upon its relative age as a result. During this period, the sur-face of the wood will change color through oxidization, the piece will change slightly in lateral dimensions, and it will become lighter and stiffer, two highly valued traits for tonewood. Drying the wood in a kiln may be a first step toward the entire drying process, but ultimately the preferred technique is to allow the wood to establish equilibrium with the moisture content of the air in sea-sonal cycles, which keeps it active and in correspondence with environmental changes. During our work, I frequently moved and stacked wood with Travis that had the years 2012 or 2013 scrawled across its surface.

However, during my work, the drying process of "torrefaction" was gaining traction as a means to artificially "age" wood.[12] Torrefied wood is heated to very high temperatures in the absence of oxygen, zapping moisture from the wood without causing combustion. The resultant wood is more brittle, but it is said to be more conductive of sound and producing tones in line with aged guitars. John was sending some tops off to a kiln in Missouri to be torrefied, knowing that there was a burgeoning group of guitar makers that preferred this wood. He said it was a missed opportunity that there was not a torrefaction kiln in West Virginia, because this method also could produce rot-resistant timber and posts. When preparing for travel to an international guitar conference in June 2017, we unpacked a crate of torrefied spruce guitar tops to grade and the scent of sugar filled the air, a sign of how the sugars had escaped the wood as the water evaporated. They were keeping some of them for sale via their website but wanted to experiment with the market at the conference, so they had some of the lower-quality tops torrefied to see if anyone would be interested in purchasing them.

While only guitar tops were being sent out for torrefaction, other pieces would dry rough-sawn until they were ready to be worked into closer specifications and sorted by grade. John and Travis would cut boards into smaller pieces with band saws and chop saws and then plane the face of the wood with a sharp jointer, revealing nuance in the quality and character of the grain. They looked for variations in grain clarity, straightness, width, color, and runout to determine the grade. Grading is a subjective process, wherein the standards are set by the tonewood producer within a basic agreed-upon system. Yet, grading changes with the perspective of the grader, as well as with the species and the market for specific kinds on tonewood. While lumber is graded based on standards of strength and clarity of materials set by professional associations, there are no such official criteria for tonewood. Producers are free to grade wood how they choose, usually sticking to a range demarcated by the series AAA, AA, A, and B, though many makers may add extra levels in between, or they may add one above as "master" grade tonewood.

Keeping personal aesthetics, agreed-upon community aesthetics, individual tree variations, and the relative scarcity of some kinds of wood in concert can create disjunctures in the grading system. For example, with red spruce, John told me, "it's in such demand that the qualities don't have to be as high as what we demand for European spruce. Our European spruce is a lot tougher on the grading than we are on the local stuff." They were much more lenient with the grading of the red spruce, generally grading it two levels higher than a similar quality piece of European spruce. This process is highly relational and constitutes one reason John prefers that people come to select wood in person at the shop. In addition to providing an opportunity for meeting them and getting to know their work, this in-person selection reduces potential misunderstandings

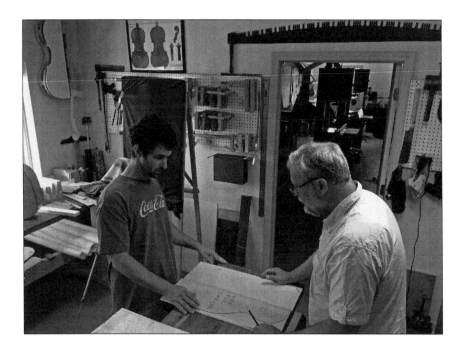

Fig. 5.6. Travis and John grading guitar tops

due to the inconsistencies in the grading system, thus reducing the change that makers will order and return wood until they find something suitable. However, without a microscope to look at the individual cells, it can be difficult to determine which species of spruce is which.

Once, while unloading wood with Travis, we tested ourselves in our knowledge. We could see some redness in the wood and felt the heaviness of the red spruce, but we ultimately found through our guesses and checks that the best indicator was how it had been graded. A "AAA" red spruce top often looks like an "A" Carpathian top in terms of the thickness of the growth, coloration, and wave in the grain. In fact, because of the premium on red spruce, John suspected that people may have been buying lower-quality Carpathian wood and passing it off as red spruce.[13]

Once the pieces had been sorted and graded, they were cleaned up for final processing, then photographed to be put on the website to sell individually to makers and musicians in the United States and internationally. During my work, however, the shop also fulfilled orders for large instrument supply companies and manufacturers. For one such order, we worked up large boards for banjo necks. This company had ordered a large quantity of the parts in quick succession, despite the fact that they had not ordered any in the past year before that. Travis and I pulled the rough-sawn blanks from a storage shelf and wheeled them up the hill to the machine portion of the shop.

We worked in a factorylike progression: Travis planed two sides of the lumber to see the grain and make it workable; I chopped them to length and cut off the end "checking" that had occurred while drying; John cut them to near specification with a jig on the band saw; and Travis planed them one last time to make each one smooth. It took "working up" about forty-five blanks to make the thirty that were of requisite quality to ship to the company. Eight were deemed inadequate, as they had defects throughout the grain or a grayish staining, and they were given to a local carpenter. Another five were resized down to mandolin neck blanks for future sale. Two were set aside for scrap. John said that the company that bought the necks would sell them as nearly finished products, only missing the varnish, so they add the "greatest value to the process." They joked that they would send the order to the shipping department as they packed the boxes and moved them outside where a shipping truck would take them to the next destination and beyond to makers and musicians.

SOURCING IN TRANSYLVANIA

While aging for years in the shop, the rough-sawn West Virginia boards are in company with the Romanian varieties that have taken a parallel (if longer) route through a commodity chain to the Old World Tonewood Company. It begins when Catalin receives photos, text messages, and phone calls from loggers and dealers when they believe they have good logs, knowing that the price will be higher for tonewood logs. He will then take large "loops," as he refers to them, through the J-shaped Carpathian mountain range that physically divides the country, visiting the log yards and cutting sites to determine if they are worth the risk of purchasing and shipping back to the tonewood factory in the town of Râșnov in Brașov County. He looks at the logs on harvest sites in the forest to large log yards for trees that will make the cut as tonewood. Instead of corporate quotas, these trees would have been cut according to volume quotas, assessed at cubic meters per hectare, and regulated by the state silviculture office, even on private land. In searching for these logs, Catalin told me, "There are a lot of details. You must balance the defects and qualities, and you cannot see what is inside. I check the bark. I check under the bark. I make a thin slice on the edge. After that, it is luck and experience."

He was referring to the luck and experience necessary to produce suitable tonewood play out at the factory of the Carpathian Tonewood Company. Its large stock is sold to customers from individual makers to large instrument factories. The company is housed in a large, expansive structure, which previously served as a barn for a dairy cooperative. It is one building out of a long line of industrial spaces, the other spaces being converted from livestock barns into other trade businesses, including a log yard, a mechanic's shop, and storage spaces for construction equipment. Outside, two large open structures are used to dry recently cut wood for guitars and violin family instruments, and families of brown sparrows flit in and out of their roofs. Depending on the season, the structures may be relatively empty or completely filled with wood, due to the seasonal regulations on cutting logs in the forest. When I visited in October 2015, the stock was relatively sparse, as the trees were not cut until the winter months. But in the spring of 2018, the space was brimming with wood stacked in neat piles bound for a range of makers and factories.

In the yard, there was also a large feed silo left over from the dairy cooperative. It was fed by a vacuum from inside that pulls sawdust from the factory floor. Catalin told me he would sell it if more was produced, but there is not enough to do anything but gift it, so it goes to a dairy farmer nearby who returns the gift with milk or helps with moving logs. Neighboring dogs occasionally slipped between the fence for scraps of yesterday's lunch or simply to lie in the grass in the main lot of the factory, escaping the sound and commotion of the log loaders and chain saws in the log yard next door. The yard was grassy but split by a long stretch of mud, which had hardened into tough ridges left by the large tractors used to deliver logs.

Beside the front doors of the factory, there was a small door with a cart and track running through it from the area where the logs were stored onto the floor for easy transport to the sawmill. The factory was split into four rough sections: a sawing floor, a break room, a storage floor, and an office. The sawing floor had a large wheeled band saw mill along the ground, as well as the large machinery needed to do the rough workup of the blanks: a large band saw, a planer, and a jointer. Tools used to move the logs and position them on the bed of the saw as well as the patterns for instrument blanks hung along the walls around the machinery. The storage floor had large piles of guitar tops, bracewood, violin blanks, and other assorted tonewood neatly stacked into cubes for storage or placed on pallets for shipment to other factories or makers. Some were already wrapped in plastic, ready to be transported in containers to factories in the People's Republic of China. In the office, they kept the finest grade instrument wood for listing on their retail website, each carefully manicured for sale. The scales and equipment needed to calculate shipping were close by, anticipating a quick shipment.

Fig. 5.7. The Carpathian tonewood factory in Râșnov, Romania

The factory employed at least four people: two sawyers, one temporary machine worker, and a worker who predominantly sorted wood and handled the storage of tonewood. They were supervised by a foreman, Mihai Filip, who managed the factory while Catalin was working from his home in Bucharest or on loops looking for logs. Mihai, known by the nickname Mișu, shared some of the financial burden of the factory and managed the online sales and every-day workings of the factory, so he and Catalin considered each other partners. While the other workers had well-defined, dedicated tasks, Mișu and Catalin often alternated between different tasks within the organization and the task of making decisions on how to cut the logs. I asked Catalin about what he calls the work, offering the term *tonewood cutter*, and he parried that "tonewood is not just about cutting, it is also about knowing the wood and producing for years."

In April and May of 2018, the factory was humming with activity, being the busy time of the year for buying logs that had been cut over the winter. I predominantly worked with John, sorting wood that he would ship to West Virginia, but we also occasionally offered advice on how to cut logs to get different kinds of instruments. While we worked, they cut several large spruces that John said would be "monster spruce in West Virginia," as well as a black alder (*Alnus glutinosa*), black poplar (*Populus nigra*), and willow (*Salix* spp.). The logs were stacked outside, though they were subject to the same concerns of staining and insects as at the shop in West Virginia. The willow log seemed to be the only one that was left in the yard, and as a testament to its ongoing biological processes, I noticed every day how the prone willow was still sending shoots toward the sun.

They used levers and wedges to maneuver the large logs (the largest at that time was about ten feet long and thirty inches in diameter) off the platform and onto the cart that ran inside. The sawyers then cut the bark off using a bark spud, leaving behind gouged marks on the surface, demonstrating that the bark was not as loose as those logs cut in the spring months and delivered quickly in West Virginia. Pushing the logs onto the carriage of the sawmill, they fixed the log into place with a series of jacks and dogs. Depending on the type of tonewood to be cut, they then drew onto the exposed face of the log the dimensions or angle needed to be cut and began to make large cuts, pushing the carriage and saw blade through the wood. The saw was loud but powered by electricity rather than the gasoline of the mill in West Virginia. As we watched the sawyers cut a spruce for guitar tops, John commented that he wished he could have an electric mill to mitigate the fumes and cost of gas, but that it is cost-prohibitive in West Virginia to transfer to the three-phase electric current needed to run large equipment.

Guitar tops are the primary tonewood for the factory. They are cut radially into pie shapes, or quartersawn, then sectioned into half-meter lengths, which are planed and resawn on the band saw with a carriage into guitar tops, and finally stacked to dry. In this process, the wood passes through the hands of all the workers in the shop before going to Mişu for a final grading. While this is the standard course for spruce logs, the hardwoods that form the body of instruments require more strategy on the "best" use of the log to maximize yield. In cutting the poplar and willow logs, which can be used for making the backs of viola, cello, and double bass, John, Mişu, Catalin, and I worked with the sawyers to determine how to cut the logs. The outside surface of the poplar log had revealed a lot of deep curling figure to it, so it would be valuable as backs for instruments. Cello backs by themselves can cover the cost of the logs, which often require hundreds if not thousands of dollars of investment.

Measuring and drawing in possibilities for boards on the face of the log, John tried to convince Catalin to cut the logs "tangentially" to the heart to maximize for one-piece backs. Catalin disagreed, wanting to take as many radially cut pieces as possible because then the figure would be more striking, and he could grade the wood higher, thus raising the price. John retorted that people making instruments with poplar instead of maple are usually concerned with making in the old Italian traditions, where poplar-backed instruments did not necessarily have deep figure.

However, after making the first skim, the sawyers put the piece through the jointer, removing the rough-sawn surface and revealing an incredibly deep curl to the wood. Once Catalin saw the figure, he decided that he would cut all radial to get the most highly figured pieces. The sawyers pulled the pieces off the rapidly diminishing log, rotating the remainder before every pass, and leaned them against a bench when they began to slightly discolor as they dried out in the air. John excitedly moved to place and trace patterns for violas, cellos, and even a double bass on the wood, configuring the boards for the best yield. Along the irregular external edges, it was difficult to determine where to place patterns, but John relied on his knowledge of instrument making, immediately recalling the measurements of the size of instruments, as well as where their arching would occur to get around minor blemishes. We also tried to trace bug holes and knots through the wood, anticipating how they would project through the unseen internal wood and might influence trying to build an instrument. In the remainder of the space on the wood, John would square off a section and scrawl *eclise*, or the sides of an instrument, to cordon off a section of matching sides.

As they cut through the second half of the log that flared out near its base, everyone became slightly dismayed by the size of the heartwood, as well as the knots and blemishes that pocked the wood. Catalin brought a bottle of ammonia window cleaner to the log and sprayed on a place where he suspected that it had begun to rot. He told me it helps to reveal the extent of the rot by coloring places where it has set in. With this knowledge, he could determine whether the wood would be usable, as it was near the heartwood, or whether it was susceptible to rot. John again lobbied to cut it tangentially as a slab, but Mișu decided to cut it as radial backs in an attempt to get two-piece double bass backs, in addition to the viola and cello backs they had already cut.

John and I returned to sorting already cut tonewood for export outside, and we were surprised to see Catalin leave in a hurry and return a few minutes later excitedly with a bottle of Pepsi and several bars of chocolate. He laughed as told us that he said he would buy everyone the treats if they got bass backs out of the log. John and I followed him inside and admired the bass back, which John said might sell for well over U.S. $1,000, essentially paying for the entire log. He joked that he and Catalin should bring it to the upcoming Violin Society of America meetings and sell it with a stamp from both companies, illustrating the collaboration and correspondence in cutting the log.

Through the whole process, John and Catalin seemed to be coming from two different places, making sense of two sets of practiced knowledge as they made decisions about how to cut the log. Though it was Catalin's log to decide how to cut, John's expertise formed a valuable aspect of the correspondence in cutting the log. However, it often appeared that John's experience in making and playing instruments gave him a different insight that prioritized a maker's needs or desires—that is, sacrificing the flame for a rarer one-piece back. At the same time, Catalin and Mişu tended toward thinking how the wood would sell, especially online, placing primacy on elements of the wood that were particularly visible and might stand out on a computer screen, such as the undulating curls of the figure in the poplar.

John and I spent most of our time at the factory either assisting in this way during the cutting or going through stacks of cut and dried wood to determine what he would send back to the States. We spent this time sorting in the covered huts where the wood sits in stacks to dry; it spends the majority of its time in the factory, waiting to join a shipment or for a buyer to come to select wood. They are stacked according type and grade and left outside to age, usually for the season before being brought inside.

One day, we selected pieces from the cello stock with Mişu and organized them based on grade as we pulled them out. We held up the bookmatched pieces and looked for the minor imperfections that might preclude the wood from traveling to West Virginia. Handling the fifty or so backs and tops that were available, our hands became tacky with the sap pockets seeping from the spruce tops and the sawdust covering the blanks. After selecting the backs, John and Mişu lightly negotiated which ones of the highest quality would go to West Virginia or the website, trusting John to adjudicate what the highest quality would be. He was quick to bring them back to the office to get them on the website as fast as possible, as individual sales online bring the best price. Mişu said that every time he handles wood, he is thinking about how he might be able to profit from it, a slight distinction from John's maker-oriented view. Sorting through a nearby pile of wood for archtop guitars, Mişu said that the entire log was really nice, and he asked John to put aside one out of five of his selections for the website. John agreed, and when I asked about this consulting, he said that is why he feels it is a partnership, albeit with no shared business. He offers a skill and added value as a maker with a maker's eye, and together they have the combined connections and ability to find the high-quality trees that others cannot.

We spent one morning looking at pieces of irregularly figured maple, as Catalin and Mişu asked John what would be the highest use from the pieces. They were large and figured like red maple, yet they had slightly irregular

Fig. 5.8. Mihai Filip and John discuss the tonal prospects of a cello top blank

shapes that made for a challenge to decide what instruments could be recovered from them. John saw a lot of possibilities and tried to get many of them, but Catalin wanted to keep some on account of the singular figure. Its remarkable figure was both desirable and problematic, as the deep curl would make it very unpredictable. The pieces showed many signs of cracking within the wood itself, and they were deeply pitted from chipping during the planing, both indications that this tonewood might be volatile in the construction of an instrument. Nevertheless, John continued to search for the best "use" one could get out of it, suggesting violin or viola backs, while Catalin pushed for guitar backs. Ultimately, they decided to give John a few and use the others for guitar backs and sides. Mișu put some up in the rafters to continue to age, and he cut others. They talked about what the alternatives were if the wood was not suitable for tonewood after all, suggesting that its lowest use would be to cut binding for guitars that would be exceptionally figured. Catalin also mentioned that he had a deal with a Korean firm to ship curly wood for pool cues, and John seemed to be excited by this process, as the pool cues would be an easy alternative for scrap tonewood.

When not going through pieces with us, Mișu was busy readying a massive order for shipment to a guitar factory in the People's Republic of China, which principally consisted of a thousand guitar tops that he had to sort and grade. Despite the sunshine and heat outside, the concrete and sheet metal structure stayed quite cool, so he sat between the large pallets of tonewood, wearing a hat and vest over his flannel work shirt, and sorting the wood. He went one by one, checking the bookmatched pieces in the dim light of the factory stockroom. As the Chinese factory wanted a range of tops but did not need the highest grading of AAA, he was pulling those aside for the factory to sell otherwise. I helped him sort the guitar tops by checking the AAA-graded wood for runout to see if they would be suitable for the website. Mișu showed me how to take a small spokeshave, plane off a shaving from the edge, and split apart the shaving to see if it split evenly. The angle of the split showed me if the wood fibers were "running out" of the face of the blanks, which would grade them down. Mișu said the other way to indicate is by pulling on the loose fiber on the edge of the wood, relaying that he "can almost feel" the runout. John chipped in, "If it [the fiber] pulls easily," then it should be free from runout. Meanwhile, Catalin asked me to use my camera to see if there was a way to use high-quality photos to inspect batches of guitar tops for runout. Having taken photos of a stack of tops, we looked at the magnified pictures for the slant of the grain fibers that might indicate runout. However, when we checked against the physical method, we could not reliably tell if any of the tops had runout, proving that the manual method was a better test.

While he sorted, I asked Mișu if he graded "master grade" as Chris had graded his best wood in the guitar apprenticeship. He responded with a laugh, "When it is the highest grade and I don't want to sell it, I call it master," referring both to his own desires to sell the higher-grade wood and to make a guitar of his own. As he inspected each piece, he would line up the pattern and trace the outline of half a guitar on each of the bookmatched pieces; he said, "You give value to it" when you put the tracing on. "Before it was a piece of wood, now it is a guitar," he added with a grin. They focus on guitar tops, the most lucrative tonewood due to the global demand for steel-string acoustic guitars and the relatively high yield of the wood.[14] In grading, Mișu would use different guitar patterns as would John—such as a dreadnought or parlor-size guitar—to determine what kind of guitar top it would be. However, with connections to the rest of Europe, they also have access to markets for large-scale production of smaller European folk instruments that makes it possible to be more productive with small pieces that will not accommodate American-style guitars. For instance, one pallet of tops was individually marked with the word *fado*, indicating the Portuguese style of music and the small Portuguese guitar associated with it.

At the factory, John and I spent hours poring over the pieces needed for violins: necks, backs, and sides from curly maple and tops out of spruce that comprise most of his stock in Lewisburg. We passed through thousands of pieces of wood stacked neatly in meter-tall piles. John assessed the wood while I assisted in triage, eliminating pieces that were definitely not of the requisite quality. We passed wood back and forth, as John tested my knowledge gleaned during the apprenticeship, and I attempted to select wood that would meet John's standards.

One day, John and I selected maple backs for violins that had been put up since 2015 and 2016 and were already graded. We searched for light pieces that had straight grain and visible figure throughout the width of the piece, though John pointed out that some with the most spectacular figure also had a defect that caused the fibers to grow in alternating patterns. This gave the wood a slightly fuzzy look on its surface, and it was visible in alternating stripes of whiter wood on the end grain. Although perhaps not discernable to the untrained eye, this makes working with the wood considerably harder, and it served to show that John's knowledge of the wood goes beyond the basic standards of tonewood.

Mişu came in to check on us and asked about the wood. "How would you say it is? Like factory grade?" He meant this in a slightly negative sense, in that the wood might be bound for factory production as opposed to a single instrument maker. Indeed, many of the recently cut violin backs had grain lines that showed over the figure, and John said that it would be more difficult to sell them and thus not worth the shipment over the Atlantic Ocean. Although he was very taken by the unusual lightness of the wood, he lamented that most makers will not think through the weight but rather look at the figure in the curl when they purchase tonewood. Once again, the wood seemed to present a choice of what is apparent in selling the wood as opposed to physically interacting with it. The choice between an easier wood to work or a more fantastic figure was again an issue of marketing of the wood's visual characteristics and its relational qualities that might be preeminent during the making of the instrument.

The violin tops, on the other hand, graded higher, and we did not struggle to meet the number that John needed. John took only the highest-grade wood, figuring that once he had "worked them up" for sale in West Virginia, some would show defects or issues that would bring them down or make them unsuitable for sale. Nevertheless, in looking for the two hundred tops John

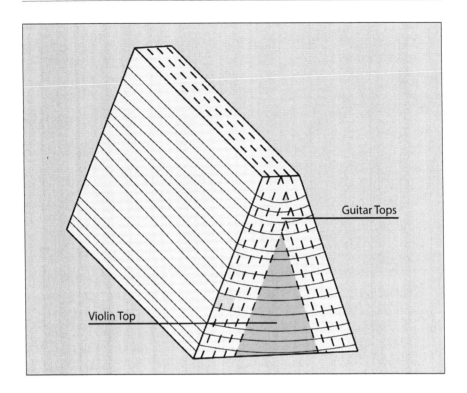

Fig. 5.9. How tonewood billets are cut for guitar tops with a violin top created from the waste

needed, we went through approximately four times that amount. This is because at the factory, violin tops are largely a by-product of the guitar tops. The guitar tops are resawn off the billet from the outside working toward the center. Once the smallest possible tops are taken, a core of spruce remains that can be turned into a two-piece violin top.

We encountered a similar process while sorting violin necks and sides, struggling to find enough to match the backs that we had accumulated. Violin makers strive to match the grain and figure of the neck, back, and sides if wood from the same tree is not available for these parts. However, at the factory, violin necks are also often a by-product of processing other pieces rather than a separate focused and concerted production. We tried to match the grain to the highly figured backs that we had picked out, but John stressed that some makers do not want curly necks because the peg box is weaker, so a balance must be struck between matching and the material requirements of the instrument. "I can understand why they would like to get a lot from the same kind of wood because it just reduces the differences they have to apply when they're making the instrument to make it sound as well." After an afternoon spent looking for sides, John was frustrated by the process, as we had mostly offcuts to go through to find matching sides. He had anticipated finding matching pieces taken from the same logs as the backs that we had chosen, as they were labeled with the year and log number. Going through the piles of wood, however, we could not find matching logs for many of them, so we had to attempt to find best fits.

After ten days of working at sorting in the yard and factory, John and I totaled up the wood that we had piled on a pallet in the storeroom and marked with an Old World Tonewood stamp to differentiate it from the rest of the stock in the room. I took a scrap of wood and marked down the numbers that we had, easily calculated by the six-to-a-level stacking method I had picked up from Mişu. Mişu told us how he would pack it up in a pallet that fit onto the airplane that would deliver it to the United States. The final step would be to look for bracewood, which they sell by volume or weight rather than piece. John and I went through one of the neatly stacked piles nearby and were dismayed to see fairly low quality wood in the squared rectangular prisms that had been sawn off a log that couldn't be used for guitar tops. Again, there was some frustration about the time it took us to go through the bracewood, not even finding 10 percent of what John needed. Looking through large piles inside and two outside that were left to dry in the sun, he said that it wasn't worth the time. Catalin showed John some bracewood that had been split rather than sawn, so the grain was running clearly through it, but John replied that they already had a lot of nice split bracewood from red spruce, and if he couldn't get the good quality, he would just rely on that. As we sorted through the wood, he told me of a difference he had encountered between makers: guitar makers prefer squared-off wood and violin makers prefer split wood. He attributed this to the machine work generally involved in guitar manufacture and said they will not buy wood that has been split or has rough edges, whereas violin makers prefer that.

Tired of looking through individual pieces of bracewood, I looked through the two-cubic-meter pallets of bracewood that they had already packed up for sale to China. Mişu said they would continue cutting and drying the wood until they had an entire lorry full to ship out. I was impressed by the size of the pallets, trying to envision how many guitars could be made with this bracewood along with the guitar tops that Mişu was still sorting. Who were the makers of these guitars? What would the factory look like? How would they feel about making musical instruments? Though the linkage between John, Catalin, and

Mişu, and thus West Virginia and Romania, was apparent through their friend-ship and collaborative understanding of the trade, these pallets of wood also drew into focus the global scale of this work.

The factory had become a global destination and source point for tone-wood customers. In early May, while we were there, the shop also hosted a Korean violin and cello maker as well as another violin maker from the United States, who was moving to Italy to make violins for a documentary. While the American stopped for one afternoon in hopes of finding the highest possible quality wood for his project, the Korean maker took time over two days to survey a range of grades of wood, from the highest to the lowest. He searched with intent, tapping the wood, scratching across the grain with his fingernails, and searching for visible defects, ultimately staying for a May Day celebration Catalin hosted at a nearby friend's house. He was visiting Europe to enter violin contests and wanted to select wood for his craft by hand in the shop while he was near Romania.

Catalin talked about his travels to China recently for a musical instrument exposition and spoke about his recent hosting of Chinese businessmen who were in Romania to buy tonewood. He is used to talking with people through-out the world to sell Romanian tonewood, having taught himself several lan-guages to do so. A survey of reviews from individual makers on his website includes makers from Romania, throughout Europe and Scandinavia, North America, South America, and East Asia, in addition to his industrial contacts in China, India, and other burgeoning hubs of manufacturing that buy in wholesale. With shipping contacts that will deliver the wood directly from the factory to the door of makers, Catalin proudly said that he could deliver tone-wood anywhere in the world. Yet, while they open doors, these international connections also create disjunctures where the aesthetics of wood choice are complicated by physical time and the space realities of shipping wood between continents.

In our first meeting in 2015, John had told me of his initial attempts to get wood into the United States and how his shipment was held up in Baltimore, the port of entry. Other countries have high protective tariffs on imported wood, and both John and Catalin mentioned Mexico as a country that would not accept their tonewood from Romania or West Virginia without cost-pro-hibitive testing.[15] While we were working at the factory in Romania, Catalin had an order from Brazil, but it turned out that the piece of wood had cracked badly while it was drying, and it was still on the website. He decided to send two lower-quality tops instead, and John agreed. Matching the exact piece would be too difficult—this is the solution they both turn to when a piece is damaged in shipping—as it is often more expensive to pay for shipping back and forth than to just replace the damaged piece. It turned out that this customer was a musician who had ordered the piece for a commission to a luthier. John and Catalin questioned this way of doing it, preferring that luthiers choose the wood they know will work rather than musicians who likely do not know the process as fully. On the Carpathian website, they attempt to draw the individual customer in, offering high-quality pictures, as well as the density and tone-tap of the wood upon request for makers who may wish to hear the sound that the wood makes in an electronic recording.

I stayed with Catalin at a friend's house when I did not stay with Mişu and his family, and on one of our nightly postdinner walks, I asked him about what the tonewood business means to him and if he would continue doing it. Catalin mentioned that he would continue doing tonewood for a long time because it was challenging and fun and fulfilling to see the whole process from logs on a log yard to the blanks he ships out. He also said that the business had grown past the point where he could sell it, knowing that the intricacies and knowledge of the business were rooted in his personality and patterns of work. Yet, the work was not without its frustrations, primarily in attempting to communicate the inexactitude and uncertainty of musical instrument tonewood. People want perfect wood, he said, but that is never possible because it is the outcome of a living process of growth and environmental response.

John has a similar point of view, which he shared in our first interview: "I have a desire to do it the way they did it two to three hundred years ago without a neural network or some kind of tooling that takes away from the experience. I believe you have a better outcome and more of your personality in it the more contact you have with the wood from the beginning."

SELLING ACROSS BOUNDARIES

In John's shop in Lewisburg in July 2018, we looked over the wood that had recently arrived from our spring trip. He had shelved it to age further, trying to keep everything matched together before he could "work up" what they need for the stock. Whatever remained without defect would be renumbered and photographed for John's website and sold around the United States and the world. John said that he does most business out of West Virginia, but I saw traces of his business at many of the instrument shops I visited during my time through business cards and pieces of tonewood emblazoned with the Old World Tonewood Stamp.

John and Travis took opportunities to get their name out and increase their presence at national and international conferences. In 2017, I attended the Association of Stringed Instrument Artisans Conference with John and Travis and saw them in action at one of the country's largest conferences for guitar makers.[16] Behind a folding table in the conference's vender section, John and Travis worked to sell Carpathian spruce and maple, as well as varieties of West Virginia tonewood. Passing guitar makers were particularly interested in the "bee's wing" cherry, whose figure undulates like insect wings through the wood; low-grade Carpathian guitar tops to sample; and rosewood backs and sides that John was moving after holding on to for several years. John was surprised about the cherry, as no one would buy it online, but when they saw it on the shelf they thought it was an exotic wood and bought it quickly. The figured walnut and ash pieces, however, did not sell, despite those woods' high value in the lumber market at that time.

They had established a contact to sell maple backs to a large supplier of tonewood to large retail companies in the United States, which would ease the burden of marketing lower-graded wood and expand potential destinations for West Virginia tonewood. Representatives from these companies and others that specialize in sourcing gave talks about the commodity chain process during the conference, explaining the sourcing of tonewood, with an emphasis on those species bound by international regulations. Through their descriptions of sourcing tonewood, largely in the Global South, these buyers typically visited places once or twice to establish connections and ensure the legality of the purchase to begin the flow of tonewood. Showing photos of workers in Central America, sub-Saharan Africa, and India, they illustrated how they comply with legal frameworks to source logs and blanks from forests and log yards. When I asked what the workers on such log yards thought of supplying tonewood, one spokesman said that they are interested in cutting wood for instruments but are more interested in cutting for slab than radial because it is less work. Ultimately, the conversation became less about the commodity chain and more about the legal predicaments and sustainability of endangered tonewoods.

Around the same time, John was experimenting with building a guitar made entirely of West Virginia wood in his shop. While other makers in West Virginia certainly embrace this practice with the body and top, John was dedicated to making all parts with West Virginia products, including the fingerboard, bridge, pickguard, and interior parts. He sanded down a sheet of walnut to the thickness normally reserved for plastic pickguards and was happy to use American persimmon (*Diospyros virginiana*) in place of the ebony that was increasingly expensive and rare, noting that they came from the same genus and had many of the same material qualities. The wood was similar in density and toughness, but it was colored a creamy gray compared to the deep black preferred by instrument makers. He had been asking if any of his clients were interested, but they had not been. This presented a larger concern for John about the use of woods and why people seemed to be so stuck in traditions that he deemed to be fairly modern and unsustainable. In our first interview, he made this clear:

A complaint I would have about people demanding these perfect pieces of wood, and that just doesn't happen, and so, you know, we shouldn't be wasting this resource, you know. I mean, you look at the most famous instrument of all, the Stradivari's Messiah, and there's a resin pocket on the front of the spruce that he patched, but yet you try to tell somebody to make a violin with a resin pocket today, and they won't do it, and I understand why not. But it's like we're too picky to me about it because [of] that. I guess that goes back to what I was saying. I wish people realized how precious and difficult this wood is, but I understand, hey, that's what the players want. But they're the ones driving it, the music stores are selling it and the players [are] buying it. The maker's in between, he's caught in between. He may want to use wood that he likes for tone, he or she likes for tone, or it has a little knot in it. There's just a lot of things I kind of wish were more appreciated. . . . Some of the people really recognize how difficult this is and I just wish everyone . . . appreciated the value of this because it's, it's a really limited resource and, I don't know, maybe that sounds bad for myself saying that. It's just when you go, when you see how much, how difficult it is, how few trees produce good wood. It's really kind of a precious commodity. Uh, I just really have a reverence for the wood, that's what I'm trying to tell you.

Adding value to something that might not have been valued otherwise constitutes a major part of making this work meaningful to both John and Catalin. Materials influence the work and lives of the tonewood producers, compelling them to travel great distances and to work against the natural processes of decomposition. The temporal relationships with the forest and its products can outlast many personal relationships. Yet, these same meshworks and processes of becoming tonewood producers also intersect with transnational personal relationships and commodity processes. The forest environment provides a physical basis for creating the raw materials by which meaningful labor can be achieved, but it is also through the meaningful relationships built through studying, producing, and exchanging tonewood that work becomes meaningful. Relationships with the forest environment extend far out into the global political economy and ecology, interconnecting instrument makers and tonewood producers both in their re-enchanting craftwork and in their disenchanting industrial work.

SUCCESSION IN CRAFT AND FOREST

CHANGING FORM AND SCALE

In the last months of fieldwork in 2018, my apprenticeships transitioned from collaborating on instruments to reflecting on the facts and forms that on-going craft as an ethnographer would take. I visited with Chris, Paolo, and John in their homes and workshops, and they were curious to hear about the work that other makers had done, how they approached the craft, and what similarities I had drawn in my study. I dropped off copies of my emerging writing for their review, and they responded with comments, suggestions, and corrections in kind. On one such visit to John Preston's workshop in Lewisburg, I decided to veer off the main highway and stop off at the home of Eddie Fletcher, the local woodworker mentioned earlier. These kinds of visits to family and friends were common throughout my time in the region. With few main roads to take me between points, I was always passing the place of someone I knew and rarely could stop myself from popping off for a chat.

Eddie was a frequent visitor to John's shop, delivering logs for John as well as bringing his own for sawing on his flatbed trailer. He had carved out his own section of forest hollow, complete with a nineteenth-century log cabin, by working for years in construction before returning to the hills he hunted, foraged, and lived in as a kid. In the little hollow, he made his living through woodwork: carving, building, and supplying logs with intense swirling burls and ornate figures salvaged from timber operations that looked for more regular material. In the group of outbuildings that surrounded his house, his stock of trees was cut and stickered, appearing like articulated illustrations found in forestry reference books. He showed me particularly interesting pieces, pulling them out into the light of the autumn sun, brushing away animal feces, dirt, and leaves that had accumulated on the boards as they aged and running hands over their unique characteristics. He mentioned that boards cut into slabs like these were very fashionable at the time, and he added that some furniture makers were using resins to fill in negative spaces in the wood to provide an interesting look.[1] However, he claimed, such configurations frequently don't hold up over time. The wood—unlike the plastic—continues to live in relationship with its environment, creating gaps and cracks between the two materials. The wood lives on after it is cut, he said, and one must consider this ongoing life beyond the period in which it is dried and processed.

Wood has three lives: as a tree in relation to environmental and economic processes, as a material bound for use as a resource for human or nonhuman action, and as a (never quite) finished craft artifact that will require diligent care and musical interaction as long as it plays. It passes through various relationships in correspondence with human and nonhuman actors, still tied into biological meshworks through its material qualities while being made into a resource and an affective thing. In the craft of wood musical instrument making, the material constantly compels makers to action throughout the creation of an instrument, driving meaningful connections through the precarious liveliness of tonewood. Makers may encounter the wood in three phases of liveliness and must act accordingly to assure a successful instrument capable of a singing tone. First, it is an organism shaped by its metabolic processes and ecological community, a tree whose material qualities are influenced by rain, wind, elevation, seasonality, and other growing conditions of forest ecology, including human actors that manage forests and monitor trees. Second, stripped of limb, leaf, bark, and root, it is wood that, while no longer living in a strict sense, still maintains an animacy as it is processed as tonewood.[2] It is subject to other living organisms and the ebb and flow of water that makers carefully manage over years of patient attendance. Finally, the wood is crafted into thin pieces of wood, articulated into recognizable lines and shapes, and imbued with the capacity to produce meaningful sound and the capacity for life as a singing instrument. An instrument's biography extends from several different tree and animal species through the shops and workspaces of makers and into life as a musical instrument—bought and sold, traded and collected, becoming and deteriorating as it produces music. Though other craft objects may compel human actors to interaction through their shifting states of becoming and unbecoming, such as the cutting board that warps over years of washing or the chair rung that annually loosens in the winter, musical instruments must contribute an added dimension of liveliness: their song.

For instrument makers, meaning is not made simply through the final instrument but also through the interventions and instances of correspondence at various scales of time and space and conditions of materiality. These scales of space and time and material conditions can be difficult to comprehend. They can be as small as the microscopic interactions of fungus spores in wood fibers and the immaterial plays of light and shadow that reveal what the human eye has missed. They can be as large as felling trees or loading containers bound for transoceanic voyages or passing through a state bureaucracy for permissions. These interactions have affective and emotional connections that are often obscured to the recipient of the instrument. Nevertheless, connections to the people and the things that make place serve to drive the personal motivation and intent that inspire makers to continue to create.

A maker's interventions in this years-long material and emotional transformation create relationships to the craft materials and instruments, make the work meaningful, and compel makers to continue their practice. Through the material they choose and work upon, makers express their philosophical, artistic, and scientific ideals and theories and are, in turn, shaped by the embodiment of the relationship of sound and wood. These material relationships extend out into the arboreal environment of maple and spruce forests that surround makers in the Alleghenies. They support local communities in various ways, giving makers the opportunity to use trees and wood imbued with the significance of place, as well as cherished sonic qualities. Though the tasks of instrument makers appear to be solitary and isolating, they extend out into constellations of meaningful relationships with organisms and communities.

Yet such attention to often overlooked participants in the craft process should not discount the human connection that is also enmeshed in its fibers. The desires of a client, the comments of a friend, and the questions of an itinerant apprentice ethnographer also become articulated through the materials. Through support and sharing ideas about practicing and refining the craft, relationships are made and remade that span the world. Paolo and his brother practiced a playful sibling competition in comparing the products of their work, and John's interest in the transatlantic trade of tonewood built kin-like networks between two mountain regions. Chris also felt that the craft as an expression of his God-given talents to make instruments and music connected him in powerful ways to people in his geographic community and beyond. Through the materials, makers connect with other people, building and strengthening bonds that enchant the work with affective possibilities.

These makers and the Appalachian region they inhabit were not fixed in space as peripheral or isolated but extended through global processes of the economic exchange and artistic expression. They weave themselves within aesthetic, political, economic, and ecological meshworks of production and consumption. While artisans may be beholden to traditions practiced in their craft, they were not traditions practiced because of isolation, but persisted because of and in spite of changes in production and consumption of musical instruments. By pursuing re-enchanted work, they were not entirely resisting forms of production that disenchant labor but rather remaking labor practices and material relationships of their own through the craft. Salvaging and making, they moved through time and place in a current of relations.

MAKING CRAFT A LIVELIHOOD

Like the wood drying at Eddie's place, the work of instrument makers has a social life of its own, flowing through time and changing with the relationships with which it is entangled. As banjo and guitar maker Pete Hobbie told me, "Having a relationship with your craft is what keeps it real." The reality is that the work is always changing, finding new expressions, unexpected stops, and leaps to new practitioners.

Chris Zambelli had begun thinking of shifting his practice to selling tonewood, while making fewer instruments. Regularly busy with responding to eBay orders, he was often preoccupied with readying sets for other prospective makers to ensure that his supply would not outlast his making career. He had kept busy with the number of orders he was getting for instruments but was feeling pressured by the pace, not sure that he would have time for his own projects. "I've got sides that have been in a mold for ten years," he told me, referencing a D-18–style guitar of his own that he never seemed to catch up with. Meanwhile, Paolo Marks continued making violins but had also picked up considerable repair work through a connection to a regional symphony and school system. He said repairs on dozens of violin family instruments were now taking up most of his practice. A life-threatening illness had caused him to pause work and consider whether he would ever make instruments again.

Near the end of my work in 2018, John Preston told me he had set aside a couple of pieces that I liked while we sorted in Romania and that I should come for them when ready to build my next violin. While looking at some of the one-piece backs we had selected, John informed me that he would not be continuing to cut the local wood and was going to scale back the work of the shop. He hoped that someone else would take up the cutting of the West Virginia wood, as it was still there and he did not want those trees to go to other purposes. He said he just couldn't manage it all anymore, and the work in West Virginia "just felt like a job" while working in Romania was like "being with family." By 2021, he had sold the rest of his tonewood business and moved to working solely on violins and making instruments, trading his shop for a space in a historical school turned studio.

In September 2021, I sat in John's new studio and talked with him and Travis Holley about how their work had changed in the three years since I had last worked with them. While John worked on a violin in the background, Travis told me that he had taken up the mantle of cutting tonewood by launching a business, Appalachian Tonewood, in late 2019. His work with John through the years had left him with the skills to identify those properties necessary for tonewood and the techniques to draw them out. John explained that initially, "I was doing all figuring [of what instruments to cut for] and everything. But then about the last maybe two years, Travis was doing it all. He had learned enough from what I was doing that he just did everything."

Travis credited the time spent with John on the sawmill and at the bench in the shop making guitars as preparing him to take on the craft himself. "[John] knew the dimensions [of the instruments] and how they were cut, and that was the hardest thing to get through my head. Making the instruments that I did really helped, getting it through my head, like, 'Oh, okay, now I see.' " This transferal of skill allowed Travis to begin to practice the craft, take on every stage of the production, and even begin teaching his partners what he had learned:

The first two years I started this company, I was doing everything. And it was just crazy amounts of work. . . . I have a partner now, and I think I've taught him a lot about it. I mean, he has cut wood in the past, but he's learned a lot. You have to teach people, especially when we're taught what to cut. There's a lot you have to know. You've got to know fifteen different instruments in your head, and how to best get the best piece out. If it's shorter, it's like 'Oh, okay, we're not going to cut this, we're gonna cut guitar necks, or we'll cut bass neck instead.'

I asked how the work had changed since he struck out on his own, and he replied that it had changed immensely in all aspects, starting with how the tonewood was selected and processed.

In the beginning, it was more individual attention to detail, the piece was a lot, it was graded with stricter grading on it. There was more attention to the details of the product that was going out. The new transition, loose grading, not because the specs aren't as stringent as—well, the retail market was what we were basically doing from the beginning. And now it's more wholesale; it's more larger factories with less stringent requirements for the wood being cut. . . . So let's just stick with red spruce. If I'm cutting a red spruce log, I'm cutting that perfect vertical grain piece out of the center. And we usually just stop there, and now I can go out a little bit and be a little off. And [our customers] are a little less stringent on the runout aspect of it, so, you know, we can buy lesser-grade trees. Before, John and I would flag like fifteen or twenty of those trees, and we would pick three or four of them. Now I would have probably bought three-quarters of them. I don't think it necessarily makes it less special, just to get more out of [it]; I mean, they're starting to realize that you can't get that perfect piece of spruce anymore. So they're like, okay, we're going to have to accept some flaws—accept a little runout or a little off quarter. . . . I think it's more that they want red spruce for a certain price and they're lowering their standards as long as it fits their need.

While small makers might still be looking for perfect individual pieces, the bulk buyers are much more likely to accept pieces with flaws unacceptable in years past. As the parameters have opened up, demand for the red spruce has increased. Travis now has larger orders to fill and more competition from emerging tonewood firms looking toward the red spruce forests of the Alleghenies: "We're starting to talk about expanding up north more just to keep the current volume that we need for the contract that we have. So we're gonna have to look a lot harder than when I first started. And everything's hard. There's more everything going against it. There's also more competition in the area for the same wood. People doing what I'm doing are here looking as well."

Travis noted that they still typically pay much more than the lumber board footage for the logs, and even though they will buy a higher volume now, they are still beholden to the loggers and the loaders who ultimately define the fate of trees. Travis bemoaned the loss of a favorite logger, who was always interested in the logs becoming tonewood and would make sure to set them aside at a logging landing. "It depends on the logger that's logging, if they're interested. They think that that's all cool. You know, it's going into music instruments, they'll make sure it gets out. But otherwise, if it's the old-timer—old school ones, it's 'let's get on the next job.' They just fly on." The foresters they had previously worked with were no longer working for the companies that owned the logging tracts, and they felt like a learning partnership had been lost, where the commodity was either not valued or hypervalued and priced out of possible use. Nevertheless, Travis still felt that they were engaged in a process of salvaging the spruce logs for a higher use:

> We used to just strictly let the forester pick logs. We didn't go flag. But I'll go flag a tract for five logs, then I'll spend a day or two with a drone, and three people on the ground, trying to get every guitar tree we can possibly find. Before we wouldn't even have looked at that tract. And if the forester pulled a log out, then we'd go up and look at it. There's a lot more [work] on the ground, looking at spruce.
>
> When you're flagging a tract, and you know it's not going to be there two weeks from now, that's a little depressing. And so you get a little [discouraged], but you know you're saving it from a fence rail or pulp. So you're torn. You're looking at this beautiful tract of woods that you would like for it to be there, but [you] know that it's going. So it's kind of exciting and then depressing all at the same time. But you're like running through the woods. 'Oh, my gosh. There's one. There's one!' And then it kind of dawns on you. You're like, 'Oh, yeah, this is all gonna be gone.' . . . You take it all in. And, I mean, when you first get there, you're sort of taking it all in and then you start laser focusing away. You can go through this really dense forest. Rhododendron up to here [motions above head level]. It's hard to even see them in front of you. I spent a week on one tract, just running from tree to tree, just like a child who was like, 'There's one, there's one!' [. . .] I don't typically ever go back to the tract that was cut. I don't want to see it. It's like a wasteland."

Though Travis and his partners will spend significant time flagging trees and building relationships with the human links in the logging chains, they also face more competition from other wood-production ventures. He told me that curly maple logs had tripled or quadrupled in price, placing the material out of financial viability for cutting into guitar, banjo, and mandolin pieces as he had been trained to do. They simply could not compete with the prices offered for full logs from firms ready to load them into shipping containers and send them out to global markets. At the same time, Travis told me that they were facing increased competition from another source: bugs.[3]

> There's a bug problem now. We never had a bug problem. But pretty much every spruce they put on the ground will have bugs starting immediately at the landing. So I'm trying to speed that process up even faster. Now it's like as they come out of the woods, I will bring the truck up on a landing site

and set two logs. Then we'll come back in a week, and they'll be in there. . . .
There's different varieties [of beetles] because there's different hole sizes.
I've pulled a few and thought about sending them off to see if this is new,
or is this a spillover from the dead standing ash?[4] Maybe they're bringing a
lot more powderpost beetles now?[5] Because it just seemed to kind of blow
up right as the ash was dying out around here, but that's speculation. I've
lost lots of guitar tops to bugs. They'll go in an inch and a half, and that inch
and half is extremely important when you are trying to get a guitar top. So
just one more layer. And then you have the staining. Everything is going
against a piece of spruce.

With the growing pressures on spruce, maples being too expensive, and
the native cherry trees being out of fashion for guitars, Travis was turning to
black walnut as the key that would open his business to tonewood markets.
With a density and coloration that comes close to the desired rosewood species, walnut was beginning to be considered for production-line instruments
by large companies. In fall 2021, Travis and his partners had secured a contract
with a large company to supply walnut backs and sides for a new line of acoustic guitars. "In order to make it profitable, we're gonna have to move toward
predried wood," he told me. They were going to buy kiln-dried lumber from
Missouri and feed it through a resawing machine to get their guitar sets. "That's
when it turns into a factory job," he said, "when you're shoving boards through
a machine—that's not going to be as near as rewarding." They ended up less
than pleased with the tonal qualities of that wood and had to reconsider buying
green logs and doing all the sawing and drying themselves. "Proper drying
is what makes tonewood *tonewood*," Travis explained. Nevertheless, he continually returned to the connection with the spruce and its extension into the
forest as what kept him returning to the work of tonewood cutting. "I think it's
that with any tonewood cutter or maker or builder, or anything at all that re-
volves around [this], it is just the obsession or the love for it. There's not a lot of
money in it. And then you wonder, 'Why are these people doing it?' " he asked
himself. "Because they like it," he earnestly answered. He added that it is the
process of finding the spruce trees standing in the woods and bringing them
into tonewood form [that is] the most meaningful aspect: "Luckily, I'll get to
continue with the spruce and finding that that's going to be from the forest all
the way."

Travis's work points to the importance of various kinds of succession
that drives the continuation of craft practices, the sustainability of forests,
and the entanglement of economic processes that impact them. The work of

Fig. C.1. A red spruce guitar made by John Preston

instrument makers is the result of generations of the transmission of knowledge about materials, how to interact with them, and moral judgments about their "best use." Travis found himself at the center of these processes as well as their entangled contradictions that create surging demand and new work opportunities while opening the materials they rely on to further exploitation.

Further, making a livelihood and finding meaningful expression while balancing the rote mechanization of processes required by the speed of production elsewhere reflect a central challenge of artisans.

While the instrument-making craft is posited as one of many possible routes to expand and diversify economies in the Appalachian region, the future of work, forest environments, and very human communities that support rural workers are all at a very uncertain crossroads. The availability of a basic income and health care may also influence the drive toward a more meaningful livelihood for people, it could have rippling effects through the landscape of work and processes of production and consumption throughout the world. The rise of collaborative work spaces and the gig economy may also present options for people to pursue craft practices as livelihoods or, alternatively, present alternatives that are not actually tenable. Work and how people relate to it are facing a moment of global reconsideration, as political, economic, and cultural struggles over how and why people work are contested through concepts like universal basic income and universal health care in the wake of the COVID-19 pandemic. Travis hypothesized that its impacts on labor in the music industry had caused the severe paucity of demand for musical instrument materials during the first year of the outbreak. As Travis pondered the material viability of the work he considered meaningful, millions of others refused wages that had not kept up with productivity and inflation in decades, pondering themselves the balance between the meaning of hours of work and the wages attached to them. When I was interviewing makers throughout the state, I often heard the claim that they pushed aside mental calculations of their hourly wage, refusing to entertain their work's financial reality.

Parsing a stack of violin backs in Romania in May 2018, John told me, "When I was twenty-five, I knew I wanted to be a violin maker. I just had to figure out how to make enough money so that one day I could be one." Likewise, Chris and Paolo stoked the fires of passion for the craft work of making musical instruments, pursuing it as a livelihood over the years before finding niches of their own. Travis was finally seeing some light opening up in the overstory for his enterprise to launch. I asked him when he was going to make his first violin, pointing toward that genealogy: "Whenever I start making a paycheck," he responded with a laugh.

LISTENING TO NEW GROWTH

Such lines of human economic engagement have been flowing through time alongside generations of tree species, each influencing the others in sometimes minute but powerful ways. To lose one may also mean losing another.

Forests will persist and craft traditions will persist, but what connections can be lost in the clattering noise of transition and succession?

Working alongside these materials and living with the trees that provide them have caused me to ask what the song of the spruce is. Is it the springing bass line fretted through a flatpicked melody in Chris's shop? Is it the rhythmic scraping of fibers off the tops of Paolo's violins? Is it the sound of a log crashing to the ground on its way to Travis's mill? Is it the gentle vibration the instrument emits when it's passed from hand to hand between generations of makers and players? A song is more than a series of sounds: it broadcasts a message, it tells a story, and it changes with the audience and performer.

I'm on top of Red Spruce Knob in Pocahontas County once more. It's quiet. The wind blows the branches of the trees, the liquid air bowing a series of tones and overtones while swirling leaves and pollen rosin give the place its timbre. I hear a song that emerges through the actions, materials, bodies, and contexts of the broad variety of actors described through this book—a vast intermeshing of the sounds of human and nonhuman life and animacy. As biologist David George Haskell puts it in *The Song of Trees* (2017), "Life is an embodied network. . . . We cannot step outside life's songs." When listening for the song that makers attempt to find in making instruments, we cannot step outside the other forms of song that are extended through the instruments—other communication signaled through the sounds of ecological melodies.

Emerging literature in forestry has pointed to the fact that trees communicate with one another, though perhaps not in the ways in which we consider human communication to take place.[6] This body of research points to the fact that the song of the spruce is always in relation to its environment: political, economic, ecological, aesthetic, or otherwise.[7] Foresters and ecologists listen to the spruce by measuring the health of individual trees and the forest communities to which they belong. The sound of red spruce falling, or the lack of it at all, is a harbinger of climate change.[8] As a species existing in fractured ecosystems that is very temperature sensitive, the spruce forests of West Virginia will be among the first to change drastically with warming temperatures in mountains forests throughout the Appalachian Mountains. Yet listening to the sounds of spruce in concert with the human and other than human life around them also sounds undertones of alternate futures. The gentle whisper of needles dropping signifies the capture of carbon in the forest floor. Spruce needles trap carbon in the soil, and their acidity enables a greater flow of carbon into the soil.[9]

The scratching sound of dibble sticks—and, ironically, tractors—delving into compacted soil is the prelude to the orchestration of broad sweeps of red spruce reforestation happening through the central Appalachians. The Central Appalachian Spruce Reforestation Initiative plants, collects seeds, and monitors red spruce and native hardwoods. Reversing years of surface mining reclamation processes that compacted soil to mitigate erosion, they have torn up soils and replanted hundreds of thousands of red spruce across thousands of acres in the Alleghenies. With partnerships that extend across state, local, and institutional backgrounds, they have aimed to replant, keeping in mind the biodiverse presences and relationships that make a forest, an effort at reforestation rather than replanation.[10] And in the notes of these foresters, we can see a willingness to accommodate more than human life into relationships. A forester working on red spruce replanting efforts, Anoob Prakash, said in a 2020 interview, "[Spruce] are like human babies: you have to care for them for a long time before you can actually see a result."[11] Prakash's advisor, Stephen Keller, admitted in the same piece that his interests were partially motivated by the climate issues described above, but they were also aligned with his love of the forest. The long life of spruce trees demanded by the aesthetics and craft practices of instrument makers thus fits into a larger concert of old trees, diverse forests, and human relationships.

Nevertheless, across the world tonewoods will continue to be threatened by changing ecological conditions coupled with increased demand—being loved to death by the instrument trade. In 2018, I invited Romanian forester Florin Dinulică to visit the tonewood factory in Râșnov while we were selecting wood to export to West Virginia. John, a trained forester himself, and Florin were eager to compare the incidence of curly maple logs in their respective home forests, trading their own estimations of the occurrence of the tree and projecting its future. Dinulică, a leading researcher at the Transilvania University of Brașov in forestry and tonewood, expressed concern that the tree was too valuable in Romania. Surmising that genetic inheritance has a great deal to do with the figure in a piece of wood led him to believe that the wood would soon be overexploited and no longer exist in Carpathian forests. While spruce is now once again growing in notoriety as a tonewood in West Virginian forests, in the Carpathians tonewood exploitation may speed its overharvest.

The fibers of tonewood trees hold a tension—a tension between the aesthetics and material qualities of sound and sight. As the tension of a wound string compels a musician to draw from it a melody, these tensions compel makers to continue to use the materials.[12] What percentage of a tree's identity as a tonewood belongs to the aesthetic traditions of lutherie and what percentage belongs to the material qualities of the wood itself? Can the two be

Fig. C.2. A red spruce sapling growing on Cheat Mountain in Randolph County, WV

disentangled, or is the desire for the wood the true defining aspect of the relationship? Is the succession of craft practice entangled in the material as genetics and environment are in the growth of curly maple bound for the sawmill?

Forest succession is a sociobiological process that relies on such tensions between material and inheritance. Grasses, shrubs, and trees succeed one another as a forest returns, until it reaches a point of stasis in which certain species of trees dominate the overstory. Yet those trees compel human beings into action, using skills to direct forests into global flows of commodities and craft materials. Those flows complicate the succession of skills and livelihoods of makers who seek to draw out sonic bounty and a lively aesthetic. Instrument makers, music players, and listeners are all part of the succession happening in forests and workshops throughout the world. The stories of forests and workshops are inscribed and sung through instruments as the background of melodies, harmonies, and dissonances that move, shape, and create the world around us.

NOTES

INTRODUCTION

1. On defining West Virginia artisan practitioners, see Morris, "Seminal Seeds and Hybrids."
2. Ethnography is the documentary craft of the humanities and social sciences. Employing a broad methodological toolkit, researchers in folklore, anthropology, sociology, and geography—to name a few—may use interviews, oral histories, observation of and participation in social events, photographs, films, and recordings, as well as extensive, in-depth notetaking to produce a representation of a given population. Since the methods tend to capture the present moment from human perspectives, historical, archival research and attention to the materials of life are important accompaniments to round out the picture.
3. On artifact biographies, see Bates, "The Social Life of Musical Instruments"; Kopytoff, "The Cultural Biography of Things."
4. Apprenticeship, as with all ethnography, requires careful attention to the intersecting positions of the ethnographer. As I found in my larger study, instrument makers in West Virginia are predominantly male, white, and speak to regional identity through their work and lives. Thus, I was mindful of showing gendered male expressions and signifiers of my West Virginia identity with my collaborators, as well as how my whiteness in relation to racialized power in the larger national context may have shaped interactions and relationships in various ways throughout my fieldwork.
5. On craft apprenticeship and ethnography, see Cant, *The Value of Aesthetics*; O'Connor, "Embodied Knowledge." On power and ethnographic apprenticeship, see Anderson-Lazo, "Ethnography as Aprendizaje"; Coy, *Apprenticeship*; Downey, Dalidowicz, and Mason, "Apprenticeship as Method."
6. This translates occasionally in this book to a form of ethnographic writing known as "autoethnography." Autoethnography embraces the perspective, biography, and positionality of the ethnographer to offer explanation, critique, and nuance to cultural analysis. In this book, expect to find my personal narrative guiding the narrative of making instruments alongside makers.
7. For more on the intersections of craft and ethnographic apprenticeship in my work, see Jasper Waugh-Quasebarth, "Learning and Labor in Ethnographic Apprenticeship," *The Anthropology of Work Review*, 2021. John Preston and I have also coauthored a piece on his work in Romania: Jasper Waugh-Quasebarth and John Preston, "Listening for

Musical Tonewood in the Appalachian and Carpathian Mountains," *Bulletin of the Transilvania University of Braşov* 12, no. 61 (2019), https://doi.org/10.31926/but.pcs .2019.61.12.35.

8. Following Weber, *The Protestant Ethic and the Spirit of Capitalism*.
9. For more on "re-enchantment," see Bennett, *The Enchantment of Modern Life*; Jenkins, "Disenchantment, Enchantment, and Re-Enchantment."
10. Harcourt and Escobar, "Women and the Politics of Place"; Ingold, "Bringing Things to Life."
11. Dudley, *Guitar Makers*.
12. Gibson and Warren, *The Guitar*.
13. This book treats the terms *maker*, *crafter*, and *luthier* as interchangeable in description as I encountered them in the field; that is, as one who makes stringed musical instruments. Similarly, I use the term *lutherie* interchangeably with musical instrument craft for mostly word economy reasons. However, for some, *lutherie*, and the less common *luthiery*, are terms reserved for specific kinds of wooden, stringed musical instruments. In the field, I found that adoption of *luthier*, *lutherie*, and *luthiery* was sometimes accompanied by value judgments about other makers. Either the term *luthier* was reserved to distinguish oneself as a specific profession or it was considered a hubristic label that would betray the humility of a crafter to embrace it.

CHAPTER 1

1. Irwin, *Musical Instruments of the Southern Appalachian Mountains*.
2. In one archival research stint, I asked to see the musical instruments in a collection and was brought out only the mountain dulcimers, despite the handmade violins, guitars, and banjos in storage.
3. For example, Sears-Roebuck's cheapest violin in 1902 (with bow, strings, and setup) cost $2.45, or about $70.00 when adjusted for inflation. A violin made from solid wood on Amazon.com today is comparable, costing at least $60.00.
4. Milnes, *Play of a Fiddle*.
5. Rohr is said to have taken up violin making as practice for his fine motor skills necessary for surgeries and would go back and forth between the two practices sometimes in his shop and office.
6. This article shares much of the same content with a later article from the *Shepherdstown Register* from April 1, 1915.
7. Gwin, "Another Allison Tries His Hand at Making of Violins."
8. Wenberg, *Violin Makers of the United States*.
9. "Evening Chat," *West Virginian*, September 12, 1916. These kinds of stories are common fascination. An article written forty years later suggests the possibility of an Amati-made violin in Charleston that was carried through the Civil War to West Virginia as the payment for saving a child from a burning plantation house: Ed Morris, "City Violin May Be Amati-Made," *Charleston Daily Mail*, December 8, 1957.
10. Smith, *Appalachian Dulcimer Traditions*.
11. "Plant to Enlarge," *Charleston Daily Mail*, November 13, 1915. I searched for the building that would have housed the factory, but records seem to suggest that it was demolished to make way for the I-64/I-75 overpass through Charleston.
12. "Buyer Visits Beckley," *Beckley Messenger*, August 8, 1916.
13. "West Virginia Takes Place in Capital News," *Clarksburg Daily Telegram*, February 23, 1916. The article goes on to claim that Cantrell gave a violin to Senator W. E. Chilton, who delivered it as a gift to President Woodrow Wilson. In a letter of February 25, 1924, from Chilton to Wilson's former aide Cary Grayson, Chilton asked for the violin back, claiming, "It was not of much value, to me, because it was a new violin made here. It has, however,

a tone which is dead to an old-time country fiddler, which I am. Of course, it has another value to me, it having belonged to President Wilson." Grayson's response regrettably informs Chilton that the violin was misplaced. Cary T. Grayson (Cary Travers), 1878–1938, "Cary T. Grayson to William Edwin Chilton," 1924 March 19, WWP16547, Cary T. Grayson Papers, Woodrow Wilson Presidential Library & Museum, Staunton, Virginia. I was not able to locate it in my research, nor could I find any example of an American Violin Company violin.

14. Through the early twentieth century, factory production in Central and Eastern Europe dominated the global market for violins. Ward ("The Mystery of Origin") estimates that between 1880 and 1914, 200,000 violins were shipped from shops and small factories in Saxony and Bohemia annually.

15. See Sennett, *The Craftsman*.

16. Langlands, *Cræft*.

17. Near-contemporary writings by other social theorists mirror the same anxieties about the loss of meaning in industrial production and reframing of material relationships. For example, the writings of Marx, "Estranged Labor," on the alienation of workers from their labor and resultant products as commodities; Weber, *The Protestant ethic and the spirit of capitalism*, concerning the disenchantment of the world by rational modes of governance and management; and Benjamin, *The Work of Art in the Age of Mechanical Reproduction*, on mechanical reproduction displacing the authenticity of art objects, have pushed scholars to consider how different modes of production create different forms of meaning around laborers and the production of material culture.

18. See Basole, "Authenticity, Innovation, and the Geographical Indication"; Cant, *The Value of Aesthetics*; Cavanaugh and Shankar, "Producing Authenticity in Global Capitalism."

19. See Kingsolver, *Tobacco Town Futures*. Contemplating and performing authenticity is especially crucial when participating in the "experience economies" in which Appalachian music and craft figure heavily. This strategy of providing cultural experiences for tourists and residents alike figures heavily into initiatives concerning economic transitions in Appalachia, such as Shaping Our Appalachian Region (SOAR), Eastern Kentucky's designated "promise zone" for economic investment, and proposed establishment of designated geographic areas that promote the ecological and cultural heritage of the region. Promoting packages of "preindustrial" and "industrial" lifeways through these projects, music and craft figure into tourist expectations of nostalgic visions of Appalachia and the kinds and quality of instruments that makers produce to fit these expectations. Placed experiences of localized music, craft, and agricultural production are central to these efforts that replace the extractive commoditization of mountain communities and environments with the commoditization of landscape and heritage.

20. Formal learning institutions include the liberal arts–oriented Associate of Science program in stringed-instrument technology at Indiana University and the Roberto Venn School of Luthiery in Arizona, among others. At the time of writing, lutherie schools were also opening across Appalachia as a revival of settlement-school models of using craft to address social issues such as addiction and poverty.

21. For more on how gender is made and unmade through everyday work, see Rolston, "The Politics of Pits and the Materiality of Mine Labor"; Lamphere, Ragoné, and Zavella, *Situated Lives*.

22. Dudley, *Guitar Makers*.

23. For an anthropological analysis of self-marketing and branding, see Gershon, "Selling Your Self in the United States."

24. Terrio explores a similar process in *Crafting the Culture and History of French Chocolate*.

25. The word "job" has become central to economic political discourse in Appalachia, as articulated through the panacea of the concept of "jobs" aimed at addressing the region's low statistical rankings in categories like per capita income, unemployment, disability

benefits, and poverty rates. As in other places in the United States, and the world, this framework posits the specific wage labor of "jobs" against other kinds of economic activity and systems of valorizing social and environmental life. In this sense, it is only capital in the private sector that creates these jobs and people's livelihoods and valorizes them against other kinds of work. Thus, work in service to capitalist enterprises becomes the central politically divisive issue. In 2016, West Virginia's legislature approved "Right to Work" legislation that was then upheld by the state supreme court. Despite this legislation and an apparent turn away from labor politics in the state, in 2018, 20,000 West Virginia teachers and public employees stopped work and shut down schools for two weeks to negotiate for better pay and health insurance coverage. Afterwards, many sought election to public office, dismayed with the political process.

26. This again resonates with Dudley's (2014) description of American guitar builders' unique brand of "self-work" that coalesces with ideas of the performance of white masculinity in *Guitar Makers*.

27. Milnes, *Play of a Fiddle*; Thompson, *Performing Community*.

28. Harkins, *Hillbilly*. Caught up in this discourse is a form of regional mythmaking that posits West Virginians as "mountaineers," captured in the masculine, pioneer visage of West Virginia University's mascot, normally wearing the buckskins, coonskin hats, and carrying the long rifle characteristic of the backwoods pioneer vision of West Virginia history. The state's motto, "Montani Semper Liberi" or "Mountaineers are always free," is a source of pride for the state and a powerful rhetorical device. Following devastating events, the trope is usually deployed as a call to symbolic action, a call to spirit and strength. For example, after the mass pollution of the water supply for Charleston in 2014, Senator Joe Manchin called for the mountaineer spirit as a rallying cry. Yet it is also a call to inaction: West Virginia mountaineers are expected to show the strength and determination to bear the impacts of such environmental and political injustices, yet not challenge the political and economic systems that give rise to them.

29. West Virginia is the only state entirely within the bounds of the federal Appalachian Regional Commission's geographic definition of Appalachia.

30. Billings, Norman, and Ledford, *Back Talk from Appalachia*; Baudrillard, *Revenge of the Crystal*.

31. Whisnant, *All That Is Native and Fine*.

32. Williams, *Great Smoky Mountains Folklife*; Conway, *African Banjo Echoes in Appalachia*; Cohen, *Folk Music*; Marshall, *Music in the Air Somewhere*.

33. Conway, *African Banjo Echoes in Appalachia;* Cece Conway's work around the history of the banjo, for instance, shows that its symbolic ties to white, working-class or hillbilly tropes bely the history of enslaved African Americans' development of the material form of the instrument as well as the musical styles that often characterize Appalachian "old-time" music.

34. See Hay, "Black Musicians in Appalachia," and Thompson and Hacquard, "Region, Race, Representation." Visitors to the annual West Virginia Black Heritage Festival or the West Virginia Italian Heritage Festival in Clarksburg would encounter different views on traditional West Virginian music.

35. More recent efforts toward social and environmental justice embrace this historical trajectory, employing music as an avenue to contest mountaintop removal coal mining, such as Stimeling's "Music, Place, and Identity."

36. West Virginia has been a major site in U.S. labor history, including Mary Harris "Mother" Jones' work to organize coal miners in the early twentieth century and the 1921 Battle of Blair Mountain that pitted coal miners wishing to unionize against a private army hired by coal operators.

37. See Batteau, *The Invention of Appalachia*; Becker, *Selling Tradition*; Whisnant, *All That Is Native and Fine*.

38. Satterwhite, "Imagining Home, Nation, World."
39. Lilly and Todd, "Could New Twists on Traditional Music Help Revive Appalachia's Economy?"
40. Rural Policy Research Institute, "2013 SOAR Summit Final Report to the Region," 58.
41. Mencken and Maggard, "Informal Economic Activity in West Virginia"; Oberhauser, "Scaling Gender and Diverse Economies."
42. See West Virginia Development Office, "The West Virginia Crafts Study," and Price et al., "The Economic Impact of Tamarack." Both studies take into account the craft and art process but ultimately transform it into terms only useful for economists and state government employees, perhaps indicative of their relatively low rates of participation as compared to heritage projects undertaken in a participatory manner. These studies represent what Susan Keefe called "Corporate Development" in that they measure success of development through economic factors and believe that the use rather than production of social resources is the prime determinant in economic development. Keefe, *Participatory Development in Appalachia*.
43. See Scott, *Removing Mountains*.
44. For more on "re-enchantment," see Bennett, *The Enchantment of Modern Life*; Jenkins, "Disenchantment, Enchantment, and Re-Enchantment."
45. Weber, *The Protestant Ethic*.
46. Taussig's *The Devil and Commodity Fetishism in South America*, an examination of how folk practices mediate and make sense of capitalist economic relationships, is relevant.

CHAPTER 2

1. West Virginia is the third-most-forested state by percentage of land area in the United States, following Maine and New Hampshire. It has a mean elevation of 1,654 feet, or approximately 504 meters. Kanawha County, West Virginia's most populous county as of 2019, boasts 77 percent forest cover.
2. This attention to scale, governance, history, and ecology is the basis of the field of "political ecology," which involves the interaction between political and economic power and ecology. This framework greatly influences the interpretations of this book. Robbins, *Political Ecology*.
3. For much of U.S. history, the Alleghenies were synonymous with the entire Appalachian range.
4. West Virginia Division of Forestry, "West Virginia Statewide Forest Resource Assessment."
5. This number fluctuates considerably during winter months due to the large ski resort in the county. It was inflated given the contentious large-scale pipeline construction project underway at the time of this fieldwork, which was the subject of considerable civil disobedience.
6. However, the proposed land was already designated as wilderness, meaning that few if any substantive changes would have been made to regulations of land use.
7. For more on the overlapping usage of forest commons, see Hufford, *Tending the Commons*.
8. Dunaway, *The First American Frontier*.
9. Abrams and Nowacki, "Native Americans as Active and Passive Promoters."
10. Emrick, "Maopewa Iati Bi."
11. Thomas-Van Gundy and Strager, "European Settlement-Era Vegetation."
12. Newfont, *Blue Ridge Commons*.
13. Rice, *The Allegheny Frontier*, 129.
14. Hufford suggests that "witness trees" also bear narrative witness to the possession and dispossession of vernacular ecologies in central Appalachia. "The Witness Trees' Revolt," 46.

15. Abrams and McCay, "Vegetation-Site Relationships of Witness Trees."
16. Marlin is the namesake of Pocahontas County's seat, Marlinton.
17. Rice, *The Allegheny Frontier*, 129.
18. Lewis, *Transforming the Appalachian Countryside*.
19. Eller, *Miners, Millhands, and Mountaineers*.
20. Clarkson and Lunk, *Tumult on the Mountains*, 37; Lewis, "Railroads, Deforestation, and the Transformation of Agriculture."
21. Lewis, *The Industrialist and the Mountaineer*.
22. Lewis, "Railroads, Deforestation, and the Transformation of Agriculture."
23. Lewis, *The Industrialist and the Mountaineer*; Harkins, *Hillbilly*.
24. Issues of extractive timbering were being addressed by two sides of a debate that still is played out today between conservationists (represented by Gifford Pinchot, the first chief of the U.S. Forest Service, who valued the forests as economic resources that were scientifically managed for sustainable exploitation) and the preservationists (represented by John Muir, who sought protection for the forests for their value to human spiritual health).
25. Lewis, *Transforming the Appalachian Countryside*.
26. Clarkson and Lunk, *Tumult on the Mountains*, 37; Lewis, *Transforming the Appalachian Countryside*.
27. Lewis, *Transforming the Appalachian Countryside*, 158.
28. "Doggin' " refers to manipulating the "dogs," or the mechanisms that secure logs on the mill carriage. Coincidentally, this would be the same role that I would play as I worked with tonewood cutters John Preston and Travis Holley in 2017. Dr. Robert P. Alexander Collection, 1880–2000, Accession No. 2012/05.0795, Special Collections Department, Marshall University, Huntington, WV.
29. It is also a great regional pride that the Wright Brothers bought red spruce from the Alleghenies of West Virginia as supplies for the construction of their flyers.
30. Remaining infrastructure of these towns features in local tourism projects, such as the operating railroad and company store at Cass, West Virginia.
31. Letters from the C.F. Martin and Co. Archives provided by Dick Boak and Greig Hutton.
32. These mandolins and guitars were used by artists who established the style and sound of the American folk music revival, rock music, blues, country and western music, and bluegrass that dominated popular music worldwide in the mid-twentieth century.
33. Also following the correspondence of the Acme Veneer & Lumber Co., Gibson and Warren in *The Guitar* (149–183) skillfully follow the decline of "Adirondack" or red spruce and transition to "Washington" or Sitka spruce through the early twentieth century.
34. United States Public Law 86–517.
35. One of the large current issues in the Monongahela, for example, has to do with the benefits that counties housing the national forests receive from the national government. Counties are eligible for Payments in Lieu of Taxes (PiLTs) to offset lost property taxes from the tax-exempt land as well as funding from the Twenty-Five Percent Act, which designates 25 percent of forest sales in the county for the use of the county school system. Recent decreases in National Forest cuttings correlate to lower federal funding for the schools. However, the Secure Rural Schools (SRS) program also provided greater funding to schools in lieu of the Twenty-Five Percent Act. For example, Pocahontas County received $461,304 from the SRS program for FY 2017 and $827,127.00 from PiLTs. The volatility of this program (allowed to expire in 2015 but renewed in 2018) contributes to the precariousness of the local schools, as tax levies in support of schools are regularly defeated in local elections, and state funding for education is a contentious issue.
36. Salstrom, "The Neonatives."
37. Beaver, *Rural Community in the Appalachian South*.

38. However, not all were happy about this change. Noted West Virginia folklorist and musicologist Patrick Ward Gainer remarked about the West Virginia Folk Festival in 1980, "I can't stand all the out-of-state hippies with guitars who think they're playing folk music. I haven't attended the festival since I quit running it, 20 years ago." Strat Douthat, *Sunday Gazette-Mail*, June 22, 1980.

39. This can result in conflicts of usage. When not productive timberland, timber companies typically do not monitor their holdings closely. Hunters on leases are protective of what they see as their private property, while local residents may be attracted to the forest commons represented by these open spaces that offer discarded tree tops as premium firewood and foraging opportunities.

40. Ingold, *A Brief History of Lines*; Ingold, *The Perception of the Environment*. See also Harcourt and Escobar, *Women and the Politics of Place*.

41. Ingold, "On Human Correspondence."

42. Ingold, "Toward an Ecology of Materials," 435.

43. This framework is not without inadequacies in addressing social inequalities and expressions of power. While it provides a structured language to describe the relationality of human-material action, it lacks in discussion as to how those actions manifest in unequal patterns and how human action may be limited as a result. I attempt to follow the relational threads through artifact biographies and multisited ethnography to push the theory into a direction that acknowledges inequalities of access and production. Theories of inequality that stress global processes as they arise in specific places are particularly useful in assessing how power and agency can tangle, unravel, tack, or mend meshworks.

44. Bates, "The Social Life of Musical Instruments"; Roda, "Ecology of the Global Tabla Industry"; Dudley, *Guitar Makers*; Tucker, *Making Music Indigenous*.

45. On "place" as a concept, see Feld and Basso, *Senses of Place*; Tuck and McKenzie, *Place in Research*.

46. Harris, *Ways of Knowing*.

47. Social theorist Walter Benjamin in *The Work of Art* conceptualizes the "aura" as a presence that brings a work of art, its author, and the spectator into a deep meaningful relationship.

48. Anthropologist Heather Paxson in *The Life of Cheese* locates a similar practice in the craft of cheese in the United States. The craft draws "meaningful lines of connection among people, culture, and landscape to invest rural places anew with affective significance and material relevance" (446), especially as it connects to the culinary concept of terroir that locates flavor in the complex relationships of a specific place that imparts a unique flavor or quality to a product.

49. Ferry and Limbert, *Timely Assets*; Richardson and Weszkalnys, "Resource Materialities."

50. Sarah H. Hill's *Weaving New Worlds* (1997) exploration of changing material techniques in the basketry of Cherokee women through a shifting forest landscape in North Carolina is an excellent example of this process linking meaning of place and changing ecological relationships. In her historical and ethnographic study of Cherokee basket weavers, she showed how knowledge and work practices in basketry were mutually influenced by the larger political ecological context as the forest composition changed due to settler colonialism and subsequent flows of introduced species, such as Japanese honeysuckle.

51. For more on multivalent understandings of forests in Appalachia, see Hufford, "Stalking the Forest Coeval"; and Newfont, *Blue Ridge Commons*.

52. For more on silencing and invisibility in narratives about Appalachia, see Kingsolver, *Tobacco Town Futures*; Turner and Cabbell, *Blacks in Appalachia*.

53. Finney, *Black Faces, White Spaces*; Kosek, *Understories*.

54. Cooley, *Cultural Sustainabilities*; McDowell et al., *Performing Environmentalisms*.

55. Allen, " 'Fatto Di Fiemme.' "

56. Carmenates, "Honduras Rosewood."
57. For more on the history, use, and conservation of rosewood species, especially in Brazil, see Gibson and Warren, *The Guitar*, 115–148.
58. Kathryn Marie Dudley, "Are Guitar Makers an Endangered Species?" *New York Times*, October 25, 2011, sec. Opinion, http://www.nytimes.com/2011/10/26/opinion/are-guitar-makers-an-endangered-species.html; Gibson and Warren, "Resource-Sensitive Global Production Networks; Greenberg, "Good Vibrations, Strings Attached"; Martinez-Reyes, "Global Wood Politics."
59. For more information on the implications of music making and environmental issues, see Allen and Dawe, *Current Directions in Ecomusicology*.

CHAPTER 3

1. Weyerhauser acquired Plum Creek in 2015 for $8.4 billion to become one of the world's largest timber management and production companies.
2. The Gibson Company moved from Kalamazoo, Michigan, to Nashville, Tennessee, in 1984 in a trend toward moving factory production to cheaper labor markets in the United States.
3. Dudley, *Guitar Makers*.
4. Ebony and rosewood species were added to CITES' Appendix III in 2011.
5. Dudley, *Guitar Makers*.
6. Martinez-Reyes, "Mahogany Intertwined."
7. Studies from other areas of the United States are producing other novel ways of working with local materials, from geographer Jared Beeton's work introducing beetle-killed western Spruce as a viable tonewood to musicologist Alex Smith's experimental "Michigan-dered Marimba" made from reclaimed Michigan alternatives to threatened percussive tonewood species.
8. Having a musical biography plays into some instrument makers' requirements of their instruments. "Cannibalizing" other instruments in this manner, as some makers say, or playing music on a radio inside a guitar before selling, for example, are ways makers assure the wood has a materiality of music before it leaves the shop.
9. The D-18—along with other Martin D-size guitars—became synonymous with American music during the folk music revivals and rise of bluegrass of the mid-twentieth centuries. Their large size provided a loud tone that could compete with the other instruments of a string band, and they were likened to the large battleship, the *HMS Dreadnought*, that inspired the name of the series.
10. *Bouts* are the curved areas at the top and bottom of the guitar body.
11. A few months later, I attended a national guitar makers' conference where I was advised by a maker and repairer to pursue repair work as a main vocation. He said that it was a more stable and dependable livelihood, but one that required that you leave no trace in the attempt to keep the instrument in its original condition. In my apprenticeship with Paolo Marks, a violinmaker, I would learn that interior signatures or stamps often accompany violin repairs as a calling card of the quality and genealogy of the instrument.

CHAPTER 4

1. This translates as "Jacob Stainer in Absam near Innsbruck [present-day Austria] 1736." Stainer died in 1683.
2. Hide glue is produced by boiling animal hides, usually cows, and processing the resultant hydrolyzed collagen.
3. Paolo often referenced the golden mean as a reference to the golden ratio, which is the numerical representation of Greek ideals of symmetry, proportion, and harmony. Paolo

equally referenced these terms in describing how instruments fit into the natural world. The numerical ratio, written as φ, has been used as a reference for principles of Classical and Renaissance design. Its prevalence in the natural world appears to be an issue of contention.

4. In the style of Antonio Stradivari (1644–1733), Giuseppe Guarneri del Jesú (1698–1744), and Nicola Amati (1596–1684), among others, who resided and made instruments in Cremona, Italy.

5. Japanese water stones are prized for their relatively soft material, which creates a slurry while sharpening that polishes the edge. Overexploitation of mining natural stones in the twentieth century led to a new market for synthetic water stones, as well as a high-end market of "natural" stones.

6. Paolo's thoughts on Japanese aesthetics and techniques and his own work recall the concepts of *ikigai*, a reason for being cultivated through self-reflection, and the *kosei*, or personality, of craft materials that Dorinne Kondo (*Crafting Selves*) describes in artisanal production in Japan.

7. In the seventy-one years Stradivari signed musical instruments (1666–1737), he produced 1,116 known instruments.

8. This is a crucial aspect of how C.F. Martin & Company depicts the history of their company, starting with the founder, Christian Frederick Martin. According to the Martin Company's historians, Martin was caught in a dispute between the Cabinet Maker's Guild and the Violin Maker's Guild of the famous Saxon musical instrument town of Markneukirchen. The violin makers sought an injunction against cabinetmakers who made guitars, writing, "The violin makers belong to a class of musical instrument makers and therefore to the class of artists whose work not only shows finish, but gives evidence of a certain understanding of cultured taste. The cabinet makers, by contrast, are nothing more than mechanics whose products consist of all kinds of articles known as furniture. . . . Who doesn't recognize that a grandfather chair or a night stool isn't a guitar?" Gura, *C.F. Martin and His Guitars*, 36–67. While today's C.F. Martin Company illustrates this as a drive away from the restrictions of guild-controlled labor, I have found that these undertones still pervade understandings of guitar craft by other types of instrument makers.

9. Blakemore, "Mineral Baths."

10. For more on this, see Hendry, "Scanning a Stradivarius."

11. A catenary is an idealized curve that is assumed when a cable hangs under only its own weight supported at its ends.

12. Nascent fronds of ferns are often referred to as "fiddleheads" for their resemblance to the violin scroll. Several species in West Virginia, such as the ostrich fern (*Matteuccia struthiopteris*), are prized greens for spring foragers.

13. *Summer* and *winter* growth are also used to describe the parts of a tree ring, with the *summer* referring to the soft primary growth and *winter* referring to the tougher, darker growth. Such a distinction points to the spruce and maple's temperate seasonalities. Exotic tonewoods growing in tropical climates may have rings based on rainy or dry seasons or lack them all together.

14. It is worth noting that Strad's hypothetical spirit lamp would have likely used alcohol obtained from the destructive distillation of wood into flammable methylene, another instance of the deconstruction of wood into various purposes in violin craft.

15. Anthropologists have suggested that "magic" in this sense is a process of mitigating uncertainty through repeating routine rituals, thereby assuring success in uncertain circumstances by gaining control over the total performance of an action.

16. Boxwood (*Buxus sempervirens*) is often also used for violin fittings due to its density and toughness. Its light color, however, is not as popular as the dark brown or black of ebony.

17. *Lycopodium* species, often called ground pine in West Virginia for their resemblance to

miniature pine trees, produce fine spores that are collectively used to repair cracks in violins. The ultrafine powder can be easily worked into the wood and finished. During my apprenticeship, Paolo expressed a desire to collect his own store of lycopodium spores from the forest nearby his house. He also mentioned that when exposed to flame, the powder flares into a bright flash, a quality prized by magicians. We joked that this was another connection to the "magic" of violin craft.

CHAPTER 5

1. Referencing the John Hartford song, "In Tall Buildings" (1976).
2. Gibson and Warren in *The Guitar* (86–110) refer to sawmills as "trading zones" where large industrial timber concerns rub up against the smaller niche products such as tonewood and craft furniture lumber.
3. The Carpathian Mountains of Romania have also recently served as a stand-in for popular media visions of preindustrial Appalachia, such as in the 2003 film *Cold Mountain* and the 2012 miniseries *Hatfields and McCoys*.
4. Dorondel, *Disrupted Landscapes*.
5. I place these terms in quotation marks as there are no agreed-upon definitions for what an old-growth forest or tree are. In the marketing of tonewood, the terms are often used as shorthand for high-quality wood, but the terminology could play into nostalgic and romantic notions of the past.
6. Albu and Dinulică, "The Woodcutting Output of the Resonance Spruce"; Dinulică et al., "Specific Structural Indexes for Resonance Norway Spruce Wood."
7. Burckle and Grissino-Mayer, "Stradivari, Violins, Tree Rings, and the Maunder Minimum"; Nagyvary, Guillemetter, and Spiegelman, "Mineral Preservatives in the Wood of Stradivari and Guarneri"; Schwarze, Spycher, and Fink, "Superior Wood for Violins."
8. Martinez-Reyes, "Mahogany Intertwined."
9. Some instrument makers, however, value wood with characteristics that may be considered defects. Fungal and insect infestations can produce novel aesthetics in the wood and are sometimes used to make singular-looking instruments. For example, "spalted" wood that appears to have ink dripped on it due to fungal growth is frequently used as an ornamental wood.
10. Splitting is probably the first way that people cut spruce tonewood, following a similar process as splitting shingles. Due to the popularity of wooden shingles to this day in Romania, John joked in an interview, "There's some houses in Romania with maybe a hundred thousand dollars of guitar tops on top." At the factory in Romania, they frequently write "șiță," or *shingle*, on guitar tops that cannot be sold and are instead used as scrap or packing materials.
11. Romanian loggers use the slang *vant*, or wind, to describe the same condition.
12. Though the wood is often known as such, John told me that it is a misnomer. "Torrefaction" better describes the process of turning wood into fuel, such as charcoal briquettes, while this process is technically "thermal modification."
13. John had also heard a rumor that Carpathian spruces were, in fact, transplanted red spruces, telling me, "There was somebody started some kind of rumor that monks brought red spruce from the U.S. to the Carpathian Mountains and planted them, and I don't know where they ever got that. I was thinking these monks must have been—I mean, we've cut trees three and four hundred years old, and were these monks over here before Columbus, when they took them? I just don't understand where they get such a story, but the woods have some similarity, so I think somebody was just trying to promote the Carpathian spruces."
14. For more on the global demand for guitars, see Bennett and Dawe, *Guitar Cultures*.
15. The Secretary of Environment and Natural Resources of Mexico requires phytosanitary

certification for wood products entering the country. John and Catalin agreed that this process was cost prohibitive at the small scales of individual pieces of tonewood.

16. Dudley's 2014 book, *Guitar Makers*, draws heavily on her ethnographic accounts of this conference, and a copy of the book was furnished for sale at the conference's silent auction.

CONCLUSION

1. "Slab cut" refers to logs that are rough cut unidirectionally, with inclusions, knots, and bark, or "live edge," included for character. Furniture and home fittings inspired by the designs of woodworker George Nakashima's (1905–1990) "free edge" aesthetic have created an immense demand for slab cut wood in recent years.

2. Mel Chen's concept of animacy complicates divides between "living" and "dead" by arguing that matter, despite how inert it appears, always has an effective and affective influence on human action. Chen, *Animacies*.

3. By playing the "biologically relevant" noises of pine beetles back to the insects, Hofstetter et al. ("Using Acoustic Technology") have had success in sparing individual trees from the "beetle kill" that decimates stands of ponderosa pine in the American West.

4. Referring to the impact of the emerald ash borer (*Agrilus planipennis*), responsible for the death of tens of millions of ash trees (*Oleaceae* spp.) across North America.

5. Woodboring beetles belonging to the subfamily *Lyctinae*.

6. See Simard, *Finding the Mother Tree*; Wohlleben, Flannery, and Simard, *The Hidden Life of Trees*.

7. Haskell's *The Songs of Trees* is an exceptional global journey through these sites of relation.

8. Koo, Patten, and Madden, "Predicting Effects of Climate Change on Habitat Suitability of Red Spruce."

9. Heyman, "Restoring WV Spruce."

10. Branduzzi, Barton, and Lovell, "First-Year Survival of Native Wetland Plants."

11. DeYoung, "A Boost for Red Spruce."

12. Kies's study of Parachan luthiers of Michoacan, Mexico ("Aesthetic Judgements of Luthiers"), gives an excellent entry into how these dynamics operate within a different global context and community of practice.

BIBLIOGRAPHY

Abrams, Marc D., and Deanna M. McCay. 1996. "Vegetation-Site Relationships of Witness Trees (1780–1856) in the Presettlement Forests of Eastern West Virginia." *Canadian Journal of Forest Research* 26 (2): 217–224. https://doi.org/10.1139/x26-025.

Abrams, Marc D, and Gregory J. Nowacki. 2008. "Native Americans as Active and Passive Promoters of Mast and Fruit Trees in the Eastern USA." *Holocene: An Interdisciplinary Journal Focusing on Recent Environmental Change* 18: 1123–1138.

Albu, Christian. and Florin Dinulică. 2014. "The Woodcutting Output of the Resonance Spruce for Semi-Products of Musical Instruments." *Revista Pădurilor* 129 (3/4): 14–24.

Allen, Aaron S. 2012. " 'Fatto Di Fiemme': Stradivari's Violins and the Musical Trees of the Paneveggio." In *Invaluable Trees: Cultures of Nature, 1660–1830*, ed. Laura Auricchio, Elizabeth Cook, and Giulia Pacini, 301–315. Oxford: Voltaire Foundation.

Allen, Aaron S., Eduardo S. Brondizio, Assefa Tefera Dibaba, and Mary Hufford. 2021. *Performing Environmentalisms: Expressive Culture and Ecological Change*, ed. John Holmes McDowell, et al. Urbana: University of Illinois Press.

Allen, Aaron S., and Kevin Dawe, eds. 2015. *Current Directions in Ecomusicology: Music, Culture, Nature*. New York: Routledge.

Anderson-Lazo, A. L. 2016. "Ethnography as Aprendizaje: Growing and Using Collaborative Knowledge with the People's Produce Project in San Diego." In *Routledge Companion to Contemporary Anthropology*, ed. Simon Coleman, Susan Brin Hyatt, and Ann E. Kingsolver, 475–494. New York: Routledge.

Appadurai, Arjun. 1986. *The Social Life of Things: Commodities in Cultural Perspective*. Ethnohistory workshop. Cambridge: Cambridge University Press.

Auricchio, Laura. 2012. *Invaluable Trees: Cultures of Nature, 1660–1830*. Oxford: Voltaire Foundation.

Basole, Amit. 2015. "Authenticity, Innovation, and the Geographical Indication in an Artisanal Industry: The Case of the Banarasi Sari." *Journal of World Intellectual Property* 18 (3–4): 127–149.

Bates, Eliot. 2012. "The Social Life of Musical Instruments." *Ethnomusicology* 56 (3): 363–395. https://doi.org/10.5406/ethnomusicology.56.3.0363.

Batteau, Allen. 1990. *The Invention of Appalachia (The Anthropology of Form and Meaning)*. Tucson: University of Arizona Press.

Baudrillard, Jean. 1990. *Revenge of the Crystal: Selected Writings on the Modern Object and Its Destiny, 1968–1983*. London and Sterling, VA: Pluto Press.

Beaver, Patricia D. 1992. *Rural Community in the Appalachian South*. Long Grove, IL: Waveland Press.

Becker, Jane S. 1998. *Selling Tradition: Appalachia and the Construction of an American Folk, 1930–1940*. Chapel Hill: University of North Carolina Press.

Benjamin, Walter. 2008. *The Work of Art in the Age of Mechanical Reproduction*. London: Penguin.

Bennett, Andy, and Kevin Dawe. 2001. *Guitar Cultures*. Oxford and New York: Berg.

Bennett, Jane. 2001. *The Enchantment of Modern Life: Attachments, Crossings, and Ethics*. Princeton, NJ: Princeton University Press.

Billings, Dwight B., Gurney Norman, and Katherine Ledford. 2001. *Back Talk from Appalachia Confronting Stereotypes*. Lexington: University Press of Kentucky.

Blakemore, Erin. 2016. "Mineral Baths May Have Given Stradivari Their Signature Sound." Smithsonian. Accessed November 1, 2018. https://www.smithsonianmag.com/smart-news/mineral-baths-may-have-given-stradivari-their-signature-sound-180961531/.

Branduzzi, Anna M., Christopher D. Barton, and Amy Lovell. 2020. "First-Year Survival of Native Wetland Plants in Created Vernal Pools on an Appalachian Surface Mine." *Ecological Restoration* 38 (2): 70–73.

Burckle, L, and H. D. Grissino-Mayer. 2003. "Stradivari, Violins, Tree Rings, and the Maunder Minimum: A Hypothesis." *DENDRO Dendrochronologia* 21 (1): 41–45.

Cant, Alanna. 2019. *The Value of Aesthetics: Oaxacan Woodcarvers in Global Economies of Culture*. Austin: University of Texas Press.

Carmenates, Omar. 2010. "Honduras Rosewood: Its Endangerment and Subsequent Impact on the Percussion Industry." PhD diss., Florida State University College of Music. https://diginole.lib.fsu.edu/islandora/object/fsu:182367/datastream/PDF/view.

Cavanaugh, Jillian R, and Shalini Shankar. 2014. "Producing Authenticity in Global Capitalism: Language, Materiality, and Value." *American anthropologist* 116 (1): 51–64.

Chen, Mel Y. 2012. *Animacies: Biopolitics, Racial Mattering, and Queer Affect*. Durham, NC: Duke University Press Books.

Clarkson, Roy B., and William A. Lunk. 1964. *Tumult on the Mountains: Lumbering in West Virginia 1770–1920*. Parsons, WV: McClain.

Cohen, Ronald D. 2006. *Folk Music: The Basics*. Routledge Student Reference. New York: Routledge.

Conway, Cecelia. 1995. *African Banjo Echoes in Appalachia: A Study of Folk Traditions*. Knoxville: University of Tennessee Press.

Cooley, Timothy J., ed. 2019. *Cultural Sustainabilities: Music, Media, Language, Advocacy*. Urbana: University of Illinois Press.

Coy, Michael William. *Apprenticeship: From Theory to Method and Back Again*. SUNY Series in the Anthropology of Work. Albany: State University of New York Press, 1989.

DeYoung, Sonia. 2020. "A Boost for Red Spruce." Northern Woodlands website (Winter). https://northernwoodlands.org/articles/article/boost-red-spruce.

Dinulică, Florin, Cristian Albu, Stelian Borz, Maria Magdalena Vasilescu, and Ion Petritan. 2015. "Specific Structural Indexes for Resonance Norway Spruce Wood Used for Violin Manufacturing," *Bioresources* 10 (4): 7525–7543.

Dorondel, Stefan. 2016. *Disrupted Landscapes: State, Peasants and the Politics of Land in Postsocialist Romania*. New York: Berghahn.

Downey, Greg, Monica Dalidowicz, and Paul H. Mason. 2014. "Apprenticeship as Method: Embodied Learning in Ethnographic Practice." *Qualitative Research* (July). 1468794114543400. https://doi.org/10.1177/1468794114543400.

Dudley, Kathryn Marie. 2014. *Guitar Makers: The Endurance of Artisanal Values in North America*. Chicago and London: University of Chicago Press.

Dunaway, Wilma A. 1996. *The First American Frontier: Transition to Capitalism in Southern Appalachia, 1700–1860*. Chapel Hill: University of North Carolina Press.

Eller, Ronald D. 1982. *Miners, Millhands, and Mountaineers: Industrialization of the Appalachian South, 1880–1930*. Knoxville: University of Tennessee Press.

Emrick, Isaac J. 2015. "Maopewa Iati Bi: Takai Tonqyayun Monyton 'To Abandon so Beautiful a Dwelling': Indians in the Kanawha-New River Valley, 1500–1755." PhD diss., West Virginia University. https://doi.org/10.33915/etd.5543.

Feld, Steven, and Keith H. Basso. 1996. *Senses of Place*. Santa Fe, NM: School of American Research Press.

Ferry, Elizabeth Emma, and Mandana E. Limbert. 2008. *Timely Assets: The Politics of Resources and Their Temporalities*. Santa Fe, NM: School for Advanced Research Press.

Finney, Carolyn. 2014. *Black Faces, White Spaces: Reimagining the Relationship of African Americans to the Great Outdoors*. Chapel Hill: University of North Carolina Press.

Gershon, Ilana. 2014. "Selling Your Self in the United States." *PoLAR: Political and Legal Anthropology Review* 37 (2): 281–295. https://doi.org/10.1111/plar.12075.

Gibson, Chris, and Andrew Warren. 2021. *The Guitar: Tracing the Grain Back to the Tree*. Chicago, London: University of Chicago Press.

———. 2016. "Resource-Sensitive Global Production Networks: Reconfigured Geographies of Timber and Acoustic Guitar Manufacturing." *Economic Geography* 92 (4): 430–454. https://doi.org/10.1080/00130095.2016.1178569.

Greenberg, James B. 2016. "Good Vibrations, Strings Attached: The Political Ecology of the Guitar." *Sociology and Anthropology* 4 (5): 431–438. https://doi.org/10.13189/sa.2016.040514.

Gura, Philip F. 2012. *C.F. Martin & His Guitars, 1796–1873*. Anaheim Hills, CA: Centerstream.

Gwin, Adrian. "Another Allison Tries His Hand at Making of Violins." *Charleston Daily Mail*, January 13, 1954.

Harcourt, Wendy, and Arturo Escobar. 2005. *Women and the Politics of Place*. Bloomfield, CT: Kumarian Press.

Harkins, Anthony. 2004. *Hillbilly: A Cultural History of an American Icon*. New York: Oxford University Press.

Harris, Mark. 2007. *Ways of Knowing: Anthropological Approaches to Crafting Experience and Knowledge*. New York: Berghahn Books.

Haskell, David George. 2018. *The Songs of Trees: Stories from Nature's Great Connectors*. Reprint edition. New York: Penguin Books.

Hay, Fred J. 2003. "Black Musicians in Appalachia: An Introduction to Affrilachian Music." *Black Music Research Journal* 23 (1/2): 1–19. https://doi.org/10.2307/3593206.

Hendry, Erica R. 2010. "Scanning a Stradivarius." Smithsonian.com. Accessed January 9, 2023. https://www.smithsonianmag.com/smithsonian-institution/scanning-a-stradivarius-13807009/.

Heyman, Dan. 2016. "Restoring WV Spruce Means Cleaner Air for the Region." 2016. https://www.publicnewsservice.org/2016-07-11/climate-change-air-quality/restoring-wv-spruce-means-cleaner-air-for-the-region/a52868-1.

Hill, Sarah H. 1997. *Weaving New Worlds: Southeastern Cherokee Women and Their Basketry*. Chapel Hill: University of North Carolina Press.

Hofstetter, Richard W., David D. Dunn, Reagan McGuire, and Kristen A. Potter. 2014. "Using Acoustic Technology to Reduce Bark Beetle Reproduction." *Pest Management Science* 70 (1): 24–27. https://doi.org/10.1002/ps.3656.

Hufford, Mary. 2001. "Stalking the Forest Coeval Fieldwork at the Site of Clashing Social Imaginaries." *Practicing Anthropology* 23 (2): 29–32.

———. 2016. "Tending the Commons: Folklife and Landscape in Southern West Virginia." Library of Congress webpage. Accessed January 9, 2023. https://www.loc.gov/collections/folklife-and-landscape-in-southern-west-virginia/about-this-collection/.

———. 2021. "The Witness Trees' Revolt: Folklore's Invitation to Narrative Ecology." In *Performing Environmentalisms*, eds. John Holmes McDowell et al. Urbana, Chicago, and Springfield: University of Illinois Press.

Ingold, Tim. 2007. *A Brief History of Lines*. London: Routledge.

———. 2010. "Bringing Things to Life: Creative Entanglements in a World of Materials." Working Paper 15, ESRC National Centre for Research Methods, Manchester, UK.

———. 2017. "On Human Correspondence." *Journal of the Royal Anthropological Institute* 23 (1): 9–27. https://doi.org/10.1111/1467-9655.12541.

———. 2011. *The Perception of the Environment: Essays on Livelihood, Dwelling and Skill*. New York: Routledge.

———. 2012. "Toward an Ecology of Materials." *Annual Review of Anthropology* 41: 427–442.

Irwin, John Rice. 1983. *Musical Instruments of the Southern Appalachian Mountains*. Westchester, PA: Schiffer.

Jenkins, Richard. 2000. "Disenchantment, Enchantment, and Re-Enchantment: Max Weber at the Millennium." *Max Weber Studies* 1 (1): 11–32.

Keefe, Susan E., ed. 2009. *Participatory Development in Appalachia: Cultural Identity, Community, and Sustainability*. Knoxville: University of Tennessee Press.

Kies, Thomas J. 2008. "Aesthetic Judgments of Luthiers: A Case Study of Mexican Guitar-Makers." *The Galpin Society Journal* 61 (April): 177–191.

Kingsolver, Ann E. 2011. *Tobacco Town Futures: Global Encounters in Rural Kentucky*. Long Grove, IL: Waveland Press.

Kondo, Dorinne K. 1990. *Crafting Selves: Power, Gender, and Discourses of Identity in a Japanese Workplace*. Chicago: University of Chicago Press.

Koo, Kyung Ah, Bernard C. Patten, and Marguerite Madden. 2015. "Predicting Effects of Climate Change on Habitat Suitability of Red Spruce (*Picea Rubens* Sarg.) in the Southern Appalachian Mountains of the USA: Understanding Complex Systems Mechanisms through Modeling." *Forests* 6 (4): 1208–1226. https://doi.org/10.3390/f6041208.

Kopytoff, Igor. 1986. "The Cultural Biography of Things: Commoditization as Process." In *The Social Life of Things*, ed. Arjun Appadurai, 64–93. Cambridge: Cambridge University Press.

Kosek, Jake. 2006. *Understories: The Political Life of Forests in Northern New Mexico*. Durham, NC: Duke University Press.

Lamphere, Louise, Helena Ragoné, and Patricia Zavella, eds. 1997. *Situated Lives: Gender and Culture in Everyday Life*. New York: Routledge.

Langlands, Alex. 2018. *Cræft: An Inquiry into the Origins and True Meaning of Traditional Crafts*. New York: W.W. Norton.

Lefebvre, Henri. 1991. *The Production of Space*. Oxford, UK; Cambridge, MA: Blackwell.

Lewis, Ronald L. 2017. *The Industrialist and the Mountaineer: The Eastham-Thompson Feud and the Struggle for West Virginia's Timber Frontier*. Morgantown: West Virginia University Press.

———. 1995. "Railroads, Deforestation, and the Transformation of Agriculture in the West Virginia Back Counties, 1880–1920." In *Appalachia in the Making: The Mountain South in the Nineteenth Century*, eds. Mary Beth Pudup, Dwight B. Billings, and Altina L. Waller, 297–320. Chapel Hill: University of North Carolina Press.

———. 1998. *Transforming the Appalachian Countryside*. Chapel Hill: University of North Carolina Press.

Lilly, Jessica, and Roxy Todd. 2015. "Could New Twists on Traditional Music Help Revive Appalachia's Economy?" Public Broadcasting website, October 23. http://wvpublic.org/post/could-new-twists-traditional-music-help-revive-appalachias-economy.

Marshall, Erynn. 2006. *Music in the Air Somewhere: The Shifting Borders of West Virginia's Fiddle and Song Traditions*. Morgantown: West Virginia University Press.

Martinez-Reyes, José. 2012. "Global Wood Politics: Gibson Guitar Style." Anthropology News website, January 10. https://www.academia.edu/3188071/Global_Wood_Politics_Gibson_Guitar_Style.

———. 2015. "Mahogany Intertwined: Enviromateriality between Mexico, Fiji, and the Gibson Les Paul." *Journal of Material Culture* 20 (3): 313–329.

Marx, Karl. 2009. "Estranged Labor." In *Social Theory: The Multicultural and Classic Readings*, ed. Charles C Lemert, 32–38. Boulder, CO: Westview.

Mencken, C., and S. Maggard. 1999. "Informal Economic Activity in West Virginia." In *Inside West Virginia: Public Policy Perspectives for the 21st Century*, ed. Bruce Keith and Ronald C. Althouse, 87–106. Morgantown: West Virginia University Press.

Milnes, Gerald. 1999. *Play of a Fiddle: Traditional Music, Dance, and Folklore in West Virginia*. Lexington: University Press of Kentucky.

Morris, Christine Ballengee. 1996. "Seminal Seeds and Hybrids: Colonialism and Mountain Cultural Arts in West Virginia." *Journal of Multicultural and Cross-Cultural Research in Art Education* 14: 66–79.

Nagyvary, Joseph, Renald Guillemetter, and Clifford Spiegelman. 2009. "Mineral Preservatives in the Wood of Stradivari and Guarneri." PLOS One website. https://journals.plos.org/plosone/article?id=10.1371/journal.pone.0004245.

Newfont, Kathryn. 2012. *Blue Ridge Commons: Environmental Activism and Forest History in Western North Carolina*. Athens: University of Georgia Press.

Oberhauser, Ann M. 2005. "Scaling Gender and Diverse Economies: Perspectives from Appalachia and South Africa." *ANTI Antipode* 37 (5): 863–874.

O'Connor, Erin. 2005. "Embodied Knowledge: The Experience of Meaning and the Struggle towards Proficiency in Glassblowing." *Ethnography* 6 (2): 183–204.

Paxson, Heather. 2013. *The Life of Cheese: Crafting Food and Value in America*. Berkeley: University of California Press.

Price, Jennifer, Calvin Kent, Emily Springer, and Serhun Al. 2008. "The Economic Impact of Tamarack." Huntington, WV: Center for Business and Economic Research, Marshall University. https://www.marshall.edu/cber/files/2021/04/2008_12_31_Tamarack 01072009.pdf.

Rice, Otis K. 1970. *The Allegheny Frontier: West Virginia Beginnings, 1730–1830*. Lexington: University Press of Kentucky.

Richardson, Tanya, and Gisa Weszkalnys. 2014. "Resource Materialities." *Anthropological Quarterly* 87 (1): 5–30.

Robbins, Paul. 2012. *Political Ecology: A Critical Introduction*. Second edition. Critical Introductions to Geography. Chichester, UK: J. Wiley & Sons.

Roda, P. 2015. "Ecology of the Global Tabla Industry." *Ethnomusicology* 59 (2): 315–336.

Rolston, Jessica Smith. 2013. "The Politics of Pits and the Materiality of Mine Labor: Making Natural Resources in the American West." *American Anthropologist* 115 (4): 582–597.

Rural Policy Research Institute. 2014. "2013 SOAR Summit Final Report to the Region." Pikeville, KY: RPRI.

Salstrom, Paul. 2003. "The Neonatives: Back-to-the-Land in Appalachia's 1970's." *Appalachian Journal* 30 (4): 308–323.

Satterwhite, Emily. 2008. "Imagining Home, Nation, World: Appalachia on the Mall." *Journal of American Folklore* 121 (479): 10–34.

Schwarze, Francis W. M. R., Melanie Spycher, and Siegfried Fink. 2008. "Superior Wood for Violins—Wood Decay Fungi as a Substitute for Cold Climate." *NPH New Phytologist* 179 (4): 1095–1104.

Scott, Rebecca R. 2010. *Removing Mountains: Extracting Nature and Identity in the Appalachian Coalfields*. Minneapolis: University of Minnesota Press.

Sennett, Richard. 2008. *The Craftsman*. New Haven, CT: Yale University Press.

Simard, Suzanne. 2021. *Finding the Mother Tree: Discovering the Wisdom of the Forest*. New York: Knopf.

Smith, Ralph Lee. 1997. *Appalachian Dulcimer Traditions*. American Folk Music and Folk Musicians, no. 2. Lanham, MD: Scarecrow Press.

Stimeling, Travis D. 2012. "Music, Place, and Identity in the Central Appalachian Mountaintop Removal Mining Debate." *American Music* 30 (1): 1–29. https://doi.org/10.5406 /americanmusic.30.1.0001.

Taussig, Michael T. 2010. *The Devil and Commodity Fetishism in South America*. Chapel Hill: University of North Carolina Press.

Terrio, Susan J. 2000. *Crafting the Culture and History of French Chocolate*. Berkeley: University of California Press. http://site.ebrary.com/id/10057111.

Thomas-Van Gundy, Melissa, and Michael P. Strager. 2012. "European Settlement-Era Vegetation of the Monongahela National Forest, West Virginia." Gen. Tech. Rep. NRS-GTR-101. Newtown Square, PA: U.S. Department of Agriculture, Forest Service, Northern Research Station. https://doi.org/10.2737/NRS-GTR-101.

Thompson, Deborah J. 2012. *Performing Community: The Place of Music, Race and Gender in Producing Appalachian Space*. PhD diss., University of Kentucky. http://uknowledge.uky .edu/geography_etds/1.

Thompson, Deborah J., and Darrin Hacquard. 2009. "Region, Race, Representation: Observations from Interviews with African American Musicians in Appalachia." *Journal of Appalachian Studies* 15 (1/2): 126–139.

Tuck, Eve, and Marcia McKenzie. 2015. *Place in Research: Theory, Methodology, and Methods*. New York: Routledge.

Tucker, Joshua. 2019. *Making Music Indigenous: Popular Music in the Peruvian Andes*. Chicago: University of Chicago Press.

Turner, William Hobart, and Edward J. Cabbell. 1985. *Blacks in Appalachia*. Lexington: University Press of Kentucky.

Ward, Richard. [2005?] "The Mystery of Origin." Ifshin Violins. Accessed November 11, 2018. https://www.ifshinviolins.com/Resources/Detail/Article/23/The-Mystery-of-Origin.

Waugh-Quasebarth, Jasper. 2021. "Learning and Labor in Ethnographic Apprenticeship." *Anthropology of Work Review* 42 (2): 108–119. https://doi.org/10.1111/awr.12223.

Waugh-Quasebarth, Jasper, and John Preston. 2019. "Listening for Musical Tonewood in the Appalachian and Carpathian Mountains." *Bulletin of the Transilvania University of Brasov. Series IV: Philology and Cultural Studies*, 141–150. https://doi.org/10.31926/but.pcs.2019 .61.12.35.

Weber, Max. 2001. *The Protestant Ethic and the Spirit of Capitalism*. London, New York: Routledge.

Wenberg, Thomas James. 1986. *The Violin Makers of the United States: Biographical Documentation of the Violin and Bow Makers Who Have Worked in the United States*. Mt. Hood, OR: Mt. Hood.

West Virginia Development Office. 2003. "The West Virginia Crafts Study: The Impact of Crafts on the State Economy." Charleston: West Virginia Development Office.

West Virginia Division of Forestry. 2010. "West Virginia Statewide Forest Resource Assessment." Charleston: West Virginia Division of Forestry.

Whisnant, David E. 2009. *All That Is Native and Fine: The Politics of Culture in an American Region*. Chapel Hill: University of North Carolina Press.

Williams, Michael Ann. 1995. *Great Smoky Mountains Folklife*. Folklife in the South Series. Jackson: University Press of Mississippi.

Wohlleben, Peter, Tim Flannery, and Suzanne Simard. 2016. *The Hidden Life of Trees: What They Feel, How They Communicate—Discoveries from A Secret World*. Translated by Jane Billinghurst. Berkeley: Greystone Books.

INDEX